Golden
Glory

The NEW WAVE of Signs and Wonders

by

Ruth Ward Heflin

McDougal Publishing is a ministry of The McDougal Foundation, Inc., a Maryland nonprofit corporation dedicated to spreading the Gospel of the Lord Jesus Christ to as many people as possible in the shortest time possible.

Published by:

McDougal Publishing
P.O. Box 3595
Hagerstown, MD 21742-3595
www.mcdougal.org

ISBN 1-58158-001-0

Printed in the United States of America
For Worldwide Distribution

Dedication

To the Harvest.

To my friend, Pastor Bob Shattles, who has always been a soulwinner and now is a great one, wielding a golden sickle.

And Simeon blessed them, and said unto Mary his mother, Behold, this child is set for the fall and rising again of many in Israel; and for A SIGN which shall be spoken against. Luke 2:34

I thought it good to show the SIGNS AND WONDERS that the high God hath wrought toward me. Daniel 4:2

He ... worketh SIGNS AND WONDERS in heaven and in earth. Daniel 6:27

And by the hands of the apostles were many SIGNS AND WONDERS wrought among the people. And believers were the more added to the Lord, multitudes both of men and women. Acts 5:12 and 14

And these signs shall follow them that believe; In my name shall they cast out devils; they shall speak with new tongues; They shall take up serpents; and if they drink any deadly thing, it shall not hurt them; they shall lay hands on the sick, and they shall recover. So then after the Lord had spoken unto them, he was received up into heaven, and sat on the right hand of God. And they went forth, and preached every where, the Lord working with them, and confirming the word with signs following. Amen. Mark 16:17-20

How shall we escape, if we neglect so great salvation; which at the first began to be spoken by the Lord, and was confirmed unto us by them that heard him; God also bearing them witness, both with SIGNS AND WONDERS, and with divers miracles, and gifts of the Holy Ghost, according to his own will. Hebrews 2:3-4

Behold, I and the children whom the LORD hath given me are FOR SIGNS AND FOR WONDERS in Israel from the LORD of hosts, which dwelleth in mount Zion. Isaiah 8:18

And I saw ANOTHER SIGN in heaven, great and marvellous, seven angels having the seven last plagues; for in them is filled up the wrath of God. Revelation 15:1

Ye men of Israel, hear these words; Jesus of Nazareth, a man approved of God among you BY MIRACLES AND WONDERS AND SIGNS, which God did by him in the midst of you, as ye yourselves also know: Acts 2:22

And the LORD brought us forth out of Egypt with a mighty hand, and with an outstretched arm, and with great terribleness, and WITH SIGNS, AND WITH WONDERS: Deuteronomy 26:8

As for the earth, out of it cometh bread: and under it is turned up as it were fire. The stones of it are the place of sapphires: and IT HATH DUST OF GOLD.　　　　　　Job 28:5-6

As for the earth, from it comes bread, But underneath it is turned up as by fire. Its stones are the source of sapphires, And IT CONTAINS GOLD DUST.　　　　　　Job 28:5-6, NKJ

Then shalt thou lay up GOLD AS DUST, and the gold of Ophir as the stones of the brooks. Yea, the Almighty shall be thy defence, and thou shalt have plenty of SILVER.　　　　　　Job 22:24-25

The king's daughter is all glorious within: her clothing is OF WROUGHT GOLD.

Psalm 45:13

Though ye have lien among the pots, yet shall ye be as the wings of a dove covered with silver, and her feathers WITH YELLOW GOLD.

Psalm 68:13

When you lie down among the sheepfolds, You are like the wings of a dove covered with silver, And its pinions WITH GLISTENING GOLD.

Psalm 68:13, NNAS

Introduction

God is positioning us for an explosion of His glory, and with that explosion will come the greatest signs and wonders the world has ever seen. There is no way we can name them because God will do things the Bible has not even previously mentioned. He will do things that we can hardly imagine ourselves.

This is the time. The greatest explosion of signs and wonders was recorded in the Bible at the birth of the Church on the Day of Pentecost. The Church had a glorious and powerful birth that swept thousands in every city into the Kingdom of God within a very short time. The whole world was affected. Were the early disciples not known as *"these that have turned the world upside down"* (Acts 17:6)? Now we are in the culmination of all things, and the coming explosion will be greater than the former and will sweep millions into the Kingdom in a very short time. It will be beyond the expectations of any of us.

I have known signs and wonders all my life. When we were still very small, our parents took us to every major revival that was being conducted around the country. We saw crippled people get up and walk. We saw deaf people hearing and blind people seeing for the first time. We saw people with oil flowing from their hands. We saw people having their teeth supernaturally filled. Seeing signs and wonders became for me an expected way of life.

Our family, in fact, lived by signs and wonders and miracles. When the gas tank was empty and there was nowhere to buy gasoline or no money with which to buy it, my parents prayed and expected God to multiply the gasoline in the car's tank, and He did. When there were bills to pay and the church offerings were too small to pay them, Mother would count the offering again, believing that God would multiply it, and He would.

Signs and wonders became such a normal part of our everyday lives that when I became a minister myself and went out to the nations, I expected to see signs and wonders following my ministry everywhere I went, and I was never disappointed. God has never stopped performing signs and wonders for those who believe, and He never will.

What we are seeing in the dawning days of the new millennium, however, is something altogether new and different. God is suddenly sending a visible glory, a golden glory, upon His people.

This golden glory is appearing on Christians of every denominational background. It comes to us as we pray and as we worship, but it is also falling on us as we drive, as we eat in public restaurants, or as we go about our daily activities — in our homes, in our offices, or in our places of business. It is happening anywhere and everywhere.

This golden glory is being manifested to those who seek it, and it is also manifested to some without their having ever sought it or even known about it. It is a sovereign act of God to show His presence and His power in these last days. It is a wake-up call for the nations.

10

God is trying to get our attention, to say to us, "I am real, and I am with you," and He is demonstrating that fact in a very visible way to the whole world — the rain of His *Golden Glory*.

Ruth Ward Heflin
Ashland, Virginia

Chapter 1

What Is This Golden Glory?

Just what is this golden glory? When it first began to appear, I called it "gold dust" because it certainly looked like gold to me. Although it sometimes appeared in larger flakes, it most often came in fine particles. Some called it "glory dust." Maybe we should call it "heavenly dust." I know that it is a miracle, and I rejoice in it.

This golden glory is the visible presence of God. It is the same glory that was seen on the face of Moses when he came down from the mountain of God. It is the same presence of God that accompanied the children of Israel through the wilderness. It was visible, to them and to their enemies, as a pillar of cloud by day and a pillar of fire by night.

The golden glory appears in various unique ways. It comes through the pores of the skin on the face or hands or some other part of the body of those who are worshipping the Lord. It rains down from Heaven, falling on either the people, their clothing or their surroundings. I have also watched as the golden glory was being created before my very eyes and fell upon the people.

We have experienced it as rain, as a mist and as a cloud

of God's presence with us. It is definitely supernatural and can be explained in no other way.

It comes on those of us who are ministering, but it also comes on many in the congregation. It comes on people of all ages, even on very small children and babies.

Not everyone receives the golden glory immediately. Some receive it after they get back home from the meetings. A lady called me in July to say, "Sister Ruth, when we got back home from Campmeeting, the gold dust fell on me and my husband." She spent the next few minutes telling me about how it happened. We had prayed for her in the camp, but the miracle had not happened to her until after she got back home.

It happens to others as they are on their way back home, or it happens to them in their offices or factories or schools. God has chosen to demonstrate His glory in our daily lives — wherever we happen to be. He gives the impartation to us when we are in a public meeting, and the manifestation of His presence begins to appear to us later.

The fact that this manifestation comes in such varied ways and under such varied circumstances shows us that God is demonstrating His sovereign power. Brother David Herzog from France was in our Campmeetings this last summer. Later he called to say that a lady was in his services, and she had on silver shoes. God covered those silver shoes with gold dust and made them appear gold. He left a few specs of silver showing through so that the miracle would be obvious to everyone.

Some people are having gold fillings replace their silver ones.

Brother Jonathan Quigley, who has been in revival in Mexico and South America and Europe, has seen many of these same manifestations — gold dust and silver dust and even diamond shavings. He mentioned that God is doing a very unusual thing. <u>He is taking peoples' costume jewelry and overlaying it with gold.</u>

Why is God doing all this? He is getting our attention. He is letting us know that He is <u>God. He is causing us to see His power and, especially, His sovereignty, in a dimension we have never known.</u>

All of this is producing a new level of faith in God's people. If we can begin to walk in this miracle flow in one area, we will find that area broadening. <u>If visible flecks of gold can appear in our midst, it causes our faith to rise until we can believe for other signs and wonders.</u>

When one of our sisters was ministering in the Royal Theatre in New Castle, New South Wales, Australia, in November of 1998, everyone present in that meeting heard the audible voice of God at the exact same moment coming across the sound system. They all looked around to see where the voice had come from, but there was no one standing near the microphones. God said, <u>"This is a revival of signs. Thank Me!" What more needs to be said?</u>

God is revealing His glory in the Earth, and He is doing it, as He always has, through unusual acts — what we call "signs and wonders." This golden glory that we are experiencing more and more in our midst is only the beginning of the greater things God has destined for His people in these last days.

Chapter 2

How We First Experienced
the Golden Glory

At Christmas time in 1997, our Sister Jane Lowder returned from a trip to South America to tell us about a Brazilian lady, Silvania Machado, who had gold dust appearing on her while she was worshipping the Lord. Jane brought a video to show us this amazing sign.

The first time Jane saw the manifestation of gold dust she was not quite sure what she was seeing. She wondered why Silvania had put gold glitter all over her face. Was this some new cosmetic fad? She had prayed for Silvania about two years before, and she was baptized in the Holy Ghost. What was happening with her now?

As Sister Jane began to inquire, she discovered that the golden dust was something that God was giving Silvania supernaturally. It was a golden manifestation of His glory, golden glory.

This visible glory seemed to flow from Silvania's scalp. Sister Jane was preaching in the church where the Machados attended, and Silvania was there every night for fourteen nights. Every night except one (when she fell into a trance on the floor), Silvania manifested the golden glory. Each night, before the service, Sister Jane checked Silvania's hair and found that her scalp was as normal as her own.

On occasion, Silvania's Brazilian pastor would open his Bible, and she would shake the golden dust from her head onto the Bible, and little piles of it would accumulate there. Sometimes the pastor caught the gold dust in his hands directly from Silvania's head. Recognizing how miraculous this gold dust was, he would take it and anoint the people with it, and great miracles were reported among them as a result.

We rejoiced when we saw the video, but we had no idea that soon God would be manifesting the golden glory in our own meetings in Ashland, Virginia. It happened within a few weeks of viewing the video. During our Winter Campmeeting the golden glory came ten or twelve times in our services. It began to appear on my face and the faces and hands of others in the congregation.

The first night of our Spring '98 Ladies' Convention, as Sister Jana Alcorn from Alabama was speaking, I saw flecks of golden glory appearing on her face. At the end of the service, I mentioned this to her, and she said she knew nothing at all about the experience. I asked Sister Jane if she would show Sister Alcorn and the whole convention the video from Brazil of the golden glory the next morning. After the service that morning, one of the ladies went into the rest room to change her clothes for the drive home. She heard something fall to the floor and thought it must be the brooch she had been wearing. She stooped to pick it up, but to her amazement, what she picked up was a gold nugget. She brought it back into the meeting so that everyone could see what God had done and rejoice. Others experienced the manifestation of golden glory as well.

A group of six very dignified ladies came to that conference from New Orleans. They were skeptical, not only of the appearance of the golden dust, but also of the laughter that was breaking out in some of the meetings. Their return flight was routed through Detroit and, because the plane they were on had some engine trouble, they were delayed there for many hours. Some of the group stayed on the plane, and the others went into the terminal. The ladies who went into the terminal began to notice that gold dust was appearing on them while they were waiting for the plane to be repaired, and after they got back on the plane, laughter broke out with several members of the group. Because they had been skeptical of these experiences, God gave them these manifestations in a most unlikely place — the Detroit airport.

In August of that year Silvania came from Brazil to minister in our Campmeeting here in Ashland. There was such a presence of God with her that I instantly began to cry when I met her.

Silvania had suffered physically for more than twelve years from a series of illnesses, including several types of cancer — liver cancer, bone cancer and leukemia. Her bones became brittle and often fractured under what would have been considered "normal activity" for anyone else. The family sought treatment for her from a series of doctors, until they had spent all they had on her treatment, liquidating all their assets in the process and going deeply into debt. In the end, Silvania became too weak to go out of the house and had to be cared for by her husband Luiz and, when he was at work, by her children. Her skin oozed bile, a condition normal only to the bodies of the dead some hours after death has already occurred.

In all this time, no one had told Luiz and Silvania that Jesus could help her. That changed one day when God sent a man from a remote part of Brazil to work in the same company as Luiz. He was there for only one month, but he and Luiz became friends. One day he passed by their house and, seeing the condition of Silvania, suggested that they take her to a certain local church where they were accustomed to praying for the sick. Luiz and Silvania gladly went.

The thing that immediately impressed the Machados was how warm and friendly the pastor and his wife were to her. Because of the bile oozing from her skin, all their friends had abandoned them, and they had felt rejected and ostracized. It was wonderful to find people who loved them and were not afraid to express that love.

The pastor and his wife first led Luiz and Silvania to Christ. Then, when he was ready to pray for her to be healed, he asked her if she would be willing to give the Lord thirty days to heal her. "What's thirty days?" she replied, "when I have suffered now for twelve long years?"

The next several days were terrible for her, and the church people prayed for her two more times on the weekend. By Monday, she was feeling so badly that she was sure the end was near. Then, when she woke up Tuesday, she knew that something had changed. She was totally pain-free. Luiz and the children noticed the difference too. Her color had changed. Several days later, she went back to her doctor and was pronounced cancer free.

About a year after her healing, Silvania was invited to an all-night prayer vigil. Having never attended a meeting like that before, she didn't know what to expect and dressed up in her high heels and her best clothes. It was that night that oil began flowing from her hands. She had no idea what it was and had to ask her pastor for an explanation, but it continued over the days and weeks ahead.

It was soon after this that Silvania first met Sister Jane Lowder. Jane prayed for Silvania and she was filled with the Holy Ghost.

About a year after the oil began to appear, at another prayer vigil, golden flecks began to appear on Silvania. She had never seen anyone with gold dust on him and didn't know anything about it herself.

At first Silvania was embarrassed by the gold flecks and washed them off as soon as possible. Sometimes, however, they would not wash off. On one occasion, she was covered with golden flecks for several days. It was this miracle that Sister Jane had witnessed and told us about, and this was the reason we invited Silvania to Campmeeting.

In Ashland that August our people witnessed the miracle of golden glory in Silvania, and others began to experience it as well. We were all blessed by her visit, and before the summer was over, this phenomenon of visible glory, golden glory, was appearing more and more among us. Nearly every time I preached, golden dust appeared on my face and on the people who were attending the Campmeeting.

When Silvania came that first time, she was accompanied by her pastor's wife (who co-pastors the church in Uberlândia, Brazil). This sister spoke to us, as well, and what she had to say was amazing and inspiring.

She told us that a member of their church had come to her and her husband shortly before they met Silvania and said that he was seriously considering leaving the church. When they asked him why, he said that he had been reading in the Bible about the early church and noticed again how many great signs and wonders were done by the early apostles. "We don't have many signs and wonders in our church," he said, "and I want to look for a church that does. If the early church had signs and wonders, we should too."

The co-pastor and her husband began to pray that God would give them signs and wonders, and it was not long afterward that God sent Silvania to their church and healed her. Her coming was the answer to their prayers for a greater manifestation of God's glory among them.

A few days after Silvania's visit, my friend Eli Mizrachi, who had served Israeli Prime Ministers from David Ben Gurion on, was visiting me one morning for coffee. He greeted me with the Hebrew *"Ma hadash?"* (what's new?), and the thing that immediately came to mind was what God was doing with the gold dust, so I began telling him about it. I told him about Silvania's visit and what God was doing in her life.

As I was talking about it, he said, "Ruth, I can see it on your face. It's coming as you talk about it." A few minutes later he said, "I see it on your hands now." He was amazed.

A few days later I was in Jerusalem and the same thing happened with an Arab businessman. "What's new?" he had asked, and as I told him, the golden glory began appearing on me for him to see. The next day he called. "I was really impressed with the gold dust that is appearing on you," he said.

This has proven to be the most wonderful aspect of this manifestation of God's presence. It draws people and opens the door to speak further about God. Although I had spoken with both of these friends about God many times, there is nothing like a supernatural work of God, a sign or wonder, to draw men and to convince them of the reality of His presence in this day.

In March of 1999, I was speaking at the Women's Conference at the Hamilton Christian Center in Hamilton, Ohio, with Diane Sloan and her ministry team. As we came into the pastor's study on the second morning, the telephone rang, and they said it was for me. A reporter was calling from Charisma magazine to ask what I knew about the supernatural manifestation of gold teeth and gold fillings and if we were having this manifestation in our meetings. Through them I learned that this manifestation had begun the week before at the Toronto Airport Fellowship Church. I told the interviewer that we had seen it in our meetings during the revival of the

1960s. It had happened occasionally during the 1970s and 1980s as well. "If that is what God is doing now," I told the interviewer, "then we will have it, too." Very soon afterward, it began to happen in our meetings in Ashland and everywhere else we went. <u>Every time we would declare it in a meeting, it would happen.</u>

Some of the people who received this type of miracle were in need of it. With others, God would replace their silver-colored amalgam fillings with what looked like shiny gold. At first, it happened to one or two, and then it began to happen to many. At first, someone got a single gold filling, but it wasn't long before some were receiving many fillings. In some cases, the person involved had every single filling in their mouth turn to gold. It was awesome to look at, and those who saw it were deeply moved.

Many of these miracles were examined by dentists, who confirmed that they were gold and found no way to explain it. It was another of God's signs and wonders to show us how much He loved us.

That June, for example, when I was at Presentation Church with Monsignor Vincent Walsh at Wynnewood, Pennsylvania, near Philadelphia, one night in the service a man stood to testify. He said, "I was here on Monday night when the lady declared that there would be gold teeth. After the meeting, my wife and her friend were looking into each other's mouths to find out if they had any gold teeth. They couldn't find any.

"The next morning, my wife and I were sitting at the table, and I started laughing about something. The way I was laughing, she could suddenly see some of my teeth

and she said, 'You're the one who got the gold tooth.' "
The ladies had been so busy looking in each other's
mouths that they hadn't thought to look in his. He went
to his dentist that day, the dentist verified that he had
gotten a gold tooth, and he was back in the meeting
Thursday night to testify

We were moving into something new and exciting.

One of the last trips my brother made before he died
was to Brazil, and he came back very excited with what
God was doing there. He had with him a jar of the supernatural oil that had flowed from Silvania's hands and
began to tell us about having met her and how God was
using her. We had no way of knowing that this would
be his last trip. Shortly after that God took him home,
but the special relationship with Brazil and with Sister
Silvania has continued, and she has visited us a number
of times for ministry.

When we brought her to our camp, it was the first time
she had been in America, so we considered it to be a
special honor from the Lord.

Chapter 3

The Glory Followed Us

The experience of the manifestation of the golden glory did not end when Campmeeting was over that year. I went that week to Jerusalem to minister with Nancy Bergen at the Mt. Zion Fellowship, and the golden glory appeared in all of the services. I was invited to speak for the Messianic congregation that meets on Monday nights at Christ Church inside Jaffa Gate, and the same thing happened there.

On the way back to America, I spoke in Denmark, and the gold dust fell there as well in the meeting of the Women's Aglow.

Then, during the weeks and months that followed, I was in meetings in major cities like Phoenix, Arizona, Charlotte, North Carolina, Atlanta, Georgia, and Mobile, Alabama and in many smaller cities. Everywhere I went that fall and winter, God manifested His glory. In November, Sister Karen Sandvick called me from Mt. Dora, Florida. She is an award-winning photo journalist who had come to the camp several years before, and God had touched her life in a very special way. She went from the camp to Jerusalem to be with us in the ministry there for a year. Then she began to travel all through the Soviet Union, photographing the Soviet Jews whom God was bringing home to Israel.

After doing this for several years, she went back home to Mt. Dora, Florida, a charming small historic town about an hour outside of Orlando. She was calling me now to ask if I would come there to help her start her ministry there. I was willing and asked her what she had in mind. "There's a little auditorium here we could rent," she said. "It seats about seven hundred." That was not bad for a town of only a few thousand people. I agreed to go. We had no way of knowing how many people might come out to the meeting, as Karen was just beginning ministry there, but the size of the crowd has never concerned us. God would work.

Karen also arranged for me to be interviewed on a program called Pinnacle on Channel 55 television in Orlando. I caught a six a.m. flight leaving Richmond and was taken right to the television station, where I met the man who would interview me. He was Brother Claud Bowers, and I did not know at the time that he was the owner of the station.

As Brother Bowers and I were talking, he looked over my biographical material. He had seen a lot of biographical material that looked better than mine, and, although he was very professional about it, it seemed that doing another program was just a duty that day.

That all changed when I asked him, "Have you heard about the gold dust we are experiencing in our meetings?"

"No," he answered, "what is it?"

I told him what God was doing supernaturally, and he instantly called an aide and said, "We will be going on live in ten minutes." The plan, until that moment, had been to tape the program for future airing, but the excitement of what God was doing had changed all that.

Brother Bowers was a very good interviewer, and the airtime passed quickly. He asked me questions about my life and ministry, and I had the opportunity to share the goodness of God with his listeners. Then, after a while, he began to ask questions about this new manifestation, and I told him what God was doing now.

Before the program ended, he switched to another subject again. Then, just as we were in the closing moments of the program, I looked across at him and I watched the Holy Spirit plant one piece of gold dust on his left cheek, right under his eye. Without thinking, I said, "Brother Claud, you have a piece of gold dust on your cheek under your left eye." With that, we went off the air.

Everybody watching the program that day saw the miracle, and it took only that one piece of gold dust on Brother Bowers' face to pack out the auditorium the next night in Mt. Dora.

Orlando is a place of many great churches and ministries. Why would the people of Orlando and surroundings drive an hour out of town at peak traffic time to go to a little town like Mt. Dora to hear someone they had never heard before? That one little piece of gold dust made the difference. That night I learned all over again what signs and wonders are about. They gather the people, and God meets them. It was a wonderful foretaste of what God was about to do.

The first night of the crusade we had a lot of gold dust in the meeting. The next morning I asked people to come forward and share their experiences of the gold dust. I thought it might take five or ten minutes. It took about forty-five minutes for them all to tell what God had done for them the night before.

One brother said that he had been out under the power of God on the floor and what was falling on him was not gold dust, but something bigger. He was being pelted by gold nuggets.

One lady said she had gold dust on her hands, and she reached over to her husband and wiped it on his coat sleeve so he could see every little grain of the gold dust that had fallen onto her hand.

When it begins to happen to us, it doesn't take God long to make believers of us. As long as it is happening to somebody else, we might remain skeptical, but when it becomes personal, it is harder to ignore.

God had moved many people in Central Florida, and He had done it with a single flake of gold dust.

I heard about a conference with pastors from the revival in Argentina to be conducted at Metro Church in Oklahoma City and felt impressed to attend. When I got there, I discovered that the organizer and convener of the conference was Pastor Randy Clark, whom God had used to help bring the Toronto Revival. I had met him several years before at a conference at Pastor Benjamin Smith's church in Philadelphia. Then I had been called up to prophesy over him, so he knew me.

On the second day of the Oklahoma City meeting, he invited me to the Upper Room, where they were having a special meeting for pastors. He talked for a while about the revival and then entertained questions from the pastors who were attending. Then he turned to me and asked me if I would like to say something about the gold dust.

"Oh," I replied, "I didn't know you knew about it."

"Yes," he said, "I've heard you are having it in your meetings."

I began to tell how this phenomenon started in our ministry, and before long another man went over to Randy Clark and began to whisper in his ear. Then the two of them stood there laughing heartily.

When I had finished, Randy Clark said, "I have to tell you what we are laughing about. Several days ago some of us were together in another church. One of our brothers came from another part of the church to where we were, and he had some glittery stuff all over him. We thought he had inadvertently gotten into some of the children's handcrafts, and we went looking through the church to see what had gotten all over him.

"It was only now, when you were talking about the gold dust, that we realized that he had received a supernatural experience and that what was on him was gold from Heaven."

Afterward, many of the ministers lined up and asked me to pray for them. As I prayed, they began falling out under the power of God. One pastor faxed me later to say that it was the first time he had ever been slain in the Spirit. When he got up, he said, his lips were covered with gold dust.

When he got home and started to undress, he discovered gold dust on his body.

That November I was in Phoenix for meetings. A man who was healed in those meetings later sent us a fax, telling us what God had done for him. Here are excerpts from the fax:

William J. Melnikas, Jr., Phoenix, Arizona:

> *Thank you for visiting Phoenix, Arizona and First Baptist Church. The presence of God I experienced Tuesday and Wednesday night has changed my life forever. Besides accepting Jesus into my life again and receiving the Holy Spirit, I received prayer for the psoriasis that covers my body and was slain in the Spirit on the floor that first night you were here. I was shaking so much and was so drunk in the Spirit that my wife had to drive home.*
>
> *I attended the Wednesday service and was prayed for again by another team member. This time I went down, and an amazing peace came over me, unlike the previous night. Later one of the ministers laid hands on me, and I fell to my seat.*
>
> *The next day I put on a new black T-shirt and went about my daily routine. That night I took off the shirt and noticed gold strands on it. My face, which is usually very dry has been extremely oily in recent days, much like my teenage years. The best news is that after two years of suffering, my psoriasis cleared up in just two days. Praise God, the Great Physician. I thank Him.*

Something new and exciting was happening.

Chapter 4

An Expectation for "the New"

After we had seen the video of Silvania and she had come to visit us, a whole new dimension of the miraculous was opened to us that we had not considered before. We were suddenly thrust into a total dependence on the Holy Spirit. As always, He did not want any of us to think we knew it all. He was removing our frame of reference and causing us to trust Him completely, for He was not doing things as He had in the past.

When we stood in His presence, we were standing totally devoid of everything that we had known in order to let Him bring forth something new by His Spirit. The only advantage we had from having served God many years was that we recognized His signature. Although He had changed His MO (His mode of operation or *modus operandi*), we could still know that what we were seeing was His doing.

When I first saw the video from Brazil, I did not need to pray about it, I did not need to fast, I did not need to do anything else to know it was God. I knew. Although I had never seen anything exactly like this, still I knew it was God.

When you know something is God, you can run straight forward into it. Some took a year or more to come around to the recognition that this manifestation was of God, and some are still pondering the meaning of all this. They are lifting the curtain to take a closer look.

Because we immediately knew the manifestation of the golden glory was from God, we were able to move straight forward in confidence. We are accustomed to new things, so this one did not shock us, as it did some.

Our meetings in Jerusalem and in our camp in Ashland, Virginia, have always been great occasions in which God was given the opportunity to declare new things He wanted to show forth. We long ago came to accept a calendar year that begins at one campmeeting and ends just before the next campmeeting. Some go from New Year to New Year, but we go from campmeeting to campmeeting because during our meetings, God always reveals new things to us and sets us on new courses in our spiritual life and ministry.

When my parents founded our campmeeting in 1955, it was in session the entire month of July. Over time the campmeeting was extended, until it lasted ten and a half weeks from early summer until Labor Day. For many weeks each summer we had the opportunity to hear the "Thus saith the Lord," of prophecy, in which God declares new things. Over the course of the years, we became a people who hunger for "the new" and who listen to God's voice constantly to hear "the new."

We have rejoiced to declare "the new" when God showed it to us, for we knew that in the very declara-

A New Thing

tion of it, we could begin to see it happen. If the Lord had said it, then He would manifest it to us.

The person who speaks and declares "the new" will ultimately cause it to spring forth before us. Then we can all begin to see the thing that God has been declaring to us.

Did not He promise:

> *Remember ye not the former things, neither consider the things of old. Behold, I WILL DO A NEW THING; now it shall spring forth; shall ye not know it? I will even make a way in the wilderness, and rivers in the desert.* Isaiah 43:18-19

> *Behold, the former things are come to pass, and NEW THINGS DO I DECLARE: before they spring forth I tell you of them. Sing unto the LORD a new song.* Isaiah 42:9-10

God is finding spiritual men and women who are willing to step into the water and carry forth the Ark, and this is causing others to follow. Some insist on standing at the water's edge. They put their toe in, then they take it out again. Then they put it in again. They are constantly testing the waters. This is not a time for testing the waters, but rather a time for stepping in boldly, carrying the Ark of God forward, and leading the people of God into "the new."

In the fall of 1998, the Lord was speaking to us about "the new." One day He said to us that He wanted us to be into "the new" by the 15th of November. We still did not know exactly what "the new" was, and I should say here that we still don't know all that "the new" is. That's why I began speaking of "the new" in this noun form.

New is usually an adjective. We speak of a new anointing, a new vision, a new dream, a new flow of the miraculous. Sometimes, however, when we don't know what the new thing is that God is about to do for us, we must speak of it in the abstract. It becomes simply "the new."

This phrase, "the new," has become an important part of my daily vocabulary over the past year. I am still using new as an adjective, but more and more I am using it as a noun. When we don't know what the new thing will be, we cannot use new as an adjective to modify something we don't yet know about. We have to say simply, "We are moving into 'THE NEW.' "

What is "the new"? We don't know fully what it is yet. It is that which we have not seen, that which we have not experienced, that which we have not flowed in, that which we have not comprehended, that which we have not demonstrated or manifested. The new is that which we have not personally seen God manifest or demonstrate. Therefore, there is no other way to describe it. It is simply "the new."

We are not totally in the dark about this current manifestation. We do know that what we are experiencing is a new wave of God's glory, and this wave is unlike any we have ever seen before. This is not like former waves. Other waves have burst upon the Church, but there has never been a wave breaking upon us in the manner of this current wave. This is something altogether new.

We know that this new wave pertains to what God is

doing in the river, that it pertains to what He is doing in the realms of glory, but that is as much as we now know. WE ARE LEARNING AS WE GO, AND THAT IS PART OF "THE NEW."

This new wave of glory will be very large, and at times we will be able to ride it. At other times, however, we will be totally inundated by it, overwhelmed, overflowed. This wave will be so large that it will take precedence over any personality. We will be in the wave and on the wave, but only the wave will be seen or known — never the individual personality. This is not a wave of personalities; this is a wave of the Spirit of God.

All that fall, every time I preached, I preached about "the new." Some preachers direct their message at the people who are present, but I find myself preaching to myself more. I kept preaching "the new" until it was mine. After all, how can we impart something we have not first received ourselves? How can we challenge people to move into something we have not yet moved into? Someone must always be at the forefront of what God is doing, someone who is not afraid of the arrows of criticism that will surely be shot their way, someone who is unafraid of what men will say.

I was well prepared for this hour, for people had always considered me to be ahead of my time, and those who know me best can verify this. I had been talked about most of my life, so this was just another chapter. When we are at the forefront of what God is doing, people will always think we are a little strange. If we have the anointing, however, if we have the touch of God, we won't even hear what others are saying.

A lovely Presbyterian pastor and his wife, Rev. and

Mrs. Charles Wonnenberg, and their family were with us during Summer Campmeeting 1998. One night Brother Renny McLean was ministering on the new song. At the close of his message he had the people walking in a great circle, singing in the Spirit, waiting for the new song.

Suddenly Pastor Wonnenberg began to sing out, as his whole body was put into motion:

> *Neeeeeeeeeew, sweeeeeeet, milk and honey, taber-nacle music, flowing, flowing.*

He repeated it, and it seemed that his hand was drawing "the new" out of his innermost being. His song brought forth great liberty and rejoicing in the service. I know that what God is doing is new, I know that it is sweet, I know that it is milk and honey, and I know that it is flowing. Since that time, I seldom use the word *new* without hearing it as that brother sang it that night.

I kept preaching what God had told us — that He wanted us to be "into the new" by November 15th. Sometimes I would draw an imaginary line on the platform and invite the congregation to join me in jumping over it. "This is 'the old,' " I would say, "and this is 'the new.' By faith we are going out of 'the old' and into 'the new.' " Then I would do it, jumping into "the new" — by faith.

We didn't know what "the new" was. We didn't know what God was going to do, but by faith we were stepping from "the old" to "the new" — whatever it was. We were stepping from that which had been to that which is and shall be. We were stepping from that which we had known into the area of the unknown, an area in which we had to trust the Lord completely.

We did not have to understand all this before we could step into it. <u>We could step in first and then allow the new thing to unfold.</u> What we are now seeing is only the first part of the unfolding. There is much more to come.

When God began to tell us about "the new," it was just a few weeks after Summer Campmeeting 1998 had finished. We had not perceived during the campmeeting that God would be giving us a date to move out of "the old" and into "the new." Now, however, there was an urgency. God was truly about to do "a new thing."

Chapter 5

The Golden Glory Falls on the Baptists

Two weeks before Thanksgiving, and one day before the November 15th deadline the Lord had given us, I got a call from a Baptist pastor in Austell, Georgia, near Atlanta. He was Pastor Bob Shattles of Friendship Baptist Church. He explained to me that his secretary had attended one of my meetings a year before and told him that he should have me in his church. He had been busy at the time and had forgotten about it, but recently the Lord had reminded him and told him that if he would have me in his church, He would bring him and his people into a new realm of glory.

I said to him, "Well, it just so happens that I am going to be in Atlanta next Thursday night," I said, "and I have the two days before that free." I had kept a couple of days open to be at home because it was the week before Thanksgiving. "If you can take me at the last minute," I told him, "I'll come down and be at your church Tuesday night, Wednesday morning and Wednesday night." He was pleased and said that they would announce it on Sunday.

On the 12th and 13th of November, I was with Mahesh

and Bonnie Chavda in Charlotte, North Carolina, and we could sense something new and wonderful happening in the services. On Friday night, the Lord spoke to me to draw that imaginary line on the platform and to jump over it. He wanted us totally out of the old and into the new. That Sunday was the 15th of November, I was back in Virginia in our camp, and it was evident that we had broken into "the new."

I began my meeting at Pastor Bob's church on the 17th. I found him to be a very warm person and his members to be very warm and friendly as well. The first night in the service, he was carried away to Heaven to the throne of God, and he had supernatural oil flowing from his hands. I would say there was at least a quarter of a cup of oil in each hand, and he had to cup his hands so that the oil would not run out of them.

The next morning he again had supernatural oil in his hands at the end of the service, and he began anointing the people in the service with it. On Wednesday night in the service, I looked and he had golden dust on his face and on his neck. When I mentioned it to him, he said, "I know. I felt it happen."

Those were wonderful meetings, and we quickly realized that we had tapped into something new and wonderful. "This is the new wave of the glory of God," I said to Pastor Bob. "This is 'the new.' This is what God is doing today." We rejoiced in it.

On Thanksgiving Day, I called Pastor Bob at Austell, Georgia, to say Happy Thanksgiving and to see how things were going, and I first got the church answering service. What I heard on the recorded message was so dynamic that it thrilled my soul: "This is Pastor Bob Shattles of Friendship Baptist Church. Come on over because we are in the midst of revival, the glory of God is falling upon us as gold dust and supernatural oil is flowing, and God is doing mighty miracles in our midst." I had never heard an answering machine message quite like it, and I called several friends, gave them the number and suggested that they call and listen for themselves. I knew that they would experience revival, just hearing what Pastor Bob had to say and hearing the anointing on his voice.

When I located Pastor Bob's home number and called him there, he began to tell me what had happened since I was with them. It was phenomenal. Gold dust had rained down from Heaven upon his service Sunday morning, and his people had all seen it. That first Sunday night after I was there, some of his members had found gold dust in their hair when they were getting ready to go back to church for the evening service. How exciting it all was for them, and for me, too!

That first Sunday when Pastor Shattles began to experience the gold dust in his church, one of his members picked up two little flecks, put them on some scotch tape and placed it inside her Bible as a souvenir. A few days later, she was visiting a friend in the hospital. This friend had a tumor on the back of her hand as large as a fist and was scheduled for surgery to remove it. The lady asked her if she had brought a prayer cloth, and she told her no, she had forgotten to bring one. Then she remembered that she had the tape in her Bible with the two small flecks of gold dust.

"Would you mind putting it on my tumor?" her friend asked.

She took out the tape with the two little flecks of gold dust and placed them over the tumor.

The ladies were busy talking for five or ten minutes, and when they looked back at the hand, the cancerous tumor had disappeared. The doctor who was scheduled to operate on the woman examined her and declared that there was no sign of cancer in her body anywhere.

Many other great miracles began to happen in Pastor Bob's church and in his ministry to other churches. Not long afterward, he began a series of revival meetings in Brunswick, Georgia, with Pastor Bill Ligon and his congregation at Christian Renewal Church. That meeting, intended for just one week, lasted for thirty weeks and brought thousands of souls into the Kingdom of God.

Several months later, while I was in France ministering at a prophetic school in Belfort, with Rev. Samuel Rhein, God spoke to me to go and spend several days with Pastor Shattles. Just as soon as we could arrange it, I flew in to be with him in the revival in Brunswick. The first night, as I sat on the platform, I was amazed to see golden dust raining down on the platform as showers four or five times during the first twenty minutes of the service. God was doing something very special for him and the people.

Since that time, Pastor Bob and I have been on several telecasts together, he preached for us at our Men's Convention in Ashland, Virginia, we did a campmeeting together with Dwight Jones at Caddo Mills, Greenville, Texas, near Dallas, and he was one of the evening speakers at our 1999 Summer Campmeeting. He has continued to move in this glory, which he calls "golden rain," and everywhere he has gone, the golden glory has been manifested.

Pastor Shattles' experience with this new wave of signs and wonders and miracles has enhanced his ministry in every way. More souls are being saved than ever, and great miracles of healing are flowing from his hands. He has been responsible for leading many others into this experience as well. His book, *Revival Fire and Glory,* which documents these miracles in greater detail, has become a bestseller, and he is already scheduled far into the future for special meetings around this country and others.

Chapter 6

Other Ministers Catch the Glory

Since the fall of 1998 at least a hundred of our friends in ministry have begun to flow in this anointing. Some of them are pastors, and their churches have been transformed by this experience, while others are evangelists — like Bob Shattles, Renny McLean, Dwight Jones, Eddie Rogers and David Piper — and they have taken this blessing far and wide.

A lady from Alaska attended one of our ladies' conventions where gold dust was appearing and people were receiving gold teeth. When she went back to Alaska, these signs followed her too, and eighty people received gold teeth. During the spring of 1999, a man flew into the camp for one of our weekend revival meetings that now continue year round. He was from Alaska, where he was the head of the Alaskan Promise Keepers. He said he had come because of the manifestation through this lady.

Dr. Eva Evans, who is an educator and also Pastor of Cornerstone Christian Center in Fairfax, Virginia, has been conducting Bible studies at the Pentagon for eigh-

teen years. She came down to speak with me about going to the Pentagon for a meeting, but, before we could
speak about the arrangements for the Pentagon meeting, she spent most of the first half hour telling us about
the gold dust, the gold teeth and many other miraculous things that God was doing in her ministry and the
ministry of other friends in northern Virginia.

Pastor Nick Pappis from Jackson, Tennessee, heard me
speak at Mahesh Chavda's conference in Charlotte,
North Carolina. Later he called to tell me that when he
returned to Jackson the children in his school had the
gold dust on them. This new wave of the glory of God
was quickly spreading across America and the world.

Here, in their own words, are excerpts from the testimonies of a few of those ministers:

✳

Renny McLean, Dallas, Texas:

> *When I came to Tulsa, the gold dust and supernatural
> oil started to manifest in the Abundant Life Church. One
> night, while we were all lingering in God's presence, the
> gold dust fell very powerfully. One man was extremely
> skeptical of the gold dust, until he saw it on his own
> hands. When he went home that night, he received a
> phone call from his attorney that a $400,000 debt he had
> incurred in his business had been cancelled. He came to
> the meeting the next night, and as he began telling what
> the Lord had done, the gold dust started falling again.
> This time even more fell, and people started getting gold
> fillings. This went on for several hours.*
>
> *I noticed that the gold dust was manifesting in the meet-*

ings as peoples' <u>hands were raised and they were doing</u> <u>a gathering motion</u>, as if they were pulling something in. As we were gathering in, the gold dust fell.

I looked at another man and said, "I see five contracts." The following day he went to work, and he had five new business contracts totalling $750,000.00.

In the same meeting, we had a lady whose neck was so short that her head seemed to be attached directly to her shoulders. While the glory was falling and the gold was manifesting, her neck grew out.

In another meeting in January 1999, I was speaking about the gold, and the gold started to appear. Prior to that, the supernatural oil was manifesting. One night we had a visitation of the living creatures while the gold was pouring out. A sister who was present, Audrey, was dying with cancer of the liver. The cancer had metasta-sized and spread to her brain. She looked like death warmed over. In that meeting, when the living creatures came and the gold fell, she froze and could not move for forty-five minutes.

Then she fell out on the floor, slain in the Spirit, and as she was slain in the Spirit, she was physically lifted up off the floor by the hand of God, and she said she physi-cally felt the hand of God touching her liver. She went back to the hospital in Tulsa, and her doctor could not believe what he saw. She asked him if he thought she was healed, and he said no. Her liver was not healed, he said; she had actually grown a brand new liver. She has been testifying everywhere since, and everywhere she testi-fies the gold comes in the meeting.

When I was ministering in Christian Tabernacle in

Houston, Texas, the gold dust started to fall as we were sharing about it. <u>As it started to fall, eyes were opened, ears were unstopped, tumors disappeared, growths of all kinds disappeared, and on the part of the body where people were healed, gold dust appeared.</u>

In that same meeting, we had a brother who was in litigation, and it looked as if he was going to lose everything. As the glory of the Lord started to fall, the gold dust came on his hands. Two weeks later he received a check for $1.5 million.

In Akron, Ohio, we were in a two-week revival, where the gold dust and the supernatural oil were appearing nightly. In one of the services, there was a seven-year-old girl whose name was Destiny. Destiny was born with no eardrum in one ear. One night I felt led to take the testimonies of those who had experienced the gold dust. As Destiny came to me, her mother ran up to the platform crying, because Destiny was listening out of the ear where there was no eardrum. When the gold dust was falling, God had created the eardrum. The doctors verified the report later.

During that same revival, when the gold dust started to fall, I saw a <u>"millionaire spirit"</u> come into the meeting. As this happened, I noticed the whole congregation was covered with gold dust. We had many financial miracles that came about after that meeting: debt cancellations and money coming from nowhere, for example. The following night a lady, Carol Hutchinson, came on the platform. She was disturbing me because I wanted to preach due to the time period remaining, but she was insistent upon telling her testimony. Finally, but reluctantly, I said, "Okay, just tell it."

She said, "Brother Renny, you don't realize this, but I own my own business. I had many contracts, lots of business that were taken away from me. Last night, when the millionaire spirit fell, God did a miracle. When the gold dust fell on my hands, it fell on my business cards as well. The next day I received a phone call from a government official, and I was given a contract for $63 million for our business. God more than restored everything that I lost."

While preaching at Praise Christian Center, in Channelview, Texas, the glory of the Lord was falling nightly, with gold and oil. One of the nights, a lady ran down to give her offering. We didn't know she was believing God for a miraculous weight loss. She ran down, dropped off her seed offering, and I noticed she was holding up her dress. Three days later, I was in another church, and she was there in the congregation. She came to me and said that while she had given her offering three nights before at the other church, she had dropped three dress sizes from the time she left the altar to the time she got back to her seat.

At Calvary Pentecostal Tabernacle, in Ashland, Virginia, one woman ran down to the altar to give her offering, and the next morning she had dropped four dress sizes. She had to fold the sides of her dress over twice into the middle.

✳

Eddie Rogers, Dallas, Georgia:

God is doing some awesome things. On Sunday night in the meetings we were conducting in Swainsboro, Geor-

gia, at Emmanuel Harvest Church, God turned a lady's silver crown to gold. On Monday night she gave her testimony, and on Tuesday we learned another lady's crown had also turned to gold. By Tuesday night the word had gotten out, and the audience tripled.

Tuesday night I had both ladies share their testimonies, and the visitors present came to the front to look in their mouths. At the close of the service I asked people to look in their own mouths and see if God was doing anything. The lady whose crown had turned gold on Monday night now had three gold teeth, and everyone had seen at the start of the service there was only one. Glory to God! The result was ten decisions for Jesus. That's what this is all about.

✳

Paul Beusnel, Olympic Peninsula, Washington:

During a recent revival, there were more and more manifestations of gold dust on people's hands. It was impossible to wash or wipe it off, and its effects would last several days. In addition, a number of people's teeth were filled with gold fillings.

On Saturday evening, a girl by the name of Mary, who by nature is very timid, came to the altar. As she was praying, gold dust began to fill her hair and cover her clothes. The more her hair was shaken or stroked, the more gold came out, covering the hands of everybody who touched her. Because this created such an interest, and she was so shy, she went home and tried to wash her hair so as to take the focus off herself. When her hair dried, the gold came back, as much as before. That evening the stairs were covered in gold dust from Mary and the many others who were receiving. Little children were in awe as their hands were covered in gold.

Sunday evening the altar was crowded. Toward the back stood a woman who felt that she had little to give to God. She had never fallen under the power and, in fact, did not do it that night. Because she was so reserved, she held back. As I began praying for her, I noticed the palm of her hands becoming moist and glistening in the light. In just a few moments, it was evident this was not perspiration, but thick oil running out of both palms and down her forearms. Whoever she touched was slain in the Spirit and ministered to in a powerful way.

Within a few minutes others began having oily palms that lasted for several hours. The oil had a powerful sweet fragrance that some said was the perfume of myrrh. It became so strong it filled the sanctuary. Two hours after the service was over it was still very strong in the balcony and, in fact, lingered till morning. Over the next day people said that the perfume could be smelled on their person as they went about their daily chores.

✳

Earl Last, Clarksville, Tennessee:

On the afternoon of August 30, 1999, I was at our church praying for the evening meeting. As I was praying, I felt prompted by the Holy Spirit to pick up my Bible and read. My Bible opened up to the chapter in Deuteronomy listing the blessing God promised the children of Israel. While I was reading, I saw a few flecks of gold on the page I was reading. I didn't think much about it, as my

Bible has gold all over it, but as I began to read the chapter over again, the gold began to increase before my eyes, and shortly my Bible pages were covered in gold.

The glory of God became so strong I fell to my knees and began to worship the Lord. Now the pulpit and chairs on the platform are covered with gold, and if you remove it, more comes to replace it.

Paula Askew, Beaumont, Texas:

About 1994, in a Sunday morning service, two ministers who write for our Harvest Times *newspaper, Bobby and Faith Hartford, had a vision, both at the same time, about the glory. They saw the glory cloud and fire, and the Lord spoke to them that His glory was coming.*

We kept hearing this for years, about the glory coming. Bobby and Faith wrote a book called Divine Revelation of the Glory *about what they saw in the vision, and because of this we all went into prayer and worship, waiting for this movement of the glory shining forth and being upon us.*

Then, in May of 1999, I was in Beaumont, Texas, ministering, and the intercessors at Church on the Rock in Nederland called me and said that the lady who wrote the book Glory *would be speaking Thursday night at Triumph Church in Nederland. I called all the ministers to come and see her and to hear about the glory.*

Later that same day, when I was in a bookstore where we get all our books for the School of Apostles and Prophets, the Baptist man who orders them for us came running up to me with River Glory *by Ruth Heflin. I looked at it and said, "This is the second confirmation I have re-*

ceived from the Lord today about hearing Ruth Heflin." The man kept trying to take the book away from me because it was selling so fast he wanted it back. I grabbed it and said, "I will be seeing her tonight, and I want it for her to sign."

We all went to Triumph that night, Sister Ruth called everyone up to receive the anointing, and all of us got the gold dust on our hands. She told us to go and impart it, and we did — to everyone we saw — and they got gold on their hands. The minister's children saw the gold dust on them and went to school and anointed the kids there, and they had many miracles.

When I was on the computer looking at Silvania's testimony and photos, the Holy Spirit spoke to me and said, "Call Ruth's camp and tell them you are willing to come there and help." I called, and they told me they needed help in housekeeping, so I went there on the 21st of June. While at camp, I got more gold teeth, several times rain fell on me inside the Tabernacle, and many times I was covered with gold dust on my face, hands and arms. Now it never leaves my hands.

My life and ministry have been eternally changed, and all of the pastors where I minister have gold on them and in their mouths. Praise God!

✳

David Piper, Poulan, Georgia

I was ministering near Brunswick recently and gold dust was appearing in the services. Many were saved and great miracles of healing took place. A forty-year-old man who had been in a bad car accident and could not walk without his walker, came into the building the next night walking on his own.

The Lord told me to go into Brunswick and stand by a certain pay phone with a copy of the book Prison to Praise in my hand. When a young man walked up, I was led to witness to him and his girlfriend. He had just gotten out of prison. As we were talking, gold dust appeared on her. I was just as surprised as they were.

"Where did that come from?" he asked.

"It is a sign that God loves you both," I told him. They wept, as they received Christ as their Savior.

In a meeting I held in Southeast Tennessee, God did many miracles. A young man who had no hearing in his left ear began to hear, and gold dust began to appear on his hands and on his wife's hands. A young lady who was in the service said that her hands not only had gold dust on them; they burned all that night and the next morning.

The brother-in-law of the pastor had been on morphine for pain for eight years. The next day he was painting a house.

While I was speaking with a fellow minister about going together to the Philippines, he told me he desperately wanted to have this manifestation of gold dust and wanted Sister Ruth to pray for him. Then he said, "You sat under her ministry; you could pray for me." I began to declare signs and wonders and miracles for his ministry, and instantly gold dust and oil began to come into his hands.

That same night I was speaking with a friend in Northwest Alabama, and she was telling me she wanted this *experience. I said, "Let's believe for it now," and we prayed. Then my friend screamed out and dropped the phone. Gold dust was coming out of her hands.*

This past Sunday night I was given an opportunity to minister in a church in Tifton, Georgia. The power of God was intense, and gold dust began showing up. Many people were healed that night. A teenage girl who had been brokenhearted said that her bed was covered with gold dust the next morning.

I was speaking in a church this past Wednesday night, September 2, 1999, and gold dust started to appear on some of the people as I was praying for them. One young man had come up to sing a special, and gold and silver began to fall on his shirt. Since the people were mostly from Baptist churches, I did not yet mention out loud from the pulpit what was happening. Several people who were there, however, saw the gold dust and believed.

The Holy Spirit had told me He would use this miracle to expand the ministry, and He has done that very thing.

Eva Evans, Fairfax, Virginia:

On October 25 and 27, 1998, Sister Ruth was with us. She and her ministry team brought us the Word, prophesied over us, encouraged us greatly, gave us personal ministry and many people were healed. The gold dust was very evident on Sister Ruth the entire time and also on Sister Jane. We believe that Sister Ruth and her team left a deposit which preceded many miraculous events. We knew that Sister Ruth had a desire to pray in the Pentagon, and on the 27th of October, we made arrange-

ments for a personal tour. She had a desire to walk in the hallway where the Secretary of Defense and his deputy were located. She also wanted to walk the corridors of the Joint Chiefs.

There were about eight people in our party. We walked prayerfully and joyfully. Sister Ruth told us not to walk lightly, but to leave the imprints of our feet. This was given to her in a prophetic word. I believe that it indicated that we were taking dominion. As we walked, I watched the gold dust appear on Sister Ruth's face and in her hair.

Suzanne Stewart, who is a vital part of our church and works at the Pentagon, was our guide. As we were walking toward the Concourse to catch the Metro, she turned to Sister Ruth and asked if we could dance. It was just past the lunch hour, and the area was crowded. We were all laughing and dancing, and the many people who passed us smiled and nodded as if this were perfectly acceptable behavior. During this time the gold dust increased on Sister Ruth and became so profuse on Sister Jane that it was falling down her back. Looking back on this it seemed to me that we were in a swirling cloud of glory. I believe that that day is significant to the revival that is coming to the Pentagon.

A few months after Sister Ruth's meetings we heard that God was blessing His people with gold teeth and gold fillings. The first chance I had to share this knowledge was in a Charismatic Episcopal seminary class. I was very excited by this miracle and asked my class if we could pray together for this. There was not a lot of response, but I insisted. Nothing happened.

That weekend we prayed in all of our meetings for gold teeth and gold fillings. Still nothing happened.

I was out of town most of that week. When I returned home, I had a voice-mail message from one of the seminary students. Her name is Kathleen, and she is a Messianic Jewish believer. That day in her car she tasted metal in her mouth. She pulled the car over and found that eight dark fillings had turned brilliant gold. I asked her if she had been praying, praising and fasting, and she said no. She had her decorator in her car, and they were discussing plans for her house. Two days later, her husband Jim, while he was at work, tasted metal in his mouth. When he went to check it, all his fillings had turned to gold.

On the following Sunday morning, fortified with Kathleen's testimony, we again prayed for gold teeth and gold fillings. Nothing happened. Sunday afternoon, Karen, who had been in the morning service, was coloring her hair in her bathroom at home. While she was waiting for the color to act, she took a small dental mirror and began to look at her amalgam fillings. She thought they were getting lighter. She brought a small flashlight and the dental mirror with her to the evening service. She was sitting with her sister and brother-in-law, Al and Ann. About fifteen minutes before starting time she called me over and asked if I would look and see if her fillings were getting lighter. As I watched, they turned brilliant gold. Within minutes, both Al and Ann had gold fillings as well. People were crowding around and looking in their mouths. It was a most explosive service. After the praise, we had Karen, Al and Ann give their testimonies, and then we prayed for miracles. In a few minutes time, twenty-six people came forward with beautiful gold crowns, gold fillings and gold teeth.

During this meeting, the children, from toddlers to highschoolers, had gold dust in the palms of their hands for the first time. It was such a wonderful thing to them that they just walked around showing their palms to everyone.

Two men each received two gold crowns on their bottom molars, and the right molar in each mouth had a decorative gold cross on it. A little boy about two who had never been to the dentist and never had cavities had a beautiful minute gold cross on a bottom tooth. He had been brought to the service by an aunt and uncle, who told me that he lives with his mother in a crack house in Washington, D.C.

Our Sunday night renewal services are attended by people from different area churches, we have had representatives from as many as a dozen. Among these have been Episcopal, Lutheran, Baptist, Methodist, Catholic, Presbyterian and Messianic. Cornerstone Christian Center and Shepherd's Heart Charismatic Episcopal Church are connected in many ways. Through Shepherd's Heart Bible College a course in Signs and Wonders was being presented at Fairfax Church of God. Ann Hammond, the wife of Father Harold Hammond, was teaching the class, which met on Monday nights. On the Monday night following the miracle service Ann did not teach the class. It was monitored by a student, Vicki. Some of the people in the class had been in the Sunday night service, and they asked if Vicki could pray for them to get gold teeth.

Immediately after the prayer, one of the church's worship leaders had all her fillings turn gold. She was so excited that she called her sister who lives in another state, but her sister was skeptical. Early the next morning she had a call from her sister, who was weeping. During the night all her dark fillings had turned to gold. The day following the class the pastor's wife, Karen Dotson, had all her fillings turn gold. Her husband said she walked around all day looking into a mirror.

I had been invited to present the college to a church in White Sulfur Springs, West Virginia. At the end of my presentation I told them that we had been having some wonderful signs and wonders, and that if anyone was interested in remaining, I would be happy to tell them about it. Twelve people stayed behind. It was not a church setting; we were in a high school cafeteria. We had no music and no prayer. I just simply told them about the gold and prayed a few sentences. Then, as we watched, nine of the twelve had dark fillings turn beautiful gold. These people were predominately Methodist.

We are closely associated with Christian Hope Center, a thriving multi-cultural church in Woodbridge, Virginia. When they heard about the miracles, they invited me to share on a Sunday morning. I just started at the beginning and related the gold stories. I know that expectation and faith are intangible, but they were so strong that you could almost see them. After we prayed and the people who got gold started coming to the front, everybody wanted to see. They crowded the platform, climbed upon chairs, and the laughter and excited comments were louder than the music. Thirty-eight people had gold in their mouths: crowns, fillings and gold teeth. From that one service many other people had gold miracles.

One of the women who received gold fillings, Brenda, owns a beauty shop. On Monday Brenda was telling a client about her gold fillings. The client, who is Baptist, asked if she could see them and then she asked if God would do that for her. Without even praying, Brenda said, "Let's look and see." They looked in her mouth, and her fillings had turned gold.

Brenda called her mother in North Carolina and prayed for her over the phone, and she got gold fillings.

Each of these individual miracles sparked others. For instance, many people left church that day and prayed for family members, and they got gold teeth and gold fillings.

A Catholic woman named Marilyn was brought to one of our Sunday evening services. She was called out and ministered to and laid on the floor for a long time. The next morning, when she was brushing her teeth, she discovered that all her dark fillings had turned gold. She went to her dentist, and he confirmed that they were gold but thought she'd had another dentist do the work. She told him it happened at church, and he said she'd better stay away from that church because only Satan did things like that. In her own words: "I knew only God could do that because since the night I laid on the floor, I stopped smoking, stopped 'cussing' and, for the first time in years, I sleep through the night." This life change is a wonderful testimony to everyone she knows. She loves to show her beautiful gold fillings.

Recently my friend Dee Zamora's brother called her from New York and asked if she knew anything about the gold teeth and gold dust. Dee told him we were having these manifestations at Cornerstone, and this resulted in my being invited to speak at the Lighthouse Church of God in Mexico, New York. Pastor Ron Russell and his wife Sue were so receptive and gracious to us. The church was full, and the praise and worship was excellent.

We heard testimonies of deliverances and healings, and by the time I was introduced, there was a haze of glory across the auditorium. I told what we have been experiencing, and then we prayed for the gold miracles.

One woman had gold dust all over her blouse, and ten people had gold fillings verified. The pastor's wife, Sue, had a remarkable filling. It was very brilliant, and it looked like a gold nugget had been laid on the top of her tooth.

There was such excitement. People were laughing and talking and trying to see into mouths. It is so easy at times like that to understand what it must have been like to be around Jesus.

Near the end of the evening, a boy of about ten came and showed me his teeth. There was a gap between the two front ones, and they were crooked. He said he needed braces, but his family couldn't afford them and he asked if I thought Jesus would fix his teeth.

I said I did and touched his mouth and prayed. When I had finished, he ran off. I moved to the next person, and a few minutes later I heard a commotion. He was running toward me surrounded by a swarm of kids. He smiled, and the gap was gone, and the teeth were straight and perfect. He had gone to the bathroom to look in the mirror.

✳

Nick Pappis, Jackson, Tennessee:

Our first encounter with the manifestation of gold dust came during a conference where Ruth Heflin was speaking. During one of her sessions, I noticed oil building up on the palms of my hands. Initially I thought I was merely perspiring, then gold dust began to appear and sparkle all over my hands. Within minutes my wife, Patty, as well as Pastors Kim and Betty Carroll, who were seated next to us, also began to see gold dust appear on their hands.

The following Sunday, while I was preaching, gold dust again began to manifest upon me, as well as on numerous members of our congregation. That afternoon one of our members came to my home and told me he felt the manifestation of gold dust must be exclusively for special people, not for him. While we were talking, gold began to appear on my hands and on his hands and clothing, and he became an instant believer.

We have had many times when gold dust appeared on every person present in our services, including visitors. On one occasion, numerous children attending a school co-op at our church were covered in gold dust so thick it looked as if it was painted on some of them. We have seen gold, silver and what looked like platinum and diamond dust appear on us in our services, while at home and even while driving. Members of our church have reported gold dust appearing during their prayer times as well as times of fellowshipping with others or simply talking about the manifestations they have seen. This phenomenon continues with us to this day.

✳

Mamie Wilson, Maiden, North Carolina:

The first time I encountered the oil and the gold dust was in 1998 at the Campmeeting in Ashland, Virginia, at the Calvary Pentecostal Tabernacle. Sister Silvania Machado from Brazil was the guest speaker. I saw for myself as the oil and the gold began to appear on her. I was skeptical when I went into the meeting, but a believer when I came out.

That has been over a year now. I have just finished conducting a Ladies Conference in Fayetteville, North Carolina at the Cedar Creek Church of God. Prior to my coming, the pastor's wife told me about what was happening at their church services. They were experiencing oil in their hands and gold dust. I could hardly wait to get there.

I began my meeting on Sunday night, October 10, 1999. During praise and worship, I noticed I was in a deeper kind of worship. It wasn't ordinary. As I yielded myself to the Lord, I felt oil in my hands. My hands were soaked in it.

I felt wonderful, but I wanted more of Him, more of His glory. So on Monday, I began seeking His face, weeping, then laughing and then dancing. It was awesome. At church service that night, after I finished preaching, I began to minister to individuals. Many of the ladies came to me and said, "I thought your suit was gold and black." (The suit I was wearing was black and white striped). I was literally covered in gold dust. It was in my hair, on my face, on my clothes, and the oil was again in my hands. Needless to say, I was excited at what God was doing in my life, allowing me to be in the presence of His glory.

✳

Larry Williamson, Baltimore, Maryland:

Gold dust came to Victorious Tabernacle in Baltimore when we least expected it. Our church was invited to participate in a shopping-center exposition with twenty-six other churches and civic groups. Our interest in accepting was to take our dance and puppet ministries to win souls for Christ and also to raise money to buy time on cable TV for our unique professional skits designed to move the watcher to seek Christ and call for help. Throughout the day, there seemed to be some spiritual warfare going on between our church and a secular group on the other end of the Mall. The clash of sound systems, between praise music and other secular styles, became very interesting.

Toward the end of the day, more and more children and families were drawn to the five ladies dancing in the Spirit and the puppets, who give a special type of witness. About this time someone noticed gold "sprinkles" on my hat, and it quickly spread to the whole team. We watched as many people, including the owner of the shopping center, were moved to give to the church. He said he had left the church years before.

We believe this is the year of the fulfillment of the vision God gave us many years ago, and as a confirmation, He sent His gold dust upon us. He is doing it even in shopping centers, and it is bringing people to Christ! Praise the Lord!

George Payne, Andalusia, Alabama:

Whatever this gold dust is, it is supernatural in origin,

and I think it's God. It happened to me first in Ruth Heflin's meetings with Mahesh Chavda. It's happening to an awful lot of folks that love Jesus deeply, so I don't tend to think it's from the devil. My little daughter Anna has gold all over her head. It not only appeared just now after we finished pizza, but it was all over her the other night at our son John's soccer game.

The other day, I got up early to have coffee with my wife Kathy (I was up late with John watching the Braves' game). There I was sitting at the kitchen table in my underwear, hair messed up, not feeling very spiritual, when I looked down and saw gold sprinkled over both of my legs.

Last Sunday before church Kathy had it all over her face. A woman came up with three young boys, and they all had it on their faces.

I feel like this is just a warm up, and I wonder what's next. I have been seeing gold now for almost a year. I have seen it in about four states and in two countries this year. I had it on me while I was at the Smithton Revival two weekends ago in Missouri. I also enjoyed seeing the gold on my hands at Arrowhead Stadium in Kansas City, as I took in the Chiefs beating the Patriots. It was a business trip with Steve Martin from Mahesh Chavda Ministries.

The gold still fascinates me as much as when I first experienced it.

We started a church in April, and we like the gold. We are not ashamed of this gold manifestation. We have a lady who came to our church for three weeks, and she came up front to say hi after the third week. Several of us saw gold immediately on her face, and we told her so. She looked at us like we were crazy. She had never heard about the gold. For some reason, God had decided to dust her real good with it.

As I was writing this e-mail, John walked up with big flakes of something gold on both hands.

✳

Debbie Kendrick, Richmond, Virginia:

In March of 1999, I went to Arkansas City, Kansas (called Ark City by the locals), where I witnessed the most amazing thing. I was staying in the home of one of the pastors of Gateway Prayer House, and I noticed several gold flakes on a tabletop. At first I dismissed them as left over from Christmas decorations. Finally when I mentioned it, the pastors, DeeAnn Ward and Sandy Newman, said, "We have been watching them. They came just after we returned from the meetings at Camp with Silvania in February."

"But let us show you this," they continued. "We have told no one," and with this they took me into the living room and showed me what was happening with their drapes. What I saw there that day was something I could never have imagined. It still has me awestruck.

The living room was the place where they most often worshipped in that home. There, in the folds of three of the six hanging drapes, was a fine, almost powdery, white gold dust. It was thick, and when I swiped at it, the gold dust covered my fingers.

We began to worship there, and for the next thirty minutes all three of us saw gold flecks falling down. They were brilliant, some of them seeming to pulsate like a beating heart. Some were almost blue.

Later that same day we were in a shop, and there was gold dust on the merchandise, including antiques from England. Gold appeared on the pages of my Bible, and when I returned home to Virginia, there was gold in my refrigerator.

When I spoke by phone with Sandy back in Ark City, she said gold dust had fallen in the workplace of one of the church members, who is a graphic artist at a bank. Hallelujah!

There is a new wave. It's a golden wave, coming out of God's heart of mercy. Just having the mist of this wave blown upon us is an experience for most of us that is beyond words. It is a wave of God's glory breaking upon the shorelines of our lives. Revelation and wisdom have come in the gold dust. In the same way as those who were caught in the Gold Rush of 1849 had to pan for gold with a sieve of separation, this experience calls us out of the old, into the new. Just as God made us out of the dust of the Earth at the dawn of creation, He is re-making us out of the dust of Heaven at the dawn of Eternity. These manifestations of gold and silver (some appear for a while, others remain) tell us that He has taken us beyond the day of the apostles in the book of Acts. After seeing the gold dust fall, it is not possible to look at anyone in need and say, "Silver and gold have I none … ."

No one knew how to react when it began to fall. We had never been blessed this way before. God is unfolding truth in the Earth in a new way. There is a new humility God is working in all of our lives through this. There is certainly no way we can take credit when it happens. Recently, while in a convention, I declared that God was pouring out the gold. A number of people received gold and silver on their hands and faces for the first time. Most had never even heard of this before. One of the song leaders was actually something of a rock in the river of God's flow. She was an attention-seeking individual, and actually kept the music from ascending to the heights of worship because of this. HER HANDS WERE COVERED IN GOLD DUST. God's light was shining brighter on my understanding. This gold dust is not meritorious. God is blowing the new into all aspects of our lives, and this wave of glory melts us. We become fluid and easily change course, like a swollen river. Now I look for God to especially bless those who need it the most.

I remember once being fairly angry with my seventeen-year-old son. Justly so, I am sure. As I was about to go into "mother overload," I beheld a piece of gold dust on his face. It is not possible to yell at teenagers and look on gold dust at the same time. A new level of grace is being ministered to us. The changes come so easily.

✳

Shelli Baker, Luther, Oklahoma:

The most dramatic testimony of the gold dust that I have yet seen in our ministry was in Malaysia in August of 1999. On the last day of our trip, the church fathers asked me to prepare the spiritual atmosphere in opening the heavens first with supernatural praise at the one-hun-

dred-thousand-seat stadium that had recently been built for the world games. Carlos Anacondia from Argentina was due there for a first-time-ever meeting in December 1999, and they desired to fill the place with healed people. Their faith was realized, as I was allowed to sing, and my voice, with no microphone, could be heard on every side of the huge stadium. We did sense the heavens open and felt the glory rain down for an hour.

As we parted and drove home, I looked at my hostess. Her neck was covered with a fine golden light-filled sheen. I asked her if she was wearing powder or a cosmetic spray, and she, emptying her cosmetic case in her purse, replied, "No! See!" She was thrilled to tears to discover that she was the first we knew of in Malaysia to be covered with the "gold dust."

As soon as we arrived at her home, her mother received it, as I prayed for her, as well as her sister. Then they called their prayer group, and a steady group of ladies kept coming all afternoon to receive the miracle. Each of them had it, to one degree or another, in their hands only, but my hostess had it all over her body.

This made them so excited that they ran out into the street in the Muslim neighborhood and held their hands to the sky to see the dust in the sunlight and they openly sang praises to the Lord Jesus. This, in turn, resulted in an immediate increase in the glory dust!

A local Malaysian newspaper published an article about a lady who, in another full-gospel church, had received a gold filling. The pastor's wife, who was from the church where we spoke, received a supernatural cleaning of her mercury fillings, and the dentist verified this the next day in amazement.

Another dramatic incident was at the White Horse Christian Center in Lafayette, Indiana, in July 1999. Ronnie and I took dust out of his Bible that had been collected from Ashland one night, and we put it on Pastor Jeff John's leg that was stiff from an accident. He was healed and leaped up a flight of stairs to show it that night. We also put the gold dust on a man with heart problems, and he testified of being healed. We also saw it forming in my hands, and I laid them on a man in his late fifties who had no eardrum and had not heard from that ear since he was seven years old. He received a miracle and left able to hear!

A lady who was living in sin saw the golden dust on my hands and, for the first time in her life, believed in the God of miracles. I had been trying to win her for years, but since the gold dust appeared, she is now a changed person. This obviously shows that the "gold dust" does not validate the person upon whom it appears or falls, but rather the God of glory, who freely gives it to show His love and mercy.

As I preach on creative miracles, they start happening without the laying on of hands. In January 1999, an unsaved Mormon lady walked out of her wheelchair, as I sang supernaturally high, long notes over her in the name of Jesus. It took twenty minutes, while the entire healing line was made to wait. Healed, she now wanted to get saved. We saw her in August, and she was still healed.

We have had deaf ears open, twelve knee joints replaced, tumors dissolved and a broken bone instantly mended in a foot that was then stomped on for hours to show off the miracle! I just preach on creative miracles, declare them and boom ... People flood the platform to testify.

In the summer of 1999, while I was at the Campmeeting in Ashland, and the gold dust was falling out of Silvania's hair, I asked the Lord to explain it to me. He reminded me of my visit to Heaven, where everything I saw was gold. Even the water was alive with an amber glow. Jesus said to me, "<u>Some believers are now pressing so close to Heaven that a residue of gold from My presence is remaining on them</u>. That is what is on your hands. Rejoice!" I did, and this golden glory has been there daily ever since.

Chip and Darlene Hill, Monterey, Virginia:

We were so blessed while attending the Waves of Glory conference in Charlotte this past week. Thank you so much for your ministry. The first night of the conference my husband had some flakes of glory dust on his pants leg, and in the next service there was more on his neck. On the last day, I had small specks all down the front of me.

Oh, what a blessing to be in those meetings! We did not realize how tired we were. You helped us so very much, and now we have been reading your books that we brought home with us and are doubly blessed.

Jane Milligan, Roseland, Illinois:

I always love to share Jesus and what He is doing for the here and now because it is so exciting. We are blessed to be living in this exciting day. I trust the discernment of

Pastor Ruth and Sister Jane Lowder. Still, when something as startling as the manifestation of gold came along, I wondered a little. I am confessing.

The first night the sister from Brazil was at camp, I stood there, praising and worshipping the Lord, saying, "Lord, really?" Suddenly He appeared over the place where some ministers were sitting on the platform. He extended both of His hands and began wiggling His fingers. As He did that, gold fell from His fingertips.

The Lord kept wiggling His fingers, but after a while it changed, and I saw what looked like jewels falling from His fingers — diamonds, rubies and emeralds.

Next the Lord reached into a box He had beside Him and began to toss out new body parts. These were not used or mended. There were new legs, new hearts, new eyes and many other body parts. I saw that the Lord was ready to do whatever creative miracle people needed.

Some time has gone by since this experience, but it still excites me every time I tell this story again.

After I left the Ashland camp last year, I went to Avon Park, Illinois, to a pastor who had asked me to come and help intercede for a prophetic conference they were having. We had been praying for about six nights when Pastor Joe Rivera came to me and held his hand out saying, "Look, sister." There in his hand was a puddle of oil. He took his finger and moved it through the oil, and there was gold underneath the oil.

Another minister had gold flecks appear on his jacket, almost the moment he came in and sat down. This happened two nights in a row. An intercessor sitting across the room was wondering if it was God. When gold dust

> *appeared on the arms of the young teen seated next to her, she was convinced. The gold dust also appeared on the arms of a pastor's wife in the car on the way to church. The lady that gave me shelter while I was in that town saw gold dust falling in her church. Some was also on her arms.*

✴

The impact of the visible glory and presence of God on men and women like these is awesome, to say the least. They go forth and turn the world upside down. Two e-mails, one from a pastor in Georgia who was blessed by the ministries of Bob Shattles and Eddie Rogers, and a second from a medical doctor in Oklahoma, whose life was changed by the ministry of Renny McLean, serve to illustrate this point:

Tim Grant, Swainsboro, Georgia:

> *I pastor in a very small town. I read your book* Glory *and later came to know that Eddie Rogers, from Dallas, Georgia, is a good friend of yours. He is my friend as well. Recently we closed out a meeting with Eddie in which God showed up and rained down His glory. We hadn't asked for it this way; He just did it!*
>
> *Recently we were having lunch with Pastor Bob Shattles. As I sat there at lunch, observing him, I saw gold and multicolored glittering flakes suddenly appearing all over his face. Pastor Eddie and I began to tell him what happened at our church.*
>
> *Sunday morning, as Pastor Eddie began to talk about signs and wonders, tiny gold-like flakes began to appear*

all over the floor in the church. One of our ladies went home after service that night and began to eat some rice her husband had cooked. She complained to him about it tasting funny and asked him what kind of pot he used to cook it in. He said, "The same old pot as always." She went to the bathroom to brush her teeth and get the taste out of her mouth, and that is when she looked in the mirror and discovered that God had turned one of her teeth totally gold. It was later verified through her dental records that no gold was ever put in her mouth by her dentist.

Pastor Bob prayed with us that day and started to leave for Brunswick. The floor of his car was covered with gold dust.

Tuesday morning another lady in our church called to say that God had turned one of her teeth totally gold. It was one that she had had filled with silver some twenty years before.

The crowd in our church, of course, has grown recently. Everyone wants to see the gold teeth. Tonight I checked each person personally. Each one had a gold tooth. At the end of the service, I turned to "the Tuesday morning" lady and told her I wanted to see her gold tooth one more time. When I looked, there were two more gold teeth in her mouth.

I praise God for what He is doing in our midst and cannot tell why He is doing it. These are signs and wonders, and the Bible says that signs and wonders will follow them that believe. Jesus performed miracles so that those who were unbelievers could believe. What I can say is that I have known these people for many years and can verify the validity of the miracles God has given. I am expecting even more miracles.

✳

Dr. Mark Gregory, Orarche, Oklahoma:

The first time I saw the gold was in April of 1999. Renny McClean was here for revival. He spoke of gold dust falling in some of his meetings. I imagined layers of gold dust that could be swept into containers and taken to the bank on Monday, knowing full well that he had to be fibbing, since anything like that would provoke much more emotion than he was showing. It was surely safe to remain hopeful though.

On the second night, after the service was over, I was looking at my wife, whom I love. On her chest was what looked like gold glitter. Before I could take a second glance, an overhead light was turned off, and I could no longer detect it. I asked her if she had used a lotion or powder with glitter in it, and she said she hadn't. I came to the conclusion it was gold.

Two days later, after the meeting had closed, about twenty of us braved the midnight hour and pulled a few hours of teaching out of Renny, and the question of the gold dust came up.

While Renny spoke, the same thing I had seen on my wife developed on his hand. First, it was just one speck of dust, then another, until it looked as if someone had brushed a gold powder along the ridge from his thumb to his first finger on the right hand. As he twisted his wrist in the light, the gold would sparkle. From time to time it would pick up enough light that it seemed that if the pieces had been any bigger, it would have blinded me.

I now trusted that the gold dust was real and pulled away from the group to try and receive the gift. Finding a bright light at the altar, I began to turn my right hand in it. When the light was just right, I picked up the first sparkle, then two, then more, until, in the creases of the palm of my hand, I saw about five specks of gold. They were just as brilliant as those seen in Renny's hands when the light was just right.

This happened on Wednesday. When I was thinking about it on Thursday, I realized why Renny had been so calm about it all. THERE IS AN INITIAL SURPRISE, BUT THEN A PEACEFUL AWE SETTLES IN AND REMAINS. ISN'T IT JUST LIKE GOD TO BRING US A PRECIOUS GIFT THAT CANNOT BE APPRECIATED BY THE WORLD?

On Friday I do nursing home and home visits. My nurse, Pam, and I were at Ada's home. Ada is an elderly patient whom I love. When I was a child, I can recall running into her store with pennies to buy candy and can still hear in my mind the screen door slam behind me. Ada has been a servant of God all her life.

We entered the home without knocking, which is our routine, since her eyesight is now poor and her legs are now feeble. She was sitting in her chair quietly, without the distraction of television, radio or a book. On her right arm was the sleeve that pumps swelling out of her arm since her triumphant battle with breast cancer.

Like a child seeing absent parents return, Ada scurried to her feet, her stature half that of mine, and we greeted and embraced and loved on each other, our normal routine. I helped her to the table so we could discuss the events of the past month and the lab results from her last blood test. As she sat back down, there, on a white sweater she was wearing, I noticed a glitter of gold. I asked Pam to confirm it, and she, too, was seeing something that glittered like gold.

We removed the sweater, and I attempted to share with Ada what I had been learning about this manifestation in recent days. I was trying to teach something I could barely understand myself.

As Pam began to take Ada's blood pressure, the light caught more dust on her left arm. Although Ada could not see the dust, due to her poor eyesight, her face was aglow as a candle in the night.

As Pam started to take a blood sample, I walked back into the living room, since it seems to make the nurses nervous if I stay. I walked to the closed front door and asked God if what I had seen was real. In a bold voice, not heard, but felt, He said, "Go pick up her Bible and let it fall open." I did as I was told, and when I picked the Bible up from the stand next to Ada's chair, it fell open, and my eyes were drawn to the middle of the right hand page to the word "GOLD" that seemed to be jumping off the page at me. With excitement, I shared with Pam and Ada what had happened and showed them the Bible in my hand, now opened to Ezra 1:4. [And whosoever remaineth in any place where he sojourneth, let the men of his place help him with silver, and with GOLD, and with goods, and with beasts, beside the freewill offering for the house of God that is in Jerusalem.] *Since I*

felt that it was the word GOLD, not the particular pas-
sage of scripture that was important, I did not note it at
the time. It was only later that I was able to find it again.
Being a man of science, I cannot explain the gold dust,
but that does not prevent me from rejoicing in it.

Since the day these men and women began to move into this new anointing, some of them now call me regularly, excited to tell me more of the miracles God is doing in their ministries.

I would not want to give the impression that only ministers are receiving this experience. Lay people of every description are receiving it as well, people like Mei Feng, to whom I was introduced by my friend Senator Stewart Greenleaf.

Mei Feng was born in China and comes from Shanghai. Several years ago, after coming to America, she was introduced to Jesus and was born again and baptized in the Holy Spirit She is a fervent Christian. In her professional life, Mei Feng is a scientist.

I prayed for Mei Feng, and now she, too, has golden glory that appears on her. At an important scientific convention, as she was speaking to colleagues about Jesus, the golden glory appeared on her, much to the amazement of everyone present. God is truly doing a new thing in the Earth, and, as always, HE IS NO RESPECTER OF PERSONS.

Chapter 7

A Winter and Spring of Signs and Wonders

Our Winter Campmeeting 1999 was glorious. Then, during the spring of the year, I did a number of conferences around the country, we did a Spring Women's Convention and a Spring Men's Convention at the camp, and we continued to do our weekend revival meetings. In every one of these services, at the camp, as well as in other places, gold dust, oil and miracles of gold teeth were witnessed. Here are some sample testimonies from that period:

Mary Hoffman, Merrill, Wisconsin:

> *A few years ago I heard about Ruth Heflin's book* Glory. *I got it and was so blessed by it that I purchased the rest of her books, and have been blessed by them as well. Many times I saw announcements in magazines or heard someone say that she was ministering somewhere, but I was always unable to go. This year, when she came to Wausau, Wisconsin, I attended both nights.*
>
> *The first evening Ruth explained about the gold dust and other signs and wonders. Somehow, I was not sure that I would get it, but I asked the Lord for it and told Him*

that I was willing to be a sign and a wonder for Him. When Ruth prayed, I received gold dust in my hands, a miracle that to this day has not left me. Every day it is on my hands and sometimes up to my elbows.

A few days after the meetings, I noticed that I had gold dust all over my purse, both inside and out. It is still there. It is on the dashboard of my car, I have seen it on my cat and in the carpeting in my home. On Friday of last week, I noticed quite a large piece of gold on the fireplace in the basement, although we haven't used it for seven years.

✳

Kathie Walters, Macon, Georgia:

A few weeks ago, I went up to Ruth Heflin's camp in Ashland, Virginia, with Joy Strang and a couple of other friends. The meetings were great. I had heard talk about gold dust, but I am one of those people who have to "see for myself," so I kept my eyes open. The second day, when Ruth ministered, I saw gold "stuff" shining all over her clothes and face.

Later, we went out to lunch with her, and I made sure I was sitting right next to her, like a foot away. Gold dust was all over her clothes and face and arms. It didn't disappear. It just stayed all over her during lunch.

That evening in the meeting I was too drunk in the Spirit to be all that observant, but at the end of the meeting, someone swept some of the gold dust on the pulpit onto my handkerchief. They said it would disappear in a day or so, but I prayed over it because I wanted to bring it

*back to Macon to encourage my prayer partners. I still
have it five weeks later.*

*When I was driving back to Georgia, I kept brushing
gold dust off my dress and coat all the way home (ten
hours). I took my coat to the cleaners the next day because I was going away somewhere else at the end of the
week. When my coat came back from the cleaners, it still
had gold dust on it. It is also still on the floor of my van,
even though I've vacuumed it.*

✳

Carol Schuster, Rockford, Ohio:

*Ruth Heflin was speaking at Hamilton Christian Cen-
ter, Hamilton, Ohio, at the Women's Praise and Worship
Conference. In one of the evening services, I saw a lot of
women facing one of the walls, examining the wall very
closely and wiping their hands all over it. I thought,*
What are those crazy women doing? *The next day I
asked someone what the women were doing. "Oh," they
said, "Gold dust came in the meeting last night, and it's
all over the wall."*

*I went and looked, and, sure enough, there was gold dust
everywhere. I took a Kleenex and wiped the wall so my
husband would believe me. I keep it in my Bible, and
every time I open it up and look at it, sure enough, it's
gold dust.*

✳

Rebecca Snipes:

*Thank you for being in the conference. I am in awe at
what God has done. I am still seeing the gold dust on my
hands. Yesterday I was at a friend's, and a power com-*

pany employee came. I was led to pray for him to get gold teeth, and he received them. How beautiful the Lord is to manifest to us His glory!

✳

Billie Watts, Phoenix, Arizona:

On September 25th, 1998, a friend from here in town was a guest on one of our local "Praise The Lord" programs. She had just returned from Sister Ruth Heflin's campmeeting. She brought with her a bottle of gold dust (more like gold flakes) from our Brazilian sister, Silvania. She told me that she wanted to anoint me and pray for me for the glory of the Lord and that God would give me the gold dust. I willingly submitted to her request.

We went into my office, and as she prayed, I fell under the power of God. She left right after praying, and I did not know what to expect. I knew that something would happen, but was not really sure what. I went about my business all afternoon, as I had work to do.

On my long commute home that evening, I noticed that my right hand began to feel sticky. I wondered what I had touched and what I had gotten on my hand. I looked at it, and, to my surprise, it appeared to be oily.

I was driving west on the freeway facing the sun, so the light was perfect. As I continued to look, I saw my whole hand sparkling with something. I looked at my left hand and saw nothing. When I got home, I called my friend. To my great surprise and delight, she told me that was the same way it had happened with her. First it came on her right hand, and later on her left hand and face.

I was so humbled and touched that God would bless me

in this way. I truly felt a change inside of me. I really cannot explain what I was feeling, but I found myself crying at the goodness of the Lord.

I was in the process of trying to move, and I well remember packing and weeping before the Lord. I cried out to him and told him "Lord, I have to have more of You. If I don't, I will utterly die."

I would drive home night after night, looking at my hands in amazement. I could not see the gold dust under just any light. It took high intensity light or sunlight.

On my drive home one evening, I heard the Lord speak to me and tell me to look in the mirror when I got home. I went into the bathroom and looked in the mirror. I saw gold on my face and neck, even on the inside of my eyelids. This was a miracle in itself. Until then, I had not been able to see gold dust on my hands in normal household light. Now I could. What a mighty God we serve!

In October of that year, my friend took me with her to Sister Ruth Heflin's women's conference in Virginia. What an experience! I began to weep as I entered the building, just standing in line for a name tag. I found myself weeping throughout the conference and searching my heart for anything that displeased the Lord. I did a lot of repenting because there was such a powerful presence of the Lord! It was so wonderful! All I can say is thanks to our wonderful Savior who has such awesome things in store for His children.

In April of 1999, my friend, Mary Jane Allen from Seattle, Washington, came to visit me. Mary Jane is the manager of the Trinity Broadcasting station in the Tacoma/Seattle area. She is a dedicated lady with a real hunger in her heart for more of God. We went to the station in the daytime and worshipped the Lord at night. Mary Jane is a marvelous musician. She is the pianist/ organist for her church. She was thrilled to hear the voices of the angels singing and to hear the instruments playing.

One evening in particular stood out in our minds. We had been singing and worshipping the Lord for some time. All of a sudden, I saw an angel come through the door. He was solid gold. His head, the helmet on his head or what appeared to be a helmet to me, was gold. His face, hands, clothing, feet and the sandals on his feet, were all gold. It was difficult to see where his sandals began and his feet were.

He came through the patio door, just walked through without opening the door. He walked to the little den just off the living room where the piano was and stood in the archway entrance to the room. At this point, I found myself on the floor on my face speaking in some strange language. Mary Jane was right behind on the floor on her face. I wanted to ask her if she saw him, but I was unable to speak a word of English. He stood in the doorway for a period of time and turned and walked out through the patio doors.

It was a while before I could speak again. Finally, I asked Mary Jane if she saw the angel. She said she did not see him, but felt an awesome presence. I am convinced that this angel comes straight from the presence of God as there is such an awesome presence about him. He is so holy that I feel just as Isaiah did, "I was undone."

My own reaction and response to his visits is difficult to explain and for me to understand. This alone convinces me that I indeed had a true encounter with this being.

One evening in late May, after praying with some friends, I went to the piano and began to worship the Lord. After awhile, I felt I really needed to get into prayer. Many times when I am seeking the Lord for specific answers, I get on the floor to pray, but this evening, I just sat in my chair. I began to pray in the Spirit and speak to the Lord of the things that were on my heart. The hand of the Lord began to touch my face, and I knew something was about to take place.

As I continued to pray, I looked up to see a big angel standing in the corner of the living room. He was stationed by the patio door as if he were guarding it or waiting for someone. At that time, I saw the golden angel that I had seen on another occasion. He just walked through the patio door just as he did before. He stopped and seemed to have a conversation with the other angel. I could see their lips moving, but could not hear what they were saying.

The golden angel then turned and began walking toward me. I really became "undone." My own reaction shocked me. I began making some kind of noise, but could not describe what I was doing. I remember that I was blowing, but do not understand why. I was aware of an awesome presence, just as I was previously, but at the same time was terrified. When he stopped in front of me, he stretched out his right hand toward me. He simply opened his fingers and gold dust began to fall. Then he wheeled around and disappeared through the patio doors as before. I sat, stunned, not understanding what had just taken place.

When I finally recovered, I thought about the gold dust that I had seen falling through his fingers. I had been seeing gold dust and platinum on my hands, arms and face for several months after my friend had prayed for me. I wondered if any of it had fallen on the floor. There were no lights in my home bright enough to see the gold dust, but then I remembered a flashlight that I bought several months before. I ran to the closet and picked up the flashlight. I looked at my hands and could see the gold and platinum on them. I sat back down in the chair and looked down at my feet, (I had been walking around barefooted), and was surprised to see gold dust on my feet, even on my legs. It was also on the carpet all around the chair where I was sitting.

I believe the gold is a reflection of God's glory. My friend has seen what we believe is the same angel, and he spoke to her twice and said that the wealth of the wicked is laid up for the righteous. This leads us to conclude that God is going to supply the finances for all of His ministers who have pure hearts before Him. I praise God for this wonderful visitation.

✳

Darlene Burkey, LaPorte, Texas

This past Saturday, March 13, 1999 at Lakewood Church in Houston, Texas the glory dust appeared. On our way to a Joyce Meyer conference, we were listening to the tape I had gotten when Sister Ruth Heflin was at Christ's Church in Texas City. We arrived at the church early and, sitting in my seat, I began to read Isaiah 52. I gave the Bible to my sister to read, and she discovered that the glory dust was appearing on the page I had open, as well as on the cover of my Bible. Then we began seeing it on our clothes and on our hands and other places around us.

I circled the places where the glory dust had fallen on the page in Isaiah 52. It said: [Therefore My people shall know what My name is and what it means; therefore they shall know in that day that I am He who speaks: behold, I AM! How beautiful upon the mountains are the feet of him who brings good tidings, who publishes peace, who brings good tidings of good, who publishes salvation, who says to Zion, Your God reigns! (Isaiah 52:5-6, Amplified)] [So shall He startle and SPRINKLE many nations; kings shall shut their mouths because of Him; for that which has not been told them shall they see, and that which they have not heard shall they consider and understand. (Isaiah 52:15)]

✳

Taveau D'Arcy, Midlothian, Virginia:

All of the people at the Mahesh Chavda conference were profoundly affected by your speaking. It moved the entire conference to a higher level. It would not have been the same if God had not sent you there. Mahesh himself was visibly affected. He staggered around like he was drunk, repeatedly mentioning "the glory" and "Ruth Heflin" at each one of the following meetings that day. The next day, at the first meeting, the gold dust appeared on Mahesh. He was like a child. You could sense how amazed and tickled and pleased he was. He even anointed everyone on Saturday night for it. Many others received the gold, including a group of seven from Chambersburg, Pennsylvania, who had it appear when they ate at Bojangles.

A big move of God began when you came, and it continued in every meeting until the last one of the conference. I had to preach in North Carolina on Sunday, so I did not go to the Sunday meeting there, but I heard that Mahesh put a red line down the center of the church and instructed everyone to cross over the line into the new thing on November 15, as you had been shown by the Lord. I was led to do the same thing in the church in which I was preaching.

Sister Ruth, many thanks for you and your giving out to the Body. I am so thankful for the many impartations that I have received through your ministry, I will never be the same.

Dolores Liberi, Raleigh, North Carolina:

The gold dust has continued to appear, off and on, on the palm of my hand, as it started to manifest during the convention. It is very light and has red dust mixed in. I brought Sister Silvania's testimony back, when I was at Camp in January and sent it to several states and encouraged many to watch. There are those who quickly believed and, of course, those who did not. Your comment that God has sent this miracle to "stretch our faith" really stirred me and this truth is setting us free. It has been a confirmation that we needed. I have found a safe haven in this Earth for a time such as this. Thank you for the camp.

Linda Pry, Houston, Texas:

The Tuesday morning meeting at Braeswood Assembly of God in Houston, Texas was wonderful. We all saw the manifest glory appear as gold glitter on a set of artificial plants located on the steps of the stage from where you spoke. I noticed a puzzling look on your face when you said something like, "I don't know why, but for some reason the gold is beginning to fall, but only on these artificial plants." Your expression stayed with me, and later the Lord showed me more.

The Lord has me constantly observing the spiritual parallels to that which occurs in the natural (from the very simple to the very complicated). The issue of the gold and the artificial plants would not leave my spirit. It wasn't long before the Lord showed me that the plants represented the church, the artificial church with its artificial Christians. God showed me that He was going to touch them with His glory.

At the conclusion of your lesson, many gathered to observe, some approached the glory, some wanted to touch the glory, some wanted to worship the glory, some denied the glory, some doubted the glory, some, with legalistic and religious hang-ups, were insulted that they could not explain the glory. It was of great interest to me to see all this.

✳

Joanie Grace Schultz, Stevens Point, Wisconsin:

Thank you so much for your ministry in Wausau, Wisconsin, April 12-13, 1999. I was able to attend, praise the Lord, and something strange happened. My friend rode with me there, and as I was taking her home, she was wishing that she had received a gold tooth or gold dust, but was just so blessed that I had told her about the meeting and that she could attend. "If God wants me to have gold fillings," she said, "then He'll make sure I have them."

I dropped her off at her home, and as I was driving to my house, she called me on my car phone to say, "The Lord is faithful! The Lord is faithful! I have three gold fillings. My husband and teenage daughters were waiting for me when I got home because they wanted to hear all about what the Lord did at the meetings in Wausau. When they heard about the gold teeth, they suggested that I look in my mouth, and there they were!" That was only one part of the miracle.

This lady is a mother of small children, as well as teenagers, and the next day was one of those "spilling-things-on-the-kitchen-floor days," and four times that day she had to get out the broom and sweep the kitchen floor. On the fifth time, she swept up something that turned out to be "this gold thing," which she described as looking like some letter of the Hebrew alphabet.

She is a "home schooler" and has resources at her disposal, so she looked it up, and, the best she could decipher, it seemed to be the Hebrew letter shen. *Later, a lady from our church heard me telling this story in a home meeting we started (so that we could share with each other the testimonies of what the Lord did for each of us at the women's seminar you did in Wausau), and when I said this, she said that she studied Hebrew letters and would do some checking. She did and told us that the lady was right.* Shen, *she said, means TOOTH! By putting His gold in our mouths, the Lord is purifying the mouth of the church,*

Another lady friend of mine from church received all gold fillings in her mouth. She didn't know they were there for a while, until one day she and her husband were talking about this miracle. They looked into each other's mouths as a joke, and were surprised by what they found. At first, she didn't believe him and called for their teenage sons, who confirmed that she had gold fillings.

The owner of the house where we have been having these weekly meetings was recently slain in the Spirit in a powerful meeting. The next morning, when he looked in the mirror, he discovered three gold fillings.

Thanks so much for your ministry.

✻

Jean Kincaid, Ada, Oklahoma:

When I got back to the hotel on Saturday night from your meeting, I had another gold filling. I prayed for the Lord to complete the work, and Monday on the way home I stopped at a friend's house where she discovered an additional gold filling completed and another further back which was turning to gold. It appears now complete. The six gold fillings I already had (five by the dentist and one by a miracle this summer in Ft. Worth) were all brightly polished and shining in the light when examined. I'm believing God for two or three more gold fillings, then all of the fillings will be gold.

When I stopped at the airport ATM for money on the way to the convention, the airport ATM was not working. I had left all my cash at home. There were only three or four quarters in my purse. All weekend long, when I'd start scrounging for change for soda, I'd find a few more quarters. At one point, I counted seven quarters, which I proceeded to spend. When Brother Keith took us to the airport I searched through my purse and found four more quarters. On my return to Oklahoma City, while driving the two hours to Ada, I became hungry. I searched through the purse again and found eight more quarters to buy a burrito. The money kept multiplying. Thanks for a great convention.

Leeon Middleton, Nederland, Texas:

I first received the touch from God, and the manifestation of the gold dust, during a Thursday night meeting at the Triumph Church in Nederland, Texas, with Sister Ruth Heflin. I only noticed three or four sparkles of gold dust that night. Two days later, on Saturday afternoon, I was sitting in the car waiting on my wife, Ginger, when God spoke to me and said "Leeon, put your hands into My bright sunlight and see all the gold dust I have given you. I want you to use it as a witness tool and tell My children that they are more precious to Me than gold. Tell them I love them so much and then lay hands on them if they want to receive this, and I will manifest My gold dust." Since that time I have witnessed to many people and everyone I have laid hands on has received this manifestation of God's glory, the gold dust.

I laid hands on my thirteen-year-old daughter, Erica, and she received a lot of gold dust, even on the tops of her hands. She was so excited as to what God was doing she went to a softball game that night and showed the other girl softball players what had happened. She laid hands on them, and they all received the gold dust too.

Another time I had talked and witnessed to a lady in our church about the gold dust. God told me to tell her, "I don't have to lay hands on you, God is manifesting His glory, gold dust, on you right now." I told her to look at her hands in the bright sunlight and she had gold dust all over her hands. Hallelujah! Isn't God awesome?

A few weeks later, God sent me and some other people to a church in Willis, Texas. God's glory was falling upon this church in an awesome way, with miracle healings, gold dust everywhere and gold teeth. Many people were receiving whole gold teeth and fillings turning to gold. It was just awesome. I went to that church six days straight. Three days after coming home, I was looking in the mirror with a flashlight to see if I had any gold teeth yet, and I didn't have any. All my fillings were silver looking. I prayed and said, "You did it for them; I believe You'll do it for me." When I awoke, some of my fillings were gold.

The Lord has been awesome and has given me some powerful witnessing tools to use.

✳

God was doing an unusual thing, and it left many amazed. In March of 1999 I ministered in Houston, Texas. On the way to the meeting the last evening, Pastor Buddy Hicks said he received a phone call in his car from his daughter. She said, "Daddy, you know the Spanish lady who cleans our church? She came into the office just a few minutes ago and had gold dust all over her face. I asked her where she had been, and she said, 'I only clean sanctuary. I only clean bathrooms.' I asked her again if she had put sparkles on her face, and she said, 'No, I only clean sanctuary,' but her face was covered in gold dust."

One lady from Hawaii, a Japanese sister, called her son from one of the meetings and was telling him about the gold dust on her.

He said, "Oh, those people are just manipulating that."

She answered, "No, they didn't come near me."

He said, "They're putting it through an air-conditioning system. That's the reason it's coming on everybody."

She tried to tell him it wasn't so, but he didn't want to listen. Later, when she opened her purse, there was gold dust scattered around the inside of the purse.

This Japanese sister is a giver and has been supporting a number of ministries. She had asked for prayer that God would enable her to give $100,000 a month, and then this wonderful sign of gold dust came on her and was scattered throughout her purse. How good the Lord is!

Another young sister came to one of the meetings where I was ministering in Houston. After the meeting that morning she went to Montgomery Ward to get herself a vacuum cleaner. As she was standing in front of the salesman, he noticed gold dust on her face and asked her about it. That gave her the opportunity to witness to him. He was backslidden, and before it was over, he had come back to the Lord.

She went downstairs to the shipping dock to pick up

her vacuum cleaner, but it had not yet arrived. A clerk from the shipping dock went upstairs to see why. When he saw the salesman upstairs, he asked, "Where did all that glitter on you come from?" As a result of this manifestation, he got saved too.

The sister finally got her vacuum cleaner, and she went home very excited about what God was doing. Here is her testimony in her own words:

Rosalinda Villareal, Houston, Texas:

> I attended Ruth Heflin's meeting at the Braeswood Assembly of God church in Houston on March 2, 1999. I had heard about the manifestation of gold dust appearing in her meetings and was excited about being in the presence of God's glory. I had not read any of her books nor did I know anything else about her ministry prior to that meeting. I purchased two of her books and noticed that she was at the other end of the table signing. I stood in front of her to get my book signed.
>
> Just then, Ms. Ruth stopped and said, "The glory has begun to fall." I looked at the tablecloth where she was indicating, but I didn't see anything. Then I noticed a speck of gold dust shining like a diamond on her purple suit. Suddenly I knew I was in the presence of God and that this was to be no ordinary meeting.
>
> We began to praise and worship God, and there was such joy and liberty present that we were all dancing. It was wonderful. Then Ms. Ruth took the podium and began to speak. The more she spoke the more she sparkled, and the glory had fallen all over the silk plants in front of the podium. We could touch it and put it on us. We all got

very excited. Eventually most of the women were covered with gold dust, looking like diamonds, shimmering and shining ever so beautifully.

After the meeting I went to Montgomery Ward to buy a vacuum cleaner. The salesman, Carl Davis, noticed the gold dust on me and I was able to witness to him and he came back to God.

He rang up my sale, and I went to the customer pick up area to get it. Another salesman, Kenneth, offered to carry my vacuum cleaner to the car for me, but he had to go back upstairs and find out what was delaying it. The next thing I know Carl came running down carrying my vacuum cleaner under his arm and calling out, "Where is that lady?" When he saw me, he came over very excited and told me, "When Kenneth came upstairs, he said, 'Man! What is all over your shirt?' It was gold dust, and you didn't even touch me."

I turned to Kenneth and began to witness to him, and he got saved that day.

Praise God!

Two days later I was in the Children's Castle, teaching the four-year-olds. Before class I was sharing with the other teachers what had happened in Ruth's meeting. Ramona came in and got in on the conversation. There was great excitement in the class, and it increased when suddenly I noticed gold dust on my left hand. I began praising God. When Ramona looked at her hands, she had it too. The glory of God fell that night in the classroom and we danced before the Lord.

✳

Here are some other testimonies from the meetings in Texas:

Norma Powers Marlowe, Kingwood, Texas:

> *One day I fell outside my garage across some furniture. The edge of the furniture was against my ribs, and in struggling to get up, I injured my ribs severely. It hurt to breathe, and I could barely move my left arm. Excruciating pain continued through the rest of that day and night. Later that week, I was in West Columbia, attending a meeting of Ruth Ward Heflin. While she was leading worship, I was still feeling pain in my ribs until gold dust in the air began to settle on my clothing. No one laid hands on me or prayed for me, but suddenly I realized that I was totally healed.*
>
> *The pain was gone. I hit myself hard in the ribs with my fist, wondering why I was doing it, but there was no pain. I was healed. It was a miracle of God. To Him be all the glory!*

✳

Wendy Alexander, Kingwood, Texas:

> *I was in one of Ruth Ward Heflin's meetings. As we entered praise and worship, I closed my eyes and began to concentrate on the Lord, blocking out everything else. When we finished, about thirty minutes later, I looked at my hands, and they were covered with gold. I was so excited to know that God did the same thing in me that He had done in Sister Heflin. He is truly no respecter of persons!*
>
> *She was also sitting on the front row, and when I showed*

her, she was just as thrilled about it as I was. God is truly doing a new thing.

✳

Sister Deborah Peregrine provided the following reports from the meetings in Humble, Crosby and Texas City, Texas.

(Reports from Crosby, Texas)
Pastor Carol Lee had gold dust on her face for three days after the meeting.

Shirley Davis went across the street to tell her daughter about the meeting and how the gold dust appeared, and while they were talking, the gold dust appeared all over her daughter, Cindi Fregia.

Joan Savavia left the meeting and unzipped her purse and found gold dust all in the bottom of her purse. She showed it to her husband at home and gold dust appeared on him. He had not been at the meeting.

Agnes Spilhaggee had more gold dust on her forehead than anyone else.

Pastor Whitehead of the Methodist church saw the gold dust and thought it to be real, but he couldn't believe about "all that oil stuff" on people's hands. Back at his church, he was looking for a bottle of oil to anoint and pray for a couple. There was very little oil in the bottle he found, but then his hand became covered with oil. He wiped it off and it appeared again. Now he believes.

The pulpit and floor were covered with gold dust after Sister Ruth left. Also, on the book table a big sheet was folded four times to fit the table. When the sheet was picked up the table under it was covered in gold dust.

(Reports from Humble, Texas)

> *Pastor Buddy Hicks had a cleaning lady come in and clean the sanctuary between meetings. She was having a difficult time vacuuming the carpet, so she went to the office to ask Sherry Hicks, the pastor's daughter, about all the glitter on the carpet. She would vacuum and more would come back. With her broken English she related that there must have been some kind of party in there.*
>
> *Sherry Hicks gave Ruth her microphone to use and when she got it back, she wiped it with her hands and gold dust appeared on her hands. She wiped the microphone on her dress to clean it off, and the gold dust was suddenly all over her.*

✳

(Reports from Texas City, Texas)

> *Pastor Delber Herrin of Christ Church Fellowship took the gold dust and had it tested. The report came back that it was pure gold. The gold dust stayed on the banners in the sanctuary that were mounted to the wall for three months afterward.*

✳

A brother from Beaumont, Texas, attended the camp one weekend in the summer. He told me, "Sister Ruth, you were only in the church in Beaumont for one night, but Beaumont, Texas, is turned upside down. The children are having gold dust in the schools, and God is sending revival to all of Beaumont through the young people who are having the gold dust."

This is a new day, and we each have the privilege of

moving into similar signs and wonders and miracles. Believe for that sovereign move of God upon your life. Believe for the gold dust to be manifested on you. Believe for the supernatural oil to flow through you. Believe for it today.

Believe for the new things that God wants to bring forth in every service. Expect it. Look for it. See what God is bringing forth by His Spirit.

Chapter 8

Signs and Wonders in Summer Campmeeting 1999

The summer of 1999 was a summer of signs and wonders. In the opening services of our 1999 Summer Campmeeting, the Lord told us that we would have five signs in our meetings, and we had them and more.

We had the gold dust in every service, and sometimes it even came down as golden rain or whirled in the air about us. Not only the preachers experienced it. Lots of the people had it on them too, even children.

We had the oil, and more and more people experienced it — on their hands, on their faces or coming from their eyes. This sign always resulted in great miracles.

We had what seemed to be a heavenly rain. Droplets of water, a literal liquid, fell on us indoors without explanation. I felt it many times during the summer. It was not raining outside, so no rain was blowing in from the outside. It was falling from Heaven. That was a different sign, but we knew it was from God. He was doing it just for us. We were hungry, and He was responding to that hunger. We were ready for "the new," and He was leading us into it.

99

We had teeth and fillings turning to gold. Over the period of weeks, from July 2 until Labor Day, hundreds of people received gold teeth, and some of them received many gold teeth. People went home and consulted their dentists to make sure they had not had a gold tooth before, and dentists confirmed that the miracle was real.

We had money multiplying. This miracle happened twice the first time and then to other people afterward. Money supernaturally appeared in their pockets. By the time they had put their offering into the offering basket and returned to their seats, a bill identical to the one they had just placed in the offering was back in their pockets. As the people sowed into the glory, they received this divine multiplication. We were seeing signs and wonders, the new dimension to this revival.

With all of this, we also experienced many miracles of healing and many creative miracles. God had told us to have an expectation for "the new." We didn't know what He was going to do in advance. He was dropping an understanding into our spirits as we were meditating on Him throughout the day and throughout the night. We had not read about some new thing we were asking God to do for us. We were hearing directly from Heaven. If not, we would not have been able to believe God for it.

When He drops such a word into our spirits, along with that word comes the enablement, the faith to believe for what God is saying. No matter how unbelievable the things He is declaring may seem, when He is speaking them into our spirits, He wants us to begin to believe for them and move into them.

Each night the signs God gave us were a little different. One night the golden dust seemed to be suspended in midair in front of us. I felt that God was doing that to let us see it more clearly.

We keep fans on the platform to cool the speaker, and I had asked that they not be used the week Pastor Shattles was with us. I didn't want the gold dust to be blown off of him. He was so covered with it that I wanted everyone to see the miracle and be moved by it.

When the gold dust was hanging in the air, my first thought was that it must be because of the fans blowing. Later I realized that the fans had never been turned on. It was a little cooler that night, and we had not needed them. The fan of the Spirit was blowing the gold dust and keeping it suspended in midair so that we could see it.

News of what God was doing spread quickly and representatives from a number of prominent revival ministries around the country attended the campmeeting, both as observers and as participants. Newspapers and magazines sent reporters to gather facts for a story. The Richmond-Times Dispatch did several pages with color photos of Silvania's ministry in a Sunday issue. The Fredericksburg, Virginia, *Free Lance-Star* ran a lovely article as well.

Charisma magazine also sent a reporter to witness what God was doing and to interview us. Since Sister Jane was the first one to meet Sister Silvania in Brazil, I suggested that the reporter interview her.

A wonderful thing happened while the reporter and her husband were with us in the meetings. He received a gold tooth. He didn't notice it until they got back to their hotel that night and he was brushing his teeth.

The reporter herself had been determined to be open and simply report what she had seen. She very much wanted not to doubt what God was doing. She said that as she sat there, she began to see little flecks of gold dust coming on my face, and she said, "Lord, I don't want to doubt, let somebody near me have some gold on them so I can see." A moment or two later, a young teenage girl nearby began to have gold dust on her.

She was still praying, "Lord, I don't want to doubt." At that moment, she looked down and saw some flecks of gold dust on her own hand. She said nobody had been near her, and nobody had anointed her. It just happened sovereignly.

Over a period of several days, one of the newspaper reporters experienced the golden rain coming down, felt the mist of it on her, and when she went forward to give a ten-dollar offering, by the time she got back to her seat, she had another ten-dollar bill in the pocket where she had removed the first one. She heard four or five people telling that they had received the same miracle that day.

This was all so amazing because just about a year be-fore this we had been out there, more or less by ourselves, on this issue of the gold dust. We didn't mind that because we knew it was of God and that everyone else would soon be following. We didn't mind waving the flag alone for God's glory. Now, suddenly, the experience was becoming almost "mainstream," as thousands of Christians everywhere moved into it.

All summer long, our camp was filled to capacity and during the final days the Tabernacle was full and the parking lots were full, making me know for the first time that the expansion program of the camp meeting facilities we had envisioned was much too small and would have to be reconsidered.

To better get an idea of what God did during Summer Camptime 1999, let me share with you some selected phrases from letters and e-mails we received and from testimonies given on tape during the campmeeting:

Dale Hood, Dallas, Texas:

> *This past July Linda and I arrived at the Calvary Pentecostal Camp in Ashland, Virginia, for a few days of revival and refreshing. We experienced a tremendous visitation of the Lord during our time there.*
>
> *Pastor Bob Shattles from the Atlanta area was the main speaker. The Wednesday service was powerful. Thursday evening, July 29, however, is when I personally received something which I did not expect, a solid gold crown on my right lower molar.*
>
> *At the close of his message, Pastor Shattles invited the congregation to come down to the front, and he began to pray and minister to the people. He called out various words of knowledge about specific individual health needs. Then he said, "Anyone having tooth problems or needing dental work, place your hands on your face."*
>
> *I wasn't in dire need in this regard or in any pain, but simply as an act of faith and obedience to the word of God that came forth, I placed my hands on my face. Brother Bob waved his hand across the congregation and prayed a simple prayer. I did not feel anything at the time. Afterward, I returned to my seat on the front row,*

and when I did, a sister asked me if I had received any gold teeth. I had forgotten about it and responded, "Well, I haven't a clue," so she looked, and there it was, as gold as could be. It had been an old grey-looking crown, but it was now turned pure gold, and it still is. Praise the Lord!

After this happened, then I really felt the powerful presence of the Holy Spirit come all over me. I asked the Lord what this really meant. What was this for? I said, "Lord, why am I to go around showing people my old ugly mouth?"

The Lord replied, "That My beauty may be seen!"

Praise His wonderful name! To God be all the glory!

Donna Clark, Camden, New Jersey:

During the summer of 1999, I was attending the Summer Campmeeting in Ashland, Virginia. I volunteered to clean Sister Ruth's house, and while I was cleaning her bedroom, I noticed gold dust on everything. It was even under the bed. I began to sweep the floor, and the more I swept it up and took it out of the room, the more there seemed to be in its place. It was an awesome experience!

I decided to mop the floor, but even after I had mopped, the gold dust would come shining through.

After camp had ended and I came home to New Jersey, gold continued to appear all around me — on my bed, on my shoes, in the car — everywhere. Before this, I had only experienced it and seen it on others inside the Tabernacle. Now God is raining it down all around me. I thank God for this miraculous impartation.

Carolyn Hall, Dale City, Virginia:

> *I just wanted to express thankfulness for the glorious weekend (12-15 August) my husband and I experienced at the Campmeeting. We learned of you through my friend who is a member at Pastor Eva Evans church. We had already purchased and passed out Silvania's videos before we saw her for the first time at the service (on Friday, the 13th). We were even more blessed to be eye-witnesses ourselves. We were sitting next to the lady who received the four or five gold teeth at the Saturday evening service. She was gracious enough to let us peer into her mouth.*
>
> *On Saturday morning, a prophecy was given that God would be healing several specific ailments, among them, sinuses and pituitary glands. I went forward for my sinuses, which had been getting worse over the past seven or eight years. When Sister Jane released the anointing for healing, the power of the Holy Spirit hit me, and I buckled to the floor. When I got up and returned to my seat, I immediately noticed that I was breathing more freely.*
>
> *I have not had a headache or gotten that yucky feeling that my sinuses usually give me. Prior to that morning I had been taking medication for my sinuses, but I have not had a pill since then. I have not had a headache, no yucky feeling, no breathing problems. I AM HEALED! I am so awed by this great move of God and the anointing of the Holy Spirit at Ashland. We had not originally planned to stay through Sunday, but we could not leave and did not want to leave. We will be back! I have not stopped burning up the phone lines, e-mail lines and*

people's ears telling the testimony of God as we witnessed it in Ashland. I want so much for those around me to get into the river of glory as we have. May God continue to bless you.

✳

Lonnie Cunningham, Atlanta, Illinois:

We wanted to first personally thank you for the wonderful hospitality that we experienced at Calvary Camp on Labor Day weekend. We enjoyed being with you in your home also, and will never forget your love and kindness. I first began to experience the gold dust when Sister June McKinney visited us.

She arrived in Illinois Mother's Day weekend this year for three meetings in my church. I have known her for over fifteen years, and she speaks in our church on special occasions. I know her ministry, and also her personal integrity. She had previously told me about sitting in to soak up the blessing in Brunswick, Georgia, under Pastor Bob Shattles' revival. I just listened, but when she arrived at the airport, she had gold dust all over her face. Knowing that Sister June would never feign anything like this, we allowed the Holy Spirit to show us His glory in the services. He was awesome, and His presence was beautiful.

Also, gold dust appeared on two babies in the church (one was in the nursery, and one in the co-pastor's home). It also came on me (the pastor) and on a friend of mine who pastors another local church in our area. It fell on the altar, on him and also on different members in our churches.

I have now experienced this wonder upon my clothing

in silver, during prayer, and also on my Bible, when reading it. It has fallen in my home in unusual places and upon my grandchildren.

Our ministry includes inner-city street ministry, and we felt called to fly to Eureka, California, to encourage the pastors of a church there to go to the streets. When we arrived, I shared with the pastors about the gold dust. They were skeptical, so I left it alone. Then it fell in their bedroom, on a comforter, and also in the car of one of the members of the church. It was very plentiful and beautiful and looked more like nuggets than gold dust. Those pastors were so touched that they flew from California to your campground in Virginia and spent the weekend there. They know that this experience is real.

I and a friend of mine also went to CPT that weekend and that was when we experienced the wonderful love and glory. When we were returning home the day after Labor Day, we went to the airport in Richmond and returned the rental car, and then as we walked through the airport, we saw gold dust all over the airport floor everywhere we walked. It was especially thick at the departure gate. When my friend returned to her vehicle at my home, she found gold dust inside it.

I constantly stand amazed at this wonder and the fruit that it brings. There are many wonderful testimonies from all over the world that magnify the Lord. From observation, I see this as a tool of harvest, soulwinning.

✳

Nancy Manno:

I was at your camp in August of this year, and while I was there the Lord showed me something very interest-

ing. When Solomon was putting the temple together, God showed him to place an altar of pure gold in it. Jesus said that we would reap what we sowed. We are now the temple of God, and anyone who will raise an altar of praise and worship before God will receive, poured out, all that Solomon sowed into the Temple dedicated to the Lord in Jerusalem by Solomon.

My husband had the gold tested, and it came back pure.

✳

Jennifer Prill, New Providence, New York:

Last spring I attended the women's retreat and was profoundly blessed by the Lord's glory. I petitioned the Lord to heal me of my bulimia, an eating disorder that I have had for twenty consecutive years (purging every day up to ten times). I wasn't healed during the conference, but twelve days later I was completely healed (body, mind, and spirit). The Lord reminded me of a prophecy one of the sisters gave at the conference: "In twelve days, your breakthrough will come." The past six months since my healing I have been in the river basking in His glory.

To top things off, when I attended the last week of Summer Campmeeting, the Lord overlaid my teeth in a silvery-gold substance. It was a profound witness to my dental hygienist, and I pray that God will use my teeth to draw my dentist to Jesus.

I praise Jesus for your ministry and your commitment to worship and to obey Him at all times!

✳

Bob Coll, Arlington, Virginia:

On July 25th I was headed to military reserve duty in

Hampton, Virginia, from my home in Arlington, so I passed through Ashland. I thought I would call to see if I could find the campground I had heard about over the years on Sid Roth's radio show. I had heard both you and your brother speak on his show.

I had also heard about the gold dust and had even had it on my hand at a church in Fairfax, Virginia, when Sister Jane Lowder and other sisters from the camp came there. Gold fillings and healings came that night, too.

I had also met Rev. Eva Evans who told of having you minister in the Pentagon. I was so blessed to think of someone manifesting holy gold dust at the Pentagon and worshipping in the Spirit there.

Someone asked me if I had been to any of the meetings in Ashland, and I said no, but thought, "I ought to go; it's so close." I had driven over a thousand miles to get to revival meetings in Tampa and Brownsville.

I called the camp and someone told me that Rev. Bob Shattles was going to be ministering that night. I had spoken with some friends in Fort Worth who had mentioned him associated with the gold flakes, so I stopped and came over to the Summer Campmeeting.

I was amazed at the volume of gold that was on Pastor Shattles' maroon jacket as he sat on the platform and was disappointed when he took it off because I wanted to see more of the gold on it. After he took off the jacket, however, the gold covered the shirt he was wearing under it. Blessed by the meeting, I went on to Hampton so I could go to work the next morning.

Then on the 27th of July, after having worked that day and still feeling the joy of the Lord from the Sunday night meeting, I was on my way to a gym to work out, when I felt in the Spirit an urging to go back to Ashland. At first I resisted because I knew I would get back late and had to work early the next morning, but I also knew that voice.

If I was going to get there in time for the meeting, I would not have time to go back to the base and change clothes, so I stopped at a WalMart and bought a pair of jeans and headed to Ashland. On the way, as I was praying, the Lord told me that because I had gone He was going to bless me.

When I got to the campground, I sat in about the third row of the Tabernacle on the extreme right facing the stage, and soon I noticed that all the people in the seats near me had gold flakes and dust on their arms, hands and clothes.

After a glorious meeting, Bob Shattles and some helpers prayed for people, and I got in line. After they prayed, one of the brothers held up a gold covered palm in my face and grinned, and I grinned back. He rubbed his hand around my chest, and as I went down on the floor, I heard someone saying, "Look, it's all over him." I didn't know they were talking about me until I began to get up. I had been covered with what looked like diamond shavings, the same thing that covered Rev. Shattles that night.

Sister Lowder had told of people who found a twenty-dollar bill in their purse, then gave it in the offering, only to have it appear again. When I got back to Hampton I noticed that a twenty-dollar bill had been placed in my empty wallet. Hallelujah! I was so blessed by that. The Lord had spoken, I had responded, and He had indeed blessed me. I felt very special.

Since that time I have been to many meetings at the camp

and am always in the powerful anointing present in the meetings.

Last week I was riding in the car with my wife and two kids toward the Skyline Drive. My wife asked me to pray for her neck. As I put my hand on her neck, I was urged by the Spirit to declare that gold dust would manifest in the car. Suddenly my wife's face – her cheekbones, around her eyes, and in the hair around her temples – was filled with gold dust. It lasted all day. She said it showed her that the Lord knew about her situation and that He was present.

✳

Laura Moore, Ashland, Virginia:

On July 28th and 29th, during Summer Campmeeting, Bob Shattles was our evening speaker, and I was one of the backup singers. During the praise and worship that evening, I was not looking for the gold to appear. I was just worshipping the Father. At the end of worship, one of the sisters nudged me and asked if I knew I had gold on my arms. I told her I didn't, but I looked, and both of my forearms were covered with shiny gold. I was told that there were flakes of gold scattered on my face also.

✳

Catherine Bruette, Baltimore, Maryland:

The Sunday afternoon after Silvania left this last time, while we were worshipping, I had a gold fleck on my right hand. Shortly after that, I was coming out of the bookstore and noticed gold coming out of the pores on the palms of both of my hands. What a wonder our Lord is!

✳

Sarah Jean Coles, Boston, Massachusetts:

The Lord woke me this morning with the realization I could not leave the campground without giving you the story of Irene Murphy's healing from liver cancer. After the placing of a handkerchief with gold flakes on the area of her body where she was receiving treatment for her cancer, she continued her medication and treatment, but she became more ill. The doctors could not understand why the treatment was making her ill and decided to do more testing. As a result of this new testing, they found that the cancer had been reduced to a minuscule dot, hardly detectable, and they discontinued the treatment.

✳

Rick Renee, State College, Pennsylvania:

I came to one of your meetings on August 21, 1999, when Sister Silvania was there. My wife and I were very blessed. While I was there, the Lord told me that the gold dust manifestation is about Jesus' feet. At the time, I did not know what He meant by that. When we got back home and shared Silvania's testimony and talked about the manifestation of the gold, someone asked me what the significance of the gold was, and all I could say was that it was part of being in God's glory.

A lady preacher spoke at our church about the woman who ministered to the Lord by cleaning His feet with her hair. In her hair, she said, was all the dirt and grime that was on the road. The Lord showed me that now He walks on streets paved with gold. All those who minister to Him, like the woman in the Bible, will end up with that which is on His feet, in this case, gold. I hope this blesses you as it has me.

✳

Marguerite Guyton, Ashland, Virginia:

About February of 1999, gold dust first appeared on the back of my jacket during a time of praise and worship after a Sunday evening service. Sister Ruth had preached, she was singing, and we were dancing. Gold dust and oil were on my hands, arms and face during service and frequently after praise and worship.

One Sunday evening that spring, Sister Ruth was walking the aisles and laying hands on people. Oil and gold dust appeared on my head and my face, and my ears had little cups of oil and gold in them.

This summer, however, during summer camp, I got my greatest blessing. When David Herzog was ministering one day, he said that God was going to open for us a new realm in the heavenlies, and the angels would come with signs, wonders and miracles. Everyone shouted, and God's power and presence was all over me and in me. David said, "Run for your miracle."

Clara Nymeyer was sitting with me and said, "You have gold teeth."

I ran down the aisle and around the outside of the Tabernacle. Someone looked in my mouth and said, "You have gold in your mouth." I ran harder, leaping, dancing and praising God, showing everyone. I had eight gold teeth.

In August, while I was visiting my daughter and son-in-law in Florida, gold dust appeared on my face. Since last summer, I have been witnessing and showing the gold teeth God gave me, and it appears to bring conviction and a melting of hearts. It creates in others a hunger for a deeper walk with God.

✳

Jeanne McCord, Bechtelsville, Pennsylvania:

>*My husband and I attended the Winter Campmeeting in Ashland, Virginia, one weekend last February to be refreshed under the anointing, not knowing who would be there. When we inquired concerning available rooms at the campground, we were told they were all full because Silvania was there. We didn't know Silvania and had not heard of her.*
>
>*The first time I saw the gold manifest and fall from Silvania's hair I just wept. We heard her speak for five services that weekend and received prayer in each service. Each time I stood in line waiting for prayer, I wept. One night while waiting for prayer, the worship team sang "And the Angels Cried Holy" over and over for thirty minutes or more. God's presence was so precious and so holy to me.*
>
>*I remembered Sister Ruth saying, "When you go home, just call the gold forth." During the days ahead, I watched the videotapes and listened to the audio tapes of the services we attended. I worshiped the Lord and just basked in His presence, remembering all that God did that weekend and thanking Him. On the twentieth day, the gold began to appear on my face, particularly around my eyes and eyebrows. For the first two days, both gold and red flakes appeared. I was so excited to have it manifest on my body that I didn't wash my face for two days. I felt God say that, just like the manna, He would give it to me fresh every day.*
>
>*We brought some gold dust home in our Bibles to give to former members of a creative praise team, of which I had been team leader for seven years. We wanted to anoint*

each person with oil and gold dust and put some in their Bible on Isaiah 61, our mission statement scripture. Ten days after I started seeing the gold dust manifest, we met in our home with the former team members to show the video of Silvania's testimony and share the gold with them.

The following morning I was about to make a phone call. As I pulled our church directory out of the drawer, I noticed there was a dusting of gold flakes all over two of the pages. I was very surprised and excited. I was to attend a women's leadership meeting that afternoon and decided I would ask the person in charge if I could show the video of Silvania and anoint the women with the gold. The next day, Thursday, I went to a local Aglow meeting and noticed gold flakes all over the steering wheel and dash of our car. That night two intercessors were at our house, and one of them noticed gold flakes all over one of our lampshades. They were too numerous to count. It seemed that every time I gave away the gold, more would appear in our house.

As I was preparing to attend an Aglow Regional Retreat that Friday and Saturday, I remember saying to the Lord that I had given out all the gold from my Bible. I didn't have any more to give away. I could take it off our church directory (but I wanted to save that to show our pastor) or I could try to take it off our lampshade. I just didn't feel led to take any from home, so I went without.

During the very first evening session, the gold manifested on my clothes, and on the palms of the hands of those sitting in my row. It appeared on all the handouts on a table near my worship flags. By Saturday morning, I was noticing gold and red flakes all over the hotel — on the floor, the chairs, on the people, on my flags. I saw it on the officers of the area board.

I sell creative praise products, and as I was showing some items to a lady, large flakes suddenly appeared on my hands. (I had told the Lord if I get it in quantities like Silvania I would put it in each bag with the flags I sell.) So the first five customers received gold flakes in the bag with each flag they purchased.

Sunday morning when I went into the prayer room I noticed I had iridescent flakes on the bottom of my feet and on my hands. I also had large red flakes on my right foot. As I was packing up the flags, banners, and items used in processionals, there was gold dust everywhere, including inside and outside the flag bags.

I returned home on Sunday around 6:00 p.m. from the weekend retreat. I went into our upstairs bathroom to remove my makeup, and I saw iridescent flakes all over the counter. They were so thick that I could write my name in them. It appeared as if 'Someone' had taken a bottle of glitter and sprinkled it all over the counter.

I spent the rest of the evening telling my husband, Gary, about the wonderful weekend I had experienced. He wondered why he hadn't experienced the gold appearing on his body yet. I said, "I think you need to repent of any doubt and unbelief." When he first saw the gold streaming from Silvania's hair he questioned if this was really from God because it was so unusual. After hearing her testimony and receiving God's touch through Silvania and Luiz, her husband, in ministry that weekend, he knew *this was truly a sign and a wonder from God. Before he went to sleep that night he repented and asked God to forgive his unbelief. When he awoke the next morning, God had put large gold flakes all around his mouth and chin. After he shaved and showered getting ready for work, all the gold was gone. I was sad that he didn't leave some of it.*

As he was getting dressed for work he called to me, "Hon, come and look at this!" He took his suit coat out of the closet and showed me the gold dust covering the right shoulder and sleeve. God is so wonderful!

A bigger surprise was yet to come. As I walked through our house the next morning, I noticed gold dust here and there. I was ecstatic. I began running to each room looking for it, and I found it in every room. It was randomly placed and different in every room. There were flakes on the wallpaper, switch plates, cupboard doors, window sills, furniture, inside drawers and cupboards, between the bedding and on room accessories. Our foyer room is decorated in a patriotic theme. It was interesting to find large red, blue, and silver flakes on the carpet and gold dust on the furniture, accessories and in the drawers. I am writing a discipleship manual on banners and creative praise. The gold dust was on various pages, in the folder, and on various resource material.

When Mt. St. Helens erupted years ago my sister-in-law, living in Oregon, commented that there was volcanic ash everywhere, even in the drawers. I remembered wondering if this was what it was like.

The biggest phenomenon was still to be discovered, on Tuesday, as I carried praise items down to our basement.

We live in a one-hundred-and-forty-year-old house with limestone whitewashed basement walls. I use the basement for a craft room that was cluttered, dusty and messy at that time. When I opened the door I immediately noticed green sparkles all over the steps. I could see fine gold and red dust on the shelves along the stairwell as I walked down the stairs. I saw green flakes everywhere and was so overcome with a sense of God's love that I started to cry. Because it was in green it was very noticeable.

As my husband and I were looking at God's miracle for us, we noticed that some of the gold flakes had clustered together to form small nuggets. We also found gold between the paper plates, on craft supplies, inside all craft boxes, inside books, between stacked books and stacked boxes and on centerpieces in the closed cupboards. We even had large green flakes on our sidewalk between the house and garage.

I'm still finding gold dust and flakes as I unpack items from storage, used cards and stationery and unroll bolts of fabric to make creative praise items. The following week after this manifestation in our house, I went shopping at a fabric store. I discovered gold flakes in many bolts of fabric that I was purchasing. It was so unusual and so noticeable that I called it to the attention of the clerk. She said, "Someone must have spilled glitter on the fabric," but I knew differently!

The flakes on the carpet have since been vacuumed away and those on the counters and pieces of furniture have been wiped away. Some new flakes continue to appear from time to time. There are still flakes in each room *around the house to remind me of that weekend when God decided to blow a rain of gold dust into our home. There is one section of our basement that I have purposely not swept. Each day since it first appeared on March 6th, I find the gold some place on my body. It seems to manifest more during worship and intercession. Many people have received the gold as we pray for them. Some have received the gold by just being in our house — stopping in for a visit. Those who stay overnight often wake up with the gold on their face.*

For the first three months I documented daily when and where I saw the gold. I was like a child in a candy store. Even to this day I get excited when I see one new flake, and I thank God for it. This experience most certainly has built our faith. We've seen the flakes in iridescent, red, blue, silver, light pink, hot pink and turquoise. I didn't know that gold could come in colors.

Besides the fine gold dust we also have seen small, medium and large flakes in our house. I have stopped documenting because it is so a part of our life that we see it regularly on our bodies or on our clothes, at home, in stores, motels, restaurants, conferences and workshops. We do not take it for granted, and we continue to thank God for manifesting His presence in such a special way. I wait in anticipation of what God is going to manifest next in our lives. We are believing for other signs and miracles.

At Summer Campmeeting God chose to turn my fillings into gold, silver and platinum. Since Summer Campmeeting, we have also seen larger pieces of gold thread 1/16 inch to 1/4 inch long. I have seen more of the silver dust on my skin and on others. When God's glory falls, people are encouraged and blessed and feel loved.

This September was the beginning of our 9th year in a creative praise ministry and teaching about the Restoration of the Tabernacle of David. After Summer Campmeeting, we changed our name to Zion's Glory, and it is our hearts' desire to truly be carriers of His glory.

✳

Billie Reagan Deck, Falls Church, Virginia:

I went to Summer Campmeeting 1999 in Ashland, Virginia, to rest after a difficult mission trip, and I received gold dust on the side of my face and later on my forehead. I had been experiencing a facial paralysis since returning from a mission trip to China, and I considered that the gold on my forehead was for a chronic sinus condition. Before going to the camp I had also experienced itching of the scalp and tingling in my face. After MRI and CAT scans were negative, I came to believe that these were preliminary to the manifestation of the gold dust.

When Silvania prayed for me, I was slain in the Spirit for over two hours, and when I got up there were gold flakes all over my right arm and shoulder. Some of the dust can still be seen on my blouse from that night. I experienced this manifestation in my room and on my clothes almost daily while at the camp. Once, while sharing with some friends in the reception office, I picked up a green and a red flake. Anytime God was being glorified He showered down His presence in a visible way.

One of the most significant appearances of the manifes-

tation occurred one Sunday in August as I was preparing to leave the camp. Sister Ruth had spoken. I went up on the stage to speak to a minister from Australia, and as I stepped down off the platform I noticed something gold on the carpet and picked it up. It was a golden thread. I went back up to show it to Sister Ruth, and everyone rejoiced because a prophetic word during the service had said that the Lord was mending broken hearts that day. As a sign, He had sent a golden thread from Heaven.

After another morning service my husband Al and I prayed for a Korean couple from New Jersey who had driven all night to get to camp. Two beautiful gold flakes appeared while we were praying for the young man to receive the baptism of the Holy Spirit.

In one morning service a shower of golden dust appeared in a section of the Tabernacle. The next day during the worship it fell again.

The week Brother Renny McLean ministered the gold manifested in each service. It appeared as dust, flakes, and gold teeth and fillings.

I was in the seat in front of Dolly Hutchison the morning she received her mouthful of golden teeth. That was also the service in which I received the miracle of multiplication of the money in my pocket. After giving my last bill in the offering, I was wishing that I could have had more to give. I felt impressed to look in my pocket and there found the same amount I had just given. It had been replaced in my pocket and I promptly gave that too. Then Brother Renny asked us all to turn to someone around us and give to others in the audience. The man in front of me gave me the same amount I had given again. I gave two offerings unto the Lord of all that I had and still had enough left over to buy tapes after the service.

Since returning from camp we have seen gold dust and flakes in almost every room of our home. It appears daily — in front of the washing machine, dishwasher, telephone, refrigerator, and coffee table, in the hall, the den and on my computer. Green and gold dust appeared on a book and tape bag I was packing for a speaking engagement. In the church where I am involved with the Intercessory Prayer Team, gold flakes appeared in front of the door as we entered the prayer room. During another prayer meeting, the manifestation appeared on the shoulder of a man I was praying for. In a Sunday night service, the glory dust appeared on the floor under my feet during the worship service and on the pew beside a friend who was writing out a check for the offering.

On the way to North Carolina to attend the wedding of a friend, gold dust appeared in our van while we were listening to a tape from the camp. During the wedding ceremony we asked the Lord to shower the couple with His glory. When we greeted the couple after the ceremony, the bride had the iridescent flakes all over her lips, and the groom had it on his chin. He said it was where she had kissed him.

I also experienced the oil on my palms and running out of my eyes.

The heavenly rain also manifested on me while I was slain in the Spirit my first night at the camp while Sister Ruth was preaching. These manifestations have brought such peace and joy to this servant.

We are continuing to experience this wonder of God's glory. As we returned from a visit with our children in Delaware, the flakes appeared in the van during the trip home.

A friend who was at camp with us has had manifestations of the glory on her hands when she plays her autoharp during times of private worship. She also had a flake of the gold appear on her paint brush when she was preparing a prophet's chamber in obedience to a word from the Lord received at camp. She came home and had the cable television removed from her home and finds her life more focused and balanced. She has given her home, family and talents to the Lord.

We have had the manifestation every day for over a month now. Just now, when we were coming home in the van, it was all over my clothes.

✳

James Baxter, Richmond, Virginia:

Some months ago I watched a tape that showed a lady with gold flakes falling from her hair. I was not sure about it at first, but as I checked my spirit, it seemed good. The lady was Sister Silvania from Brazil. She was invited to the campground in Ashland, Virginia, and my wife and I attended the services.

The first night I watched as she brushed her hair with her hand, and a stream of gold, blue and silver flakes fell from her head. As I sat watching, I greatly desired this manifestation because I felt that with this sign and wonder more souls could be won into the Kingdom.

I attended several seminars where the gold dust appeared,

but I did not personally experience it, and I wondered why. Was I doing something to displease God? I learned that the more one worships Him and talks of His signs and wonders, the more it happens.

On Labor Day 1999, I was again visiting Pastor Ruth Heflin. I took Dr. Clark and Brother and Sister Carlton William and their children to the meeting. Sister Ruth ministered to us that night, and I was blessed with the gold dust.

On Monday, September 13, I was discussing some business with Pastor Ruth. She prayed for me, and the gold dust appeared all over my face and hands. When I arrived home, my wife and son could still see it on me.

I am believing God for this to happen when I am at the store and on the street so that I can use it to proclaim the glory of God and to bring others into the Kingdom.

❋

Susan Merry, Anchorage, Alaska

Since Campmeeting 1999, I have had many wonderful experiences in God's glory. I got gold dust all over my body in all the colors of the rainbow: red, pink, orange, yellow, green, blue and purple. I looked in a new blue purse and saw a green speck and knew I didn't have glitter. Later I heard a lady tell how she found red, purple and green gold. Then I knew what it was. Since then I have had all the colors appear.

I have had fragrant oil appear on my hands and head. I have smelled the fragrances of Heaven.

Late one night, after campmeeting had ended, several of us ladies were talking in our camp dorm room about wanting gold teeth. A lady in the next room overheard us and came over to show us the gold tooth she had received and to pray for us. Three ladies got gold teeth instantly that night.

Two of my Jewish friends had all their black fillings turned to gold instantly in a prayer meeting.

I prayed for my mother that on her birthday she would receive dental surgery by the angels to fill patches and smooth fillings with gold. She received it all that very day.

From the campground in Ashland, I was speaking on the phone with a lady in Queensbury, New York. She received gold dust on herself, her husband and her baby as we spoke.

I prayed that people I saw in the supermarket would get gold. As I was talking to a lady in a supermarket office, a huge gold flake appeared on her forehead. My mouth was wide open as she smiled and said, "Have a nice day."

✳

Chris Jamison, Medford, New Jersey:

My friend Donna and I went to Ashland Campground, not seeking signs, but seeking to worship God. He told us when to go and for how long. We did not know Silvania would be there until after our plans were made.

The first time I heard of the gold dust was through friends who had just returned from a trip to Argentina with Cindy Jacobs and the Generals of Intercession. It was reported that gold dust was falling on the Argentinian intercessors as they prayed, so much so that they swept it up and had it analyzed. I was so excited and awed by this sign. How wonderful our God is to give us a tangible glimpse of Heaven, literally a piece of Heaven.

There are no words adequate enough to express how wonderful it is to be lost in worship, caught up with our Lord, wrapped in His arms, and to come down from those high heights only to find ourselves covered in gold dust — our faces, hands and clothing. One night there was even gold dust on my foot, under my stocking, and I had never taken my shoes off. When you swim in the ocean, there is a remnant of the salt water left on your skin, and when you dive into the river of God, there is a remnant of His presence left on you.

Donna and I just wept off and on for four days while in Ashland, as we found the gold dust on our faces and hands not just at the meetings, but in our room. In the morning while we worshipped, the gold would fall.

The oil also started to come onto our hands, Donna's right and my left, then both. The fragrance of the Lord lingered for hours. The gold just fell.

We saved some of the gold dust by wiping it up with tissues and placing it in our Bibles. After bringing the gold dust home and passing it on to others, many wonderful miracles have transpired. We have seen it multiply on Bibles right before our eyes. One couple was led to anoint a woman who is pregnant, and her level of amniotic fluid had dropped to a level of 7 from a level of 10. The doctor said she would have to have a C-section, that the fluid could not be restored naturally. This couple went to pray for her, anointed her with oil and with gold dust. Two days later the amniotic fluid was back up to a full level of 10.

Twice the gold dust has appeared on my face while telling people about it. Both times this happened we were in a public restaurant. Donna was sharing with others about Silvania and the gold dust, looked down at her hands and found them covered with the gold dust and some oil. As this report has been written, the gold has appeared on my face. We are so awed of Your love, Your grace and Your mercy, Lord. Thank You, Father.

✳

Judith Miller, Ashland, Virginia:

After Silvania was here in the fall of last year, I was really skeptical about what was happening. My first question was: "God, is this really you?" My next questions were: "Why is this necessary?" and "What is the purpose behind it?" The first time I experienced a gold flake on me was after a shower. My husband spotted it on the back of my leg, and was more excited about it than I was. I didn't know what to think of it, but there it was.

The next morning, as I was putting on my knee highs, I noticed many gold flakes around the toes of my left foot. This amazed me, and I wondered why God would put them there instead of on my face or hands. The more I looked at the flakes, the more they seemed to spread. They increased across my toes and even between them.

I finished getting dressed and didn't tell a soul about this experience. I still wasn't sure why God would do all this. I didn't want to come against what God was doing, but I also didn't want to appear foolish before others. I learned quickly that Ashland Campground is not a place to expect the ordinary.

Several weeks later, while sitting in the snack bar with some sisters, Sister Sandra Justus asked me if I wore eye shadow. My response was, "No, why?" She seemed to ignore my response for a few minutes and then came back with the same question again. "No!" I said again, "why?" Again she seemed to ignore my response, and when the other sisters left the table, she asked me the same question again. When I finally had convinced her that I never wore it, she said, "You have gold dust all over your eyes." It looked, she said, like brushed gold.

I thought she was seeing things, but she convinced me to go and look in a mirror. When I did, I was truly amazed. Sure enough, there was gold dust on my eyelids, under my eyes and all the way to the end of my eyebrows. That really was amazing. I wondered why.

After experiencing the gold in this manner, I began to look for it. For several consecutive days, I would see the gold dust all around my eyes. Most people wouldn't have noticed because I wear glasses, but I knew it was there, and I began to look for it on a daily basis.

"Why the eyes, Lord?" I asked Him. As I waited for His response, the Holy Spirit reminded me that twenty years previously I asked Him to anoint my eyes that I might see as He saw. Could this be the time of Him anointing my eyes? By this time, the gold dust was falling more frequently at camp and more people were experiencing it. One night, after washing the dinner dishes, I let the water out of the sink and then went to get a dish towel to dry my hands. When I looked down at them, I saw that gold dust was covering the palms and fingers of both

hands. I was excited and showed my husband. We both agreed that this was definitely of God.

I took my shower and didn't expect any more gold to appear, after all the water just washed it all away. Before I could get out of the bathroom, my left hand had the gold all over it again, and my right hand had the oil.

Something supernatural was happening, and I was getting excited, but I was still hesitant to tell my friends and family about it. I did it anyway, not knowing what to expect from them. Some of my friends just looked at me and asked, "What is the name of this place you are attending?"

One evening I went to get a pair of blue shoes from my closet and had difficulty finding them because they were buried under other shoes. When I finally found them and started to put them on, I noticed something sparkling on them. I looked a little closer, and there was gold dust in my shoes. It had gotten there while they were under a heap of other shoes. That experience truly amazed me, and I had to share it with many others. I simply could not keep quiet about that miracle.

On two different occasions, I went to get my sneakers from the closet, and as I lifted my orthonics from one pair to use in another pair, I was startled to find gold dust under the orthonics. That was a great faith builder for me.

The same day that happened the first time I went to press a jacket, and when I put it on the ironing board, I noticed something shining from it. I looked closer and saw flakes of gold all over it. I showed it to my husband and told him that I wasn't going to iron it or wear it; I was *going to preserve it as evidence of what God was doing, and I hung it back in the closet. I took out another jacket to press, and the same thing happened to that one. Gold flakes were all over the back of it and the sleeves of it. This one, too, went into my archives. But after I had pulled out the third jacket to press for that night's service, the same thing happened again. It was covered with gold flakes. I pressed it anyway, and wore it that night. When Brother Shattles was in the camp in the spring, one Tuesday night, as we were praising the Lord, Sister Janice Clark noticed gold flakes falling in front of Sister Ruth. Those of us who were on the platform that night got very excited and wanted to see more. God blessed me to see it. I was hurrying to where she told us it was falling, and the Lord allowed me to see an enormous amount of it. It formed a cylinder about ten feet in height about six to eight inches off the floor. The circumference of the cylinder was about as big as the circle I can form with my arms and hands, fingers barely touching. It was an awesome sight!*

All I knew was that I had to get in it. I saw where it was, stepped into the middle of it, raised my arms, and just turned around in the middle of it. When I stepped out of that spot, the teal-colored dress I was wearing was covered with the gold. God is so good! It was the most amazing event I have experienced with the gold.

I have been experiencing a gradual increase of the gold dust and oil as I worship the Lord. Last Sunday morning, as I was getting ready to leave home, I picked up a purse I don't normally carry and out fell a rock. I had carried that purse when visiting my daughter's family and my grandson had given me the rock as a memento (he always gives me something, a rock, a feather, a little box that I treasure). When I turned the rock over, I saw that it had gold dust on it. In that moment, I felt so much of God's love. I thanked Him and could not wait to tell some of my friends this wonderful miracle. God had put His gold dust in my purse and on the little rock as a reminder that He will take care of us — whatever life's circumstances may be.

※

Anna Marie Peereboom, Sussex, New Jersey:

I am a frequent visitor to the Ashland Camp. I come with two friends from New Jersey. Since the impartation by Silvania in February, the gold has been showing in my family in many small but precious ways.

While I was still at camp, I felt I should make a banner for a Spirit-filled church in New Jersey. When I returned home, a design came to mind. It was similar to your banner, but the world was magnified in size, and the glory was pouring on the East Coast, particularly on the tri-state area where we are praying for revival. Crystal hearts were then placed on Virginia, Pensacola, Toronto and New Jersey, with large words, "Pour Out Your Glory." As my daughter Michele and I were making the banner, we received gold on our cheeks. For this reason, we specifically did not use any gold or silver glitter on the banner at all. We used a golden net to look like gold was pouring on the East Coast. The humble minister anxiously received the banner, each week he hangs it, and each week, after the people praise and worship the Lord, silver and gold dust is found on the floor around the banner.

※

Michele Torpay, Kingsman's Ferry, Pennsylvania:

I am Anna Marie's daughter. Making the banner with my mother was my first experience with the gold. Since then, I visited the camp during Summer Campmeeting of 1999, and Silvania prayed for me.

We came home to a very hectic schedule with school starting that week. Although we live in Pennsylvania, we made the prayerful decision to drive our three children to a Christian school in New Jersey. We knew we were taking a leap of faith financially, not to mention the one-and-a-half-hour drive twice a day (on some days, it's three times). This proved to be very stressful, both physically and emotionally, for myself as well as my four-, five-, and seven-year-old children. Although I knew deep down that we had made the right decision, after only two days of "the ride" I began to wonder if it was really worth the torture.

The next morning all three of my children ran into my bedroom very excited to wake me up because they all had gold and silver "sparkles" on them. Although some might question where those "sparkles" came from, there is no doubt in my mind.

※

Hope Chapman, Inman, South Carolina:

I am a young pastor's wife from South Carolina who has been affected by your ministry mightily in the last year.

I had never even heard your name until last year, but now your name and your words will forever be embedded in my mind and spirit. You have guided me into a new level of relationship with our Father.

I never knew what walking in the glory was like until I began to read your books. I now have been teaching "Getting in God's Glory" at my church, and I use the precepts of your books. Afterwards, we actually put into practice what we have learned. These meetings have lasted hours, as we have "stumbled" into God's glory.

I have such a hunger to see people get closer to our Father and brush up against His glory. I am praying and believing for a great encounter for my church, community and state. I grew up as a pastor's daughter and, although I had strong Pentecostal roots, I never was told to pursue God's glory. I am believing for the latter rain to flood our churches. As my family has made efforts to get into the river of God, we have traveled to Brownsville, to Augusta, to Brunswick, and of course to Ashland. This past July, we were privileged to attend your campmeeting. I have attended campmeetings all of my life, but never have I experienced campmeeting on the level of yours. God stretched my family, as we witnessed the gold dust.

We spent hours debating and trying to explain why God would do this. Each night we would come and move a little closer into the river. We were thoroughly convinced on the fifth night we were there. Perhaps you may remember the testimony I gave that night.

My husband and I came believing for a miracle in our two-year-old son. He has had chronic ear infections since he was six months old. We were in the doctor's office almost every week with him, and it seemed that nothing was working. The doctors told us before we left for Ashland that he would need another set of tubes in his ears. Although this is a very simple procedure, I was not ready to put my son through another surgery, especially since the first set of tubes did not seem to work. We arrived in Ashland, believing for a creative miracle. We believed that God would supernaturally grow his eustachian tubes so that they would drain properly.

On the night our son was healed, you preached on "The Sounds of Glory." Toward the end of the service, as we were singing about the sounds of glory, my husband prayed that the sounds of glory would penetrate our son's ears and that he would be healed. Immediately, our son grabbed his ears and held on to them for several seconds. When he pulled his hands down, he had gold dust all over his hands and arms.

I testified that night, believing that God had healed him. Since that night, he has not had one ear infection.

It was through our son that God showed us that the gold dust was from Him, and since we have come home, we have experienced this manifestation regularly.

Pastor Shattles will be coming to our church in December, and we are looking forward to revival fire and glory. I am writing to thank you for who you are and how you let the Lord use you. You are an inspiration to me. I have been reading Harvest Glory, *and God is challenging me through your life's story and giving me a hunger for the nations. Because of you, I am beginning to walk in the glory. I never knew I could experience God in these ways. I am seeing visions, dreaming dreams, hearing God's voice, singing a new song and prophesying. Because of you and your teachings, our church has entered a new realm of praise and worship. We sat under your ministry and were anointed by you, and we have taken it to our church.*

Although you have never lost your figure due to pregnancy, or labored in pain in childbirth, or held your own likeness, or kissed the brow of your own flesh, you are yet a great mother. For you have carried many pregnancies, many times for longer than the usual nine months. You have birthed many revivals into the world and a mass of souls into the Kingdom. When I have looked onto the skies recently, I see your inheritance like that of Abraham, numbered with the stars. You have a large family — children that you will never know until you reach the portals of Heaven.

I am so deeply moved by you, your ministry, your books, your meetings. I have never felt so connected to someone. I have never sat across the table from you for tea, or reclined on my sofa with you as my guest, but you have discipled and mentored me and have assisted me along a most wonderful journey, which has led beyond the veil. Thank you.

✳

Mary Ellen Materna:

I attended the 1999 Summer Campmeeting at Calvary Pentecostal Camp in Ashland, Virginia, and sought prayer to take a bit of the gold dust so the Lord could touch my husband and autistic son when I got home.

Well, He touched ME first! He healed my broken heart, gave me a psalm-like poem about it and what He would be doing. This was amazing since I am not very musically inclined or poetic. He has given me joy and confidence, and I bubble over with people. Last night, when I was watching an anointed TV program, my hand began to shake and it got so strong that I staggered to the bed and silently prayed for my husband. Never has this happened before!

Also, I was watching a TBN praise program and heard the praise leader say, "Put your hands together if you love Jesus." I heard my nonverbal son get quiet and watched him push his fingers together. When the leader said it again, my son stopped rocking and stopped spinning something in his hand and pushed his hands together tightly and closed his eyes. I laughed and cried! What a present.

✳

Dina Michel-Jeune, Staten Island, New York:

Your teaching on miracles, signs and wonders has enlarged my faith. I only received my gold fillings at CPT Camp because you birthed it in me through your own faith. Keep speaking the gold till all believe and then speak it some more.

✳

Lori Brinshi, Fulton, New York:

On May 30, 1999, in the morning service at the Mexico Church of God, my pastor, Ron Russell, mentioned hearing a report about someone with a "gold filling." I immediately spoke with him after the service and told him that I had never heard of such a thing and wasn't exactly sure that this was godly. He and I agreed that we had explicit trust in each other's walk with God and that if such a thing occurred to either one of us, we would know it was truly a move of God. I spoke with a precious sister, Jeannie, on the phone that afternoon about that conversation with my pastor. Jeannie attends a church twenty-two miles away but has been an intercessor with me diligently for two years.

That evening was slightly unusual in this way: at the evening service, the pastor asked my daughter Marissa (18) to sing on the worship team with the adults. She had never done this before. My other daughter Mallori (16) was also asked to help serve communion. I began weeping profusely while I pondered seeing my two daughters serving God. Last summer, they both were missionaries to Venezuela.

When I got home that evening around 10 p.m. (we live sixteen miles from the church), Jeannie phoned me nearly screaming, "Lori, I have gold all over my hands. Lori, I have gold!" I immediately looked at my hands and began exclaiming the same thing!

I ran to my children, who were in their rooms preparing for bed, and they were covered in a fine gold dust as well: hands, faces, arms, legs, and chest. We all were marveling and speaking on the phone extensions at once.

I then made a conference call with all of us to my pastor, who was still at the church, and he announced that a couple of women had just shown him gold on their hands too. We all greatly wondered. None of us had ever heard of gold dust, just the one mention earlier in the day of a gold filling.

The next day was a Monday, and I went to a picnic with an acquaintance who often invites me to their family gatherings. I went swimming with the children in their pool and, after I got out and toweled my hands, the gold reappeared. I kept toweling, and the gold just kept popping back up through the pores of my skin. It truly was amazing.

My brethren were at first skeptical that this was from God — even though they saw the phenomenon. Later I received a call from a brother who was at the picnic, and he said he now sees the gold on his fiancee's hands. His first response had been to tell me I should see a doctor.

Over the next two weeks at school, where I teach Music, French and Drama for grades seven through twelve, I began to experience gushes of gold and oil. I was completely mesmerized and stared at my hands for hours. I wrote a note to a man I deeply respect, asking him if he had ever heard of this phenomenon. He said he vaguely recalled reading something on the Internet and urged me to put "gold dust" on a search engine and see if anyone was writing about this. He immediately drove thirty miles to see my hands and the steering wheel of my car, which was catching all the dust and glittered.

I found your website and devoured every bit of it. I knew I had to come to camp. Once I read about Silvania and the metal analysis and jeweler's statements, I almost exploded with joy. I realized I was seeing the manifest presence of God.

This past June, the gold was so glittering on my hands

that one day I literally ran through the halls of the school stopping colleagues and showing them. One student, Jennie, was with a teacher in the hall and told me that she has been getting "the same glitter stuff on her hands too!" I signed out of school and ran (literally) to the local jeweler's shop down the street. I showed her my hands. She definitely could see the gold but said that they would have to be bigger for her to test them. She told me to come back.

The next day I was staring at my hands in school again when another of my students told me he gets that often too. He showed me his hands, and he had a very fine dust of gold from his pores also. Neither of the students, to my knowledge, attend church but both have a remarkable rapport and relationship with me. I wondered if they received the gold when I did?

In July I attended the opening of Campmeeting at CPT, and on Monday night July 5, I prayed with the congregation with my hand on my mouth and asked for a gold tooth, as you prayed aloud. I returned to my motel in Ashland and checked my mouth. The next morning, I about screamed when I discovered that sometime during the night one of my fillings developed a gold streak or arch through it. My roommate confirmed the difference in my tooth from the day before. The next day I received a gold dot right in the center of another filling. I returned to upstate New York rejoicing.

In August I brought two of my daughters (the third is married) down to Ashland to see Silvania. On Friday night of that meeting, I was seated next to a woman who never saw any phenomenon like this. I showed her my hands and the children's. She wanted this, too. I told her to close her hands into a fist, I placed my hands over hers and prayed, asking the Father to give His blessed manifest presence, and when she opened her hands, there was a puddle of oil and gold. We both wept and wept.

I returned to New York that weekend and saw that Silvania was going to be at a meeting in New Jersey on Wednesday, August 18. Toni Greurio, a funeral home director and friend of Silvania's, was hosting the private, invitation-only meeting. When I phoned her to ask about attending, she informed me that it was private. A few minutes later in our conversation the Lord told her to invite me and my three guests (Jeannie and the two women from my church who have the gold) to be the intercessors for her gathering. We traveled to New Jersey and met our precious sister personally, and we interceded for the meeting as well.

I returned to CPT for the last week of Campmeeting. Many glorious restorations in the miraculous occurred as Renny McLean preached. During one of the meetings, I went to the platform to declare a miracle of restoration in my life. Since those meetings, one such notable miracle of restoration has taken place.

On January 1, 1998, I was in a severe auto accident and the C5 vertebrae of my neck was separated. This was extremely painful and required daily or semi-daily medical attention with chiropractors and physical therapists. One day a pastor called and suggested that I attend a healing service in his home. There were just a few of us present. After three hours of prayer, I was instantly healed, and was able to take the neck brace off forever. This miracle

*was documented by the doctor, who at first couldn't be-
lieve it and had me come in three times the next week
just to keep verifying the healing.*

*My daughter was also healed of the results of a serious
accident in which she suffered a fractured skull, chipped
tibia, blown apart eardrums, concussion, broken foot,
stitches, cuts, bruises and staples in her head. Every one
of her eight doctors, all specialists, declared her healing
miraculous. All of them had predicted that it would take
at least six months for her to recover from the accident.*

*I was at the doctor's office two weeks ago for a routine
yearly mammogram and was testifying of God's miracle-
working power for my daughter, when the technician
began to double over and declare the presence of God was
so strong she could no longer function. She began to
weep. Although we were in the middle of the x-ray process, I went to her and began to pray. We were detained
about an hour and twenty minutes, as God's glory filled
the room.*

*As I left the room, I saw a very ill man seeking medical
attention. The glory of God was so great that I began to
preach to him, and he came weeping to repentance and
was gloriously saved.*

*I went to the hair salon, and the women that work there
had heard about my experiences with the gold. I showed
them my hands and teeth and prayed for them, and they
were slain in the power of God right there in the salon.
One of them, my own hairdresser, came to church this
past Sunday with her estranged husband, who is in a
drug rehab center, for healing of their marriage.*

✳

One day during campmeeting, Brother James Baxter brought Dr. Elsie Clark to visit me at my house. He and his wife had met her at a cookout the weekend before, she was doing some great things for God, and he wanted to put the two of us together. As she sat in my home, I began to share with her a little about the gold dust. She had never heard about it.

After we had spoken for a while, I laid hands on her and prayed for her. When I opened my eyes, it looked as if she had a milk mustache on. Most Americans have seen the ads on TV where celebrities, wishing to show how healthy milk is for you, are pictured as having a milk mustache, a circle of milk above their lip.

A wide band of white gold dust outlined this sister's lips. I told her about it, and she went into the bathroom to look in the mirror. She got very excited, almost beside herself, as it came out more and more on her face. The patch of it got bigger and bigger.

Several ladies who were there as well that night discovered, when they got back to their rooms on the camp, that one had gotten two gold teeth and the other had gotten one. Sister Clark later wrote:

Dr. Elsie Clark, Ashland, Virginia:

> *Through Brother James Baxter and his wife, I met this wonderful woman of God [Ruth Heflin]. She prophesied over me that God would enlarge my ministry and would lead me into new signs and wonders and miracles. Immediately afterward, my face had gold dust on it, the glory of God spilling over from her. I had a patch of it above my mouth, like a milk mustache, and it was on other parts of my face.*

A week later, the prophecy began to come to pass in a conference I was conducting. A lady who had bones out of joint had them pop back into place. Several people who had had back problems were healed and were able to touch their toes. God removed arthritic conditions. He healed people who walked with a limp and they were able to straighten up and walk normally. God performed surgery on some after they had been slain in the Spirit, and they got up off the floor totally healed and set free. One lady fell into a deep sleep and stayed on the floor for some time. She was shocked when she woke up, but she was healed. Glory to God! I thank Him for the manifestation of His divine anointing.

We were not having an official prayer meeting. It was just a time of fellowship with a little prayer to close out the evening, but God is doing it differently now. He is doing it by His Spirit. What God is doing is so exciting.

Chapter 9

Golden Glory in Dallas and Orlando

I slipped out of camp only a few times during the summer for a service in some other city. I always hurried back because I didn't want to miss anything God was doing.

When I flew to Dallas for the annual convention of the End Time Handmaidens, God sent gold dust and other great signs into the meetings. It was the first time many of them had experienced it. Bob Shattles was also one of the speakers, and his ministry made a great impact.

I left early another day that same week and flew to Orlando to do a book signing with my publisher, Harold McDougal, at the annual Christian Booksellers' Association Convention.

Harold had begun to experience a few flakes of gold dust while sitting in my house in December of 1998, working with me on my book, *River Glory*. Next, the gold dust began to appear on his trousers or on or near his computer when he was sitting in his office back home in Maryland, working on the book.

A few months later, he and his wife Diane attended

our Winter Camp Meeting in February of 1999 and there witnessed, for the first time, the gold dust from Silvania's hair. He was on the platform during one service and saw dust that looked like it was falling from the ceiling onto and around the platform.

Later, when they had gone to their room for the night, Diane discovered gold dust under her clothing. From then on, she had gold dust on her neck and shoulders nearly every evening at home.

One evening, a few months later, as their son and his mother-in-law were with them in the publishing warehouse in Hagerstown preparing their exhibit for the CBA International, they were telling them about this manifestation. "Let's see it," someone said. When they looked, the gold dust was there, as it had been regularly.

Harold called me one day a few weeks before the convention and asked if we could provide some photos of the gold dust that could be displayed prominently in the booth on days I would not be there. "Let's believe for the real thing," I told him, and that's what we did.

Because of the sudden passing of my Uncle, Dr. William A. Ward, I was unable to attend the convention on Monday as scheduled. Bob Shattles agreed to go down early in my place, autographing his just-released book, *Revival Fire and Glory*, which also documents this phenomenon. He was covered with gold dust that day and the next, and many people he prayed for received the experience.

When I got there on Tuesday morning, the gold dust was already on me, and it increased throughout the day, as people came by the booth to get a copy of my book and to be prayed for. There was a little ceramic dog sitting under the table where we signed our books those two days. After the two of us were gone, people came by the booth to see the gold dust that had fallen on the dog and to get some to take with them. Many people were blessed and healed in that booth.

Flecks of gold came upon most everyone who worked the booth, even the McDougals' thirteen-year-old son. A McDougal Publishing salesman began to experience both oil flowing from his hands and the appearance of gold dust on him during those days, and it has been happening to him ever since.

When *Harvest Glory* was off the press, the McDougals took a copy home for Diane to read. She had seen bits and pieces of the story as it was in preparation but had not yet read the entire book straight through. Usually, she sleeps first, and Harold reads late, but that night she was enjoying the book so much that she read on and he fell asleep. Before long, however, he was startled awake by her shout. "Look at this!" she said excitedly. Gold dust had covered her right hand with which she was holding the book and was cascading down her arm. It was an experience she said she could never forget.

This summer, when Harold spoke at Campmeeting several Sunday mornings, there was gold dust both on him and on those he prayed for. One evening when he was sitting on the platform and Bob Shattles was preaching, he saw the gold dust come like a whirlwind and settle over the area of the platform where he was sitting. He still had it on his face when he got home to Maryland at three the next morning.

The McDougals continue to find gold dust in their home and in the McDougal Publishing office and warehouse. They have taken it as a visible symbol of God's presence with them for the work they are doing.

This was my first time to attend the CBA Convention, and I was amazed to see how many of the great names in American Christendom were there. As I sat and signed books, many prominent Christians leaders passed by the booth to greet me. Steve and Kathy Gray from the Smithton, Missouri revival, Phil Driscoll and many others came by during the course of a few hours. While Phil was there, God rained down gold dust on his shoulder.

As I said, even after we were gone, people came by to get some of the gold dust that had dropped on the carpet and furniture of the display while Bob Shattles and I were there signing.

Chapter 10

Children and Young People
and the Golden Glory

One of the most remarkable things about the golden glory is how it appears on small children, even babies. Young people get it quickly and easily. Here are a few recent examples of this phenomenon:

Katy O'Brien, Conyers, Georgia:

My daughter Amanda (6) had been hearing Granddaddy and Bubbie (Bill and Connie Wilson) talking about the woman with the gold. In February 1999, some of my friends and I went to see Silvania at Bob Shattles' church in Atlanta. In March, I went to the Spring Women's Convention in Ashland, Virginia, with a group of friends. The manifestation of gold and oil appeared on four of us. Amanda read my testimony about the special manifestations of gold appearing on Silvania and other people and she saw the gold in my Bible and in Granddaddy's as well. Then as Amanda and I listened to an audio tape one day of Barbara Richmond, gold appeared on Amanda. On the tape Mrs. Richmond was explaining how the Jewish bridegroom goes to prepare a place for his bride. When he is ready for his bride, he sends a gift of gold. Our Father is preparing a place for us, and He is sending the gold to let us know that Jesus is coming soon for His Bride.

After Amanda and I watched Silvania's testimony from CPT's Winter Campmeeting, I wanted to share it with friends. Amanda, however, was afraid we would lose the tape of "the lady with the gold" and didn't want to let it out of her sight.

In July Amanda was finally able to attend the Camp-meeting. Bob Shattles was preaching. After the service and during the ministry time, Granddaddy took Amanda to Bob Shattles and asked him to pray for the imparta-tion of gold for her. Gold immediately appeared on Amanda's arms and face.

After we went home, Amanda was very excited and told her friends at school about her experience. "It looks like glitter," she told them, "but it's not. It's really gold that comes from God."

In August, we took Amanda back to CPT with us, this time to see Silvania. Amanda couldn't believe she was going to see her in person. She sat right up front with Granddaddy praising and worshipping God.

Nan Richardson went with us that week. She is the Min-ister of Children's Education at Prospect United Methodist Church, where we attend services regularly. Amanda was so excited when she saw gold on herself and gold and oil on "Mrs. Nan" and asked Nan, "Can we tell everyone in Children's Church about the gold?" Bubbie explained to Amanda how she could pray for the children and see the visible evidence of God's presence by having the gold appear on them too.

After returning home this time, Amanda often listened to praise music with me. On certain songs, she would feel God's anointing and rewind the tape and just sit there listening in the presence of God.

When we learned that Silvania would be at a church in Eatonton, Georgia, about forty-five minutes from home, about thirty people from our Prospect church went with us to the meeting. As Silvania prayed for everyone, Amanda whispered to me, "I don't want her to knock me down" (she saw many others falling as they were prayed for). Amanda didn't get "knocked down," but she was covered in gold twice — from head to toe, and she glittered.

The entire next week gold was everywhere — in the van, in the bed. No matter how much Amanda's head was scrubbed, there was still gold in it. It was also on her face and on her arms. She had to go to school like that. She said some people believed her, and others were sure it was just glitter.

The next Sunday Amanda and "Mrs. Nan" talked about the visible evidence of God's presence — gold and oil — in Children's Church (ages 3-6). "Mrs. Nan" asked who would like to be prayed for, for the evidence of God's presence to appear on them, and eight children went forward. Amanda laid hands on the first child, then she looked at "Mrs. Nan" and said, "I forget what to say," so "Mrs. Nan" prayed for each child, while Amanda laid hands on each one. Each child immediately received the manifestation of gold on his or her body, and Amanda, as well as the other children, were telling everyone they saw about God's presence in Children's Church.

✳

Lonnie Cunningham, Illinois:

> *My grandson Chad, twelve years old, was in his room praying and worshipping, and gold dust in different colors fell on his bed with the glory. He called Chelsea, his nine-year-old sister and prayed for her ankle that had been hurt. It was immediately healed, and his mother was touched also. Chad had attended a Brunswick, Georgia, meeting. His parents are pastors, and Chad has had a calling to be in ministry since he was eight, when he went to Heaven and talked with the Lord.*

Cyndee Pillow, Arkansas:

> *Several weeks ago, my nine-year-old daughter had some little Christian girlfriends spend the night for her birthday. We were out in our yard after sunset. Often I have smelled roses in our yard, although there are no roses on my block. I began to smell them that night, so I told the girls it was the Lord's angel protecting our property. When I said that, they began to praise the Lord and sing songs out of their spirits. (Two of them are filled with the Holy Ghost.) I noticed my daughter swaying back and forth, singing, "I'm dancing with Jesus. I'm dancing with Jesus," over and over. I could see the Lord all over her. We began to sing with her.*
>
> *Suddenly, one of the girls noticed something on my daughter's hands that appeared to be gold glitter. When we looked, it was on all of us! I believe in miracles, I had visited your website many times and believed every word that I read there, but now it was happening in Arkansas in my own yard!*

"Was it real?" I wondered. I rushed into the house and scrubbed my hands, making sure there was no more 'accidental' glitter on my hands. Then, when I began to praise the Lord, the gold dust reappeared. EVER SINCE THEN, WHEN WE SING TO JESUS, IT HAPPENS. I have watched the gold dust appear. It looks like it is coming from the pores of our hands, and it gets thicker and thicker the more we worship and adore the Lord. Then it just vanishes.

This experience has boosted my faith that the literal Kingdom of God IS within us, and my faith level is way up for the laying on of hands. Christ is indeed IN US, the hope of glory!

I am having our first public meeting next weekend in a building the Lord provided. I am excited and anxiously awaiting to see the Lord be magnified.

❋

Gary and Rhonda Osborne, Elizabethtown, Tennessee:

During the service on Friday night our seven-year-old son, Daniel, who was playing with matchbox cars and coloring and, seemingly, not paying any attention to the service, held his hand out and showed us some gold dust on his hand. Later, during the same service, he asked if the wetness in the crevices of his hand was the oil. While we just thought he was playing, he was really listening to what God was doing in the service and believing with the faith of a child to receive it. He did. Glory to God! Since we have returned home, our five-year-old son Caleb has been singing over and again "Miracles, Signs and Wonders" like he heard it at the camp, and last night, while the boys were brushing their teeth for bed, Daniel told Caleb to hush up, that he was obsessed with that song. I defended Caleb because I thought his singing was cute. Then Caleb reached up his hand and showed me the gold dust on his hand. I looked at both of mine, and they were covered as well. Maybe we should all sing "Miracles, Signs and Wonders" and expect to receive them in our lives, just like Caleb did.

Thank you for the atmosphere you create at the camp that encourages even little children to expect to receive something from the Lord. So many times we stick them away somewhere in a side room to be baby-sat while we enjoy the presence of the Lord in the service, when they probably have more of an ability to receive than we do because of their lack of unbelief!

✳

Jennifer Lech, Jackson, New Jersey (16):

The gold first came upon me when I was at a meeting at Calvary Pentecostal Tabernacle in Ashland, Virginia. Sister Silvania was ministering, and I was so in awe of what was happening with her that I was not thinking about getting the gold on me. I looked down at my hands and saw tiny specks of gold appearing on them, until they were covered in gold. It happened again this summer when I was at the 1999 Summer Campmeeting. Gold appeared on my hands and arms.

The most awesome occurrence of God's glory happened to me two weeks ago, on October 11. I was feeling depressed and alone. I seemed to be failing at everything. I cried to God for His love and presence to fill the empti-

ness I was feeling. I was sitting outside my house on the steps, listening to a song that said, "You surround me like a winter coat. Sometimes You're closer then my skin." "Jesus," I prayed, "I want to feel You surrounding me. I want to know you closer than my skin."

I took a shower and was getting ready for bed, when I noticed that my arms were sparkling. I placed them in the light and saw that they were covered in gold. It was also on my hands, chest, face and legs. I felt oil begin to come out of my hands. I went into my parents' room, woke them up and showed them, because it was so amazing.

The gold was not only on me. It was all over my floor, my dresser and the papers beside my bed. God's glory and presence came down in that room and surrounded me. It came out of me. I felt God's presence "closer than my skin."

Chapter 11

Receiving the Golden Glory through Reading a Book, Listening to a Radio or Television Program or Having a Telephone Conversation

We have many testimonies of God pouring out His Spirit on people as a result of their reading one of my books or of hearing me on a radio or television program or as the result of a phone call from someone who has come into contact with the golden glory.

One of the most notable of those testimonies is of a sister from South Dakota who came to our 1999 Summer Campmeeting. In the course of an operation, something went wrong, and she became paralyzed in her hands and arms. She spent ten months in a nursing home for rehabilitation and used a wheelchair for the next five years. She was able to get a copy of my book, *River Glory*, and began reading it.

When she came to the part where I mentioned the gold dust that was falling on us, it fell on her paralyzed hands, and they were covered in gold dust for forty-eight hours. When the gold dust lifted, her hands and arms were totally healed. A few weeks later, she was out of the wheelchair and was running up and down on the platform here at the camp. Here is her story in her own words:

Krystal Kitchin, Sisseton, South Dakota:

I gave my life to Christ when I was nine years old, and Jesus told me He had a special plan for my life. I could never have imagined the pain and suffering that the future would involve and the wonderful miracles that God would do through it all. While I've always experienced some health problems, throughout the past twelve years I was very sick most of the time.

In 1986, I met, fell in love with and married my wonderful husband, Carl Kitchin. Both of us were older (Carl was thirty-nine, and I was thirty-four), yet neither of us had been married before. I was a diabetic, with the complications of high blood pressure and asthma. Three days after we were engaged, Carl and I sat across from the doctor, as he explained my health situation to Carl and added the devastating news that I also had sarcoidosis, a potentially-fatal disease. There is no cure for this illness. The prescribed treatment to keep the disease from doing severe damage, especially to the lungs, is cortisone therapy. The doctor explained that because of my other disease, cortisone could only be used as a last resort. It has dangerous side effects.

Carl and I left the doctor's office with heavy hearts. I turned to him and said, "I'll understand if you want to call the whole thing off."

He replied, "I proposed to you in sickness and in health and will marry you." So, on September 27, 1986, we began our journey together.

During our first year of marriage, I became very ill, and we had to begin therapy for the sarcoidosis. The doctor had to give me massive doses of cortisone, and the side effects were devastating. I already had a weight problem, but it was now compounded.

The cortisone treatments also caused rapid degeneration of the bones in my spine and left me with advanced degenerative arthritis of the spine, which dramatically changed my life. I couldn't walk very far without pain.

From 1987 to 1997, my health continued to deteriorate, and I spent a lot of time in hospitals. My medications cost me $1,000 up to $1,500 a month. My weight climbed to over four hundred pounds, and I rarely left the house. In March of 1997, during a routine visit to my doctor, she confronted me with the knowledge that my body could not continue to withstand the excess weight and that my body systems were breaking down. She said she didn't know how much longer I could live if something didn't change. We agreed for me to go to the Mayo Clinic in Rochester, Minnesota, for evaluation. While we were there, the doctors confirmed the following medical diagnoses: severe diabetes (I required over 300 units of insulin per day); morbid obesity; hypertension; congestive heart failure; severe asthma; sleep apnea (this required me to use a machine so I wouldn't stop breathing while sleeping); pulmonary circulation failure (the blood would pool in my legs and not return to my heart); sarcoidosis; severe depression; severe advanced generative arthritis; fibromyalgia; frequent urinary tract infections; frequent body yeast infections; and peptic ulcer disease. Each of these conditions required medications.

The doctors at the Mayo Clinic told me they felt my only medical option was to have a surgical procedure called a gastric bypass. In my case, they would do a radical procedure and leave only three feet of the large intestine, so that I could lose weight. Having the weight off, they judged, might improve some of my medical problems. They felt this was my only hope.

By now, I was unable to do anything. Carl was doing all the housework, maintaining his full-time job and caring for me. All I could do was move from the bed to my chair to the bathroom. Any more than that, and we had to use a wheelchair. I could only walk about five steps.

October 23, 1997 was a crisp, fall day that would dramatically change our lives in ways we could never imagine. My surgery was scheduled for 7:00 a.m. At 6:30 I hugged and kissed Carl, as he held me for the last time for almost a year. He prayed for me, and then they wheeled me away for a three-hour procedure. Alone, Carl waited. Finally, at 4:30 p.m. the doctor came out and told him that things had not gone well. I had experienced respiratory failure, and when he saw me, I would be on a respirator. When he finally saw me, he was horrified. I was blue-gray in color, a machine was breathing for me, and there were tubes everywhere. I was in acute critical condition and placed in Intensive Care.

After two days, I woke up a little, in excruciating pain, and was aware I couldn't move my hands and arms. I was paralyzed! I had no feeling in them. Finally, on day 6, I was able to breathe on my own with just the aid of oxygen, and I was moved to Intermediate Intensive Care. I remained there for fourteen days. Carl had to return to work after a week, and I was alone, unable to do anything.

The doctors finally decided I would have to be transferred to a rehabilitation center for intensive therapy. We found a nursing home care/rehab-center that was fifty miles from Sisseton where we lived, so we made arrangements for the transfer. I was transferred to the Whetstone Valley Care Center in Milbank, South Dakota. What we thought would be a six-week stay turned into ten long months, during which time I required two more major surgeries because of infections. I developed severe malnutrition and low hemoglobin problems. I required a feeding tube and many blood transfusions. I was shifted from hospitals back to the nursing home a couple of times. These were very dark days for Carl and me both. Every day he would drive to the nursing home, have supper with me, help me eat, get me ready for bed and then finally head for home at 8:00 p.m.. He told me later that sometimes it was so painful he would cry all the way home. He was crying out to God for help, wondering if I would ever come home again. Still, he remembered God's promise to him that He would heal me.

Finally, on August 15, 1998, I was released to go home. I was still on a feeding tube, and Carl still had to do everything for me. I had lost 140 pounds, and I was very weak. Gradually, I gained enough strength so that, with Carl's help, I could get dressed and we could go to church, but we still had to use the wheelchair. My recovery moved along very slowly. I was not able to do any household work or bathe or dress myself. The Lord began to do some healing work in my emotions, and I was drawn to God's Word and the concept of praising Him in all things.

Then, toward the end of March 1999, I became aware of Rev. Ruth Ward Heflin's books. I called McDougal Publishing and got all three. When they came, I read River Glory *first. When I got to the chapters on "Signs and Wonders in the River," something began to change. I could feel my faith begin to rise. "All things are possible." When I read the part about Silvania's testimony and the gold dust, I felt a strange sensation move through my body, and I noticed my arms and hands were covered with a soft-looking glitter. I showed it to my husband.*

My hands were washed over and over, but still the gold-like substance stayed. It was there for forty-eight hours. On the third day, I woke up and immediately noticed I could freely move my hands and arms. I was once again able to do the simplest tasks for myself. I also began to realize that I was no longer depressed and that I was experiencing new strength in my body. My health returned very quickly, and we were continuously praising God for His goodness toward us.

I began to cook meals, clean the house and care for myself. Strength returned to my back, legs and feet. On May 22, 1999, we realized I no longer needed to use the wheelchair, and I could walk freely anywhere.

We decided that we wanted to go to Campmeeting in Virginia and see for ourselves what God was doing. We had been so hungry for the glory of God for so long. We traveled by car to Virginia. It took us three and a half days of driving, but we arrived for opening night of the 1999 Summer Campmeeting, where I was able to give my testimony and dance with joy before the Lord.

I no longer have any symptoms of the following illnesses:

1. *Congestive heart failure – gone*
2. *Hypertension – gone*
3. *Obesity – I've lost 200 pounds*
4. *Asthma – gone*
5. *Sleep Apnea – gone*
6. *Severe Diabetes – I currently use 15-24 units of insulin a day, down from 300*
7. *Pulmonary problems – gone*
8. *Sarcoidosis – gone*
9. *Depression – gone*
10. *Fibromyalgia – gone*
11. *Frequent infections – gone*
12. *Peptic ulcer disease – gone*
13. *Frequent allergies – gone*

Through this testimony God has been glorified, and many people's lives have been touched by the power of the Holy Spirit. I still continue to experience the manifestation of the gold dust. It always gives honor and glory to Jesus.

✳

There is a second part to Krystal's amazing testimony. She sent it to us separately:

A week ago I returned from Kansas City, where I went to care for a friend of mine who is paralyzed. I was there two weeks. His wife had to go to the hospital, and the family needed some help. Just think, a few months ago, I was in a wheelchair myself.

The most amazing thing happened. One day I was bathing Bob. I've never given an adult male a bath, but I could feel the anointing as I did it. His daughter came into the room and began shouting at me, "You're covered in gold." Sure enough! It was all over me.

When I asked the Lord why this had happened, He answered me: "This (servanthood) is the purest form of worship. This type of servanthood breaks the yoke of the oppressor!" Taking care of an invalid is hard work, but I was so blessed. Many marveled at my ability to do it — another demonstration of God's glory and miracles in our lives.

Here are testimonies from people who received by hearing me on radio:

Sharon Walker, Atlanta, Georgia:

I first heard you on one of Sid Roth's radio broadcasts. You were talking about how to worship God and how important it is. You began to sing a song about the river: "Let the river flow, Let the river flow," and you sang it over and over again. I began to sing along with you in the Spirit, and when I did, oil began to bead up on my fingertips. I also felt the presence of God as never before. When the program went off the air, I continued to sing in the Spirit, and the oil continued to come from my fingertips. I showed my daughter. I never imagined I could receive such an anointing through a radio broadcast.

I asked God "What am I to do with this precious oil?" The answer I got was, "Just worship me, there is so much more."

I was listening to Sid Roth's program again two weeks ago, and he had Pastor Bob Shattles on with him. He said that oil flowed from his hand like liquid gold, and he mentioned your name and that you had been to his church. I got excited all over again at the mention of your name, but I wondered how I could have missed your visit to this area. At the end of the broadcast, Sid Roth spoke of your book River Glory. *I went right out to get a copy, and since it wasn't yet in the stores, I special ordered it. I was hungry for more of God.*

Margaret Weninger, New Hope, Minnesota:

About a year ago, I heard Sid Roth on the radio interviewing Ruth Heflin. She was talking about her book, River Glory, *and speaking of the signs, wonders and miracles that God was doing. The interview so arrested my attention that I recorded it and listened to it over and over. A spiritual hunger was placed inside me, and I knew I had to read the book. I was gripped by the testimony of Silvania and moved to tears over her miracle of healing.*

I went to my church bookstore and, fortunately, they had one copy, which they sold to me. I devoured that book, highlighting nearly every paragraph as I read because it spoke to my spiritual hunger. At the back of the book I found a phone number for the Ashland camp and called to see if Ruth might be coming to the Minneapolis area. They gave me the name of Ruth's friends, Ron and Joan Rousar, and from them I learned that she was indeed coming to our area in October. God was leading me.

Joan had videos of Silvania and offered to loan them to me. I watched them and wept and laughed and praised God for such mercy. The next day I had gold dust on my skin. At first I attributed this to my cosmetics, since some blushes contain glittery substances, but although I scrubbed my skin over the next three days and wore no makeup at all, it would not come off. It was even on the soles of my feet.

In the coming days, I held five showings of the gold dust video in my home, and the women who saw it were deeply touched. At least two of them also had gold dust appear on them. It also appeared on my two children. Now God is not just for me, with me, upholding me, in me, surrounding me and going before me; He is on me. Praise God forever!

✳

Here is an amazing testimony from Brother David Herzog of France about what God is doing through television. These miracles happened while he was ministering here in this country:

David Herzog, Paris, France:

I did a TBN interview in Phoenix. The Lord told me to pray for the people. People later came to our meetings and testified of their teeth being filled watching the re-runs of the television interview.

Here are some examples of people who received a miracle through a telephone call:

Steve Lockard, Washington, DC:

When I called the camp one day, I was able to talk with Connie Wilson, and she was telling me about your services down there and the different signs and wonders that were manifesting. She told me about the oil and manifestation of gold. I had just sent you my latest newsletter update, and as soon as it finished and I closed the program, the word "GOLD" appeared on the bottom of my computer screen. I called my wife down to see it, and I even took a picture of it.

That word GOLD attached itself to my Bible program. I am very knowledgeable about computers and the programs I use, and there is absolutely no natural explanation for this. This, too, is a sign and wonder, one for the books!

✳

Ruth Bauman, Schattdorf, Switzerland:

Thursday, the 18th March, I phoned home to Switzerland from the camp in Ashland, Virginia, and told my daughter the testimony about the gold which appeared in my hand. At the same moment, it appeared also on my daughter's hand, when I was talking to her — a miracle from the Lord.

✳

Darnell Tharp, Baytown, Texas:

In 1996, when Peter Wagner came to our church, he was telling about the manifestation of gold dust in Argentina. When I looked at my hands, they were sparkling with fine particles of glitter.

On another occasion, in 1997, Hector Jimenez from Argentina was testifying about the manifestation of gold dust in our Sunday morning service, and the same thing happened to me. I showed it to my husband and one other friend. Then I never spoke of it again.

When my friend Paula Askew went to Ashland, Virginia, and told me about what God was doing there, I confided in her what had happened to me in 1996 and again in 1997. She brought a book and gave it to me, and it helped me to understand why this thing happened.

Every time Paula would call me, gold dust would appear on my hands. I have three boys and a husband to care for and my time is hectic, but I always enjoyed her calls, telling me of the awesome things God is doing. One day, about thirty minutes after Paula had called, my husband called. While I was talking to him, I looked down and wondered, What did I get into? *There were big flakes of gold all over my clothing, and I started to get upset because they were new. After I hung up, I began thinking about it, and I realized what it was and where it had come from. I got so excited that I told everyone I could about it.*

Every time I told this story, a spirit of joy came over me, for this experience brings great joy. That same joy returned to me, just now, while I was writing these words. We must be nearing the coming of the Lord for Him to manifest His gift of gold just before He comes for His Bride.

✳

If it were not enough that many have received the golden glory through reading a book, through listening to a radio or television program or through a phone call, this next testimony is truly extraordinary. Max Greiner, a Christian artist in Texas, heard about the manifestation of gold dust in our meetings in Houston through a friend. The next morning, when he went down to his studio and entered the bathroom he had converted into a prayer room, as he was praying, gold dust began to appear on the floor, on the walls, on the counters and on the door. This has continued until now.

Gold dust soon began appearing on him, on his wife and on his fourteen-year-old daughter as they prayed for and ministered to people who were hungry for God or just as they witnessed to others. On one occasion, nine people watched as large flecks of gold appeared on his wife. This also has not ceased.

The artist was one of the exhibitors in the Christian Booksellers' Association annual exposition conducted in Orlando, Florida, in July of 1999. During the days of exhibition, gold dust appeared in and around his display, and on the people who visited it, as it did with ours.

This man and his wife were not in any meetings I conducted. They didn't read my book or hear me on radio or TV. They just heard about the golden glory, and it began to happen for them. Isn't our God great?

Chapter 12

The Golden Glory Affects the Nations

Directly and indirectly, we have seen the golden glory affecting many nations. During June of 1999, for example, we had two lovely families that came all the way from Colombo, Sri Lanka, to be in our weekend revival meetings. The group was lead by a professor at the University of Colombo. His wife had been given a copy of my book *Glory,* and as she read it, she developed a great desire to come to Virginia to meet us and be blessed. As a special treat, her husband brought her and his daughter, and another couple came with them.

The second night they were with us, the daughter suddenly had oil flowing from her hands. It was as much as a quarter cup of oil, and she had to cup her hands because so much oil was flowing in them. When the man saw this miracle in the hands of his daughter, he was broken, and the sight of a great university professor weeping before the Lord was moving. Before the service was over, his wife and the other lady in the group (as well as the daughter) all had gold dust from the tip of their fingers all the way to their shoulders. It seemed to be coming out of every pore. By the next night the man had gold dust all over him as well.

After they went back home to their country, they sent these wonderful reports:

Lalith and Hiranthi Mendis, Sri Lanka:

Since we came back from the camp, we are continuing to have oil and gold dust at family prayer times. Tonight, at our vigil, almost all present, even two little children, received the gold dust. Another missionary's wife had the oil pouring out. Bless the Lord.

Sister Ruth's ministry is given to passionately pursue the Lord in worship till you meet Him in glory. In recent times this has manifested as oil and gold dust on the face, hands and elsewhere. I fully believed the sign when I read about Silvania on the Internet. Her description of her disease − smell and all − were true as far as medical pathology goes. With liver cancer, bile ducts get obstructed, resulting in jaundice and stercobilin, giving the stercoral (faeces like) odour.

I nearly did a summersault when Teeny, our daughter, got the oil on her palms first and then the gold dust. Rasika, Roshan's wife, also had oil and gold dust all over her neck. I found this sign, indicating the immediate presence of the Lord, broke my besetting sin of self-importance.

Calvary Pentecostal Tabernacle is God's appointed place for important people like me to bite the dust. Praise moves from worship to glory, and worship often begins with tongues. No human being is recognised or promoted. Only one Person is sought − the Lord Jesus Christ. We were greatly blessed. We moved "from glory to glory" until we hit gold-glory.

Since the word seraphim means "burning bright ones" or "shining ones," and they are shining with God's glory presence, could it be that the gold dust is the result of our being rubbed upon by the realms of God's nearness in which seraphs live?

Since this experience, I have perceived the Lord speaking to me and saying, "If you would talk to Me instead of speaking to the people, I will do in them what does not happen when you speak to them." Since the major in my ministry form has always been teaching and preaching, I will need a complete overhaul to do the Lord's bidding. Our heart's desperate desire is to have revival in Sri Lanka and South Asia, and I dream that the close proximity of our campsite to Colombo's International Airport might be God's design. It seems that revival flus are more easily caught by churches near airports.

Do not be deceived by the devil's lie that manifestations are only superficial and have no lasting internal change. We are commencing twice-a-day revival meetings in our Colombo tabernacle with whoever is available. Every first Friday evening and Saturday there will be glory meetings at campsite. These will be titled "Taste and See that the Lord is Good" and subtitled "See My Glory."

Today at 9 p.m. oil began to pour from our daughter's hands.

✳

Roshan Gurusinhe, Sri Lanka:

We stand in awe at the presence of the Lord. When we came back from the camp, Brother Mendis started daily revival meetings at our campsite, and the river of God is flowing. We are experiencing the manifestations of the Holy Spirit, as we experienced in Ashland, and He is pouring the oil and the wine. His love is restoring our souls. We continue to have gold and oil when we worship, and when we were in Vancouver, Rasika received a gold filling. Glory to God!

Last Friday, at our vigil, one of our sisters received six gold fillings. Praise the Lord! We are so excited at what He is doing and at the exciting times that are ahead of us.

The spirit of dancing is breaking forth, and people who did not move their feet are dancing in joy before the Lord. We take this opportunity to thank you and all the beloved brothers and sisters for welcoming us with love and taking care of us when we were there. We were really blessed to be in your midst.

Brother David Herzog, who was with us from Paris, France, called me regularly after he went back to tell me of the great things God was doing in his ministry in Europe. He said, "Sister Ruth, I learned so much this summer. One of the things I learned is that as soon as the gold dust begins to fall I should start believing for miracles and declaring them. When the gold dust comes now, I begin to declare miracles. I would not have been that daring before, but as soon as it comes I know that God wants to give us miracles. I have seen such amazing miracles. I prophesied over a man that he would raise the dead, and in a very short time, it was happening. I am excited about what God is doing."

Recently, David sent this report:

In the south of France, in Toulon, we had gold dust come upon the walls of the church for three days. People came from all over with Scotch tape to take samples back to their friends and families. Fourteen people received Jesus as a result. The walls had been red. The Lord was signifying by this that the base of holiness was the foundation so we could handle the gold and other signs and wonders. When an artist paints a picture frame gold, usually he paints red under it first and then the gold over top of it. They say the gold comes out better and purer over red.

In Amsterdam, Holland, in May 1999, gold dust came for the first time in the church all over the people during my message. A woman who teaches in a public school had a surprise the next morning. It came upon the students, and she used it as a platform to preach the good news of Jesus Christ. In that same meeting in Holland, we saw teeth filled and crowned.

We have seen the gold come upon hair, hands, clothes, Bibles and even cars. In Strasbourg, they reported that their cars still had gold dust for one month after the meetings we held there.

In July of this year we saw a new manifestation. A lady's shoes that were totally silver when she walked in turned entirely to gold with only a small trace of the silver left by the Lord to testify of the miracle. The same lady had a watch that was silver on the back side. It turned to bright gold. In this same church we have seen many gold and silver teeth fillings.

In Ireland, we saw the gold dust and gold teeth fillings and crowns come upon the people for the first time in that country, or so we were told by the leaders. We actually watched as a woman's jewelry turned from silver to gold right before our eyes. It was breathtaking to watch. We have seen gold and silver fillings and crowns. Some people received up to eight teeth filled and/or crowned. Often the teeth are filled in the shape of a cross.

We have noticed that the gold dust and teeth and other gold signs point toward the fact that other miracles will take place. We have seen other miracles in our "gold meetings." For instance, we have seen paralytics walk, deaf ears open, spots on the skin disappear, instant weight loss and many other miracles. When the gold dust and teeth are in operation, it is a sign that the realm of miracles, signs and wonders is at hand. Anything under the category of miracles, signs and wonders can happen, not just gold. The gold is a sign pointing to the next level.

I prophesied over a man in Montreal, where we were having the gold dust for the first time in French Canada. I told him that he would see greater things and that he would raise the dead soon. One week later, he raised a dead person.

That which we have been longing to see is upon us. God is willing and ready to restore the book of Acts and do the "greater works" that Jesus prophesied. The "former" and latter rain glory is here.

Here are excerpts from other letters and e-mails that show what God is doing among the nations:

Chantel, Grasse, France:

One day, in our little prayer meeting, one of the girls told me I had golden dust on my face. When I looked, I didn't see anything and did not pay much attention to the event because I couldn't imagine our Lord doing that. Then, another day, after I had led the praising with my guitar, I returned home, and my room was full of God's glory, heat, perfume and golden dust in the air. I didn't know what to do, so I called the two people who were present in my flat that day, and the three of us stayed in the room, abandoning ourselves for half an hour.

The Lord was encouraging me, and He started to give me perfumes from Heaven. Sometimes other people would smell them. It started first in the middle of the night. Jesus woke me up at 2 o'clock in the morning and sent a very strong and sweet perfume. Since then, I've had many different perfumes, such as: exotic fruit, incense, cedar, vanilla, etc. On that very first night, I seized my Bible and read the Song of Songs, understanding its real meaning for the first time. Six months earlier I had wanted to take the Song of Songs out of the Bible, thinking it had been put there in error! God was my husband! What a revelation!

Others in the prayer group have experienced the perfumes as well. The strangest thing is that we live in Grasse, the perfume capital of the world! Our God has a good sense of humor.

As for the dust, the first sparkles were very big (one centimeter long) and green or blue. They didn't last more than a few minutes, and could be anywhere on us or in the house. Later, they became smaller, and have come in all colours: blue, green, red, silver and gold. Five months ago, the particles began to remain. They were very tiny. The biggest measured 3 millimeters. My hands and others' were covered with it. Then it spread among the group because it's contagious. Some six of our group experienced it.

One of my pupils, Saana, a poor Moroccan, was converted. Twice, when she came to our house to receive her lessons, we gave her something, and when she returned home, the smell of perfume was on her hands, on the things we had given her and even in the plastic bag she carried it in. We received a phone call from her mum, who was very puzzled and asked us for our secret. We had to explain that it was from the Lord.

Both of them were Muslims. Now the girl is baptized in the Holy Spirit, and the mother prays to Jesus and has approached Him. Thus our little group is getting bigger. Every time somebody comes to visit us from another town, they are blessed and go away with the dust on their face or hands. Some are healed physically.

Last Monday I had the gold dust on my feet for the first time. The oil doesn't happen to us as often. It sometimes comes into my hands, but more often on my forehead. We feel the Lord's presence in so many different ways.

✳

Helen Whitehead, Ontario, Canada:

The night before Sister Silvania came the first time, I had a vision of a large shiny pail, like what we call a coal shuttle, and two large hands were pouring gold flakes out of the pail in a great and seemingly-endless stream. I had only heard this new manifestation spoken of as "gold dust," so I wondered if I had really seen correctly. When Silvania came, however, the tiny flakes of gold appeared on her, just as I had seen them in my vision. Most wonderful of all, God gave me some of the gold dust.

A couple of ladies were in the camp with me, and we took videos home of Sister Silvania's testimony and showed them to several people. We have a small prayer group that meets regularly, and now everyone who attends those meetings has had the gold dust on them, including those who were not able to attend the camp-meeting. One young couple have children, and their children have all had the gold dust on them. It has already spread to many areas of our province.

During the summer of 1999, God put red and green flakes on my cheek one night.

In another vision the Lord gave me, I saw a river and an eddy, a place where the current turns to run back upstream for a while, then turns and mixes in with the rest running downstream. That part of the eddy was gold. At least it was on the surface. I couldn't see how deep it went.

I saw us in that golden eddy, swimming, diving and playing as an otter does, plunging in and out of the water. As we rose up, we were completely covered with gold, and there was a great joy in us, a great happiness. Together we were playing and loving the Lord in His golden river.

❋

Ian and Jeannette Turton, Hobart, Tasmania, Australia:

It is so exciting seeing children receiving gold dust on their bodies and seeing other signs, wonders and miracles. We are midway through two weeks of meetings in Melbourne and regional cities. The Lord is showing up in awesome power. There have been many healings including one guy who had not been able to straighten his leg since an operation. He was totally healed during the preaching. A number of rededications and of course much gold and silver fillings and gold dust. In one of Jeannette's meetings on the peninsula a lady demonically manifested, was delivered, filled with the Holy Ghost and hit with uncontrollable laughter almost at the same time. Many people are being delivered from evil spirits very easily under the anointing that blows into the meetings. In Bendigo, in Ian's meetings, people were falling under the power of the Holy Spirit without anyone praying for them. People told of incredible heat coming into their bodies as the Holy Spirit moved. People are continuing to be powerfully touched by the Lord, many testifying of completely revived lives and healed bodies.

We have been hearing about what God has been doing overseas filling people's teeth with gold, silver and platinum, even braces turning to gold. At River Christian Church in Hobart, Tasmania, Australia, we have been believing the Lord for miracles, signs and wonders like we have never seen before for awhile now. He led us into a time of intense warfare for a few months and then began to put on our hearts the real desire to see the miracles happen, that souls would be added because of what He is doing. It happened this way in Acts 4, where the dis-

ciples asked the Lord to give them boldness to preach the Gospel by stretching forth His healing power and that signs and wonders be done in the name of Jesus.

Last Sunday night (14th March 1999) we asked all present to lay hands on their mouths, and we prayed that the Lord would fill the teeth with gold. By Monday night we were amazed, as we actually saw fillings change into gold before our eyes. Personally, gold fillings appeared in my mouth, my wife also and others are getting blown away by their fillings changing before their eyes. God is awesome.

✳

June McKinney, Jacksonville, Florida:

I have ministered for the past ten years in the nation of Swaziland in Africa. It began when the Lord spoke to me while praying over a world map in 1989. He said, "June, I want you to go to Swaziland and take a message to King Mswattl. If you will be obedient to My call, I will give you the nation of Swaziland." I didn't even know that a nation existed called Swaziland; the Lord had to point it out to me on the map. I did not have a clue how to spell King Mswattl; the Lord showed me how to spell it. When I responded to the Lord's request and went to Swaziland for three days, God supernaturally opened the door for me to deliver the message to King Mswattl, who then received the baptism of the Holy Spirit.

King Mswattl invited me to personally teach his wives and family the Word of God, and this led to a series of twenty trips to Swaziland, three by special invitation from the King. He invited me to address the nation on Easter, Good Friday and during the National Independence Day celebration last year. This was all a prelude to the gold dust visitation there this year.

Early this spring, you and Bob Shattles were at our local TBN station in Jacksonville, Florida, where my friend Marcia is the Program Director. Marcia knew that I had operated in the gold dust manifestation when I ministered in LaPaz, Bolivia in 1997, and she told you a little bit about my ministry and asked you to lay hands on me before you left the studio.

When you met me, you said, "Are you that lady Marcia was telling me about?"

I said, "Yes."

You then said, "I have heard some wonderful things about your ministry."

I said to you, "I am a desperate woman. I want to operate in the gold dust again."

You prayed a very brief prayer and laid hands on me, and three weeks later the gold dust was again manifesting in my meetings. I began to accumulate the gold dust that remained on my clothing after meetings. I also kept some that fell in Bob Shattles' meetings in Brunswick, Georgia. I added the gold dust to olive oil from Israel, and the Lord instructed me to take this mixture with me to Swaziland, as a first fruits from the manifestation here in America. The Lord instructed me to charter a small private plane and to fly to each of the borders of Swaziland and pour it out on the border. I did this at each border gate, as well as at the palaces, government buildings and many other historical spots within the nation. This took about seven hours to accomplish.

I was invited as an international speaker for a Government Praise and Prayer Breakfast in Swaziland. It was a private prayer meeting with six hundred and sixty-five invited guests. There was one other international speaker seated at the head table, the Prime Minister, several senators, two pastors and several princes and princesses. Gold dust fell on the head table and on the carpet under it in such a way as to cover every other fiber of the carpet. All who were present witnessed it.

One of the King's wives was also present at the meeting, and she began to pick up the gold flakes and place them in a napkin. She said, "You mean to tell me this is from Heaven!" She is an attorney who no longer practices since she wed the King.

During the days I was there, gold dust fell often in our room, throughout the days and nights. The family who owns and runs the hotel were so in awe of God's presence that they did not charge us for our room, phone calls or food and would not allow us to pay anything when we checked out. They also experienced the personal touch of gold dust on them when I prayed for them.

I planted a flag of Swaziland on the altar at Christian Renewal Center in Brunswick, Georgia, and it became covered with gold dust. I took the flag to Swaziland, and it is now on display in a glass case in the foyer of the Mountain Inn Hotel.

Your obedience to embrace the gold dust visitation here in America changed my life, and your brief prayer over me at the TBN station in Jacksonville gave me the necessary jump start to once again see this outward manifestation of God's presence. This gift of gold dust *has been to me like a child visiting a candy store. It is the awesome tangible evidence of our Lord's presence. It is like vitamins that strengthen the fruit of the Spirit within me. It is like a smorgasbord that all who are hungry can share in.*

✳

Lonnie Cunningham, Atlanta, Illinois:

The Lord graciously allowed me to be a part of a wonderful harvest with June McKinney in Swaziland, Africa, when the gold dust showered in the meetings. It was such an awesome experience that it is difficult to explain. It rained down on one of the pastors and six members of the church at lunch after the first morning meeting in an Anglican Church.

✳

Onex, Switzerland (Translated from French):

This evening, Friday, February 26, 1999, from 8:00 p.m. and on, some fabulous things happened. Lee Lacoss from the U.S. and another minister accompanying him really edified us. The movement of the Holy Spirit was especially strong so that healings were numerous. Some who were mightily touched by God had gold dust on their hands as a divine sign. Others had oil flowing from their hands. I have never seen a sign like this. Although the crowd was no more than seventy people, they were from at least nine different Christian denominations. God is pouring out His Spirit in a new and special way. This must mean that He is coming soon, and the harvest is ready.

Jerusalem, Israel:

On Rosh Hashanah, Jewish New Year, a busload of visitors from Capetown, South Africa, arrived at the Mt. Zion Fellowship in Jerusalem to join others from many nations for the morning worship service. During the service, many gold flakes appeared on the floor in multicolors, and almost all of the visitors received gold dust for the first time. Only a few had ever heard of this manifestation. Sister Nancy Bergen noticed the gold on one of the African ladies in the early part of the praise service. The lady did not even know what it was. By the end of the service, all of the visitors had received it. They left very excited that day to bless their respective nations.

✷

Ruth Bauman, Schattdorf, Switzerland:

When Alois and I arrived in Switzerland the 22nd of March, we worshipped the Lord with our four daughters. The gold appeared on all of our hands, also on the youngest, who was at the neighbor's house to get her pet. Our grandchild also had gold on his face.

Through all of this, the Lord has given to my husband and me a new fire of love in our marriage.

On March 23rd, we visited my dear parents and blessed them, and my father was convicted of sin for the first time. The same evening, during the Bible reading, oil appeared on my husband's forehead. We thank the Lord. Every day we have gold in our hands.

✷

Kathy Lemmert, Port Perry, Ontario, Canada:

We first experienced the manifestation of gold and oil

when we visited the camp at Ashland, Virginia, in May of 1999. We were on our way to meetings in Canada and thought we would stop in and check out what was happening. When we hear God is moving in a special way, we always want to know firsthand. My husband and I and our ten-year-old daughter all had gold dust and flakes appear on us during worship. At one point, my eyes were filled with golden oil. The thing this did for me was to increase my faith for the miraculous.

From Ashland we went into Northern Quebec to minister. During the meetings there, the gold was poured out. One man testified to having given up going to church because of the terrible pain he had in his side. After one service, he placed a gold flake on that side, and the pain left. He went off his painkillers and attended every service with his wife.

About fifty people responded to the altar call for salvation in that place, having been drawn to the service by the miracles God was doing.

From Northern Quebec we went to minister in Port Perry, Ontario, where again the gold manifested and continues.

We thank God for the increase in salvations, healings and miracles since we visited Ashland and experienced His glory in those meetings.

✳

J. Aaron Raj, Adaman and Nicobar Islands, India:

I am very happy because I received a new anointing in your campmeetings. My wife received Holy Spirit fire, and when she prays for people they receive it too. I told the people about the gold dust, and the same miracle happened in our church. Thank God.

✳

Debbie Kendrick, Richmond, Virginia:

While traveling between meetings in France recently, we came upon a motorcycle accident. The rider was lying in the road, waiting for the ambulance to arrive. We stopped and spoke with him, told him Jesus was there and prayed for him. Gold dust appeared on his eyelid. For us, it was God's signature. This wind that blows in the evidence of Heaven also blows doubt and unbelief apart. We left knowing God heard and answered.

✳

Wallace Justus, South Africa:

Earlier this year, when I went to minister in Chile, God manifested His power greatly. I arrived on Thursday afternoon and was supposed to minister through Sunday. God told me to minister on praise. When I got to the service, I knew why. No one raised their hands, clapped or danced. I ministered Thursday, Friday and Saturday. During the Saturday service God walked into that place. It began when the bishop, sixty-seven years of age, fell on the floor shouting in Spanish. I asked my interpreter what he was saying. He said the bishop was shouting, "I want this! I want this!" Just then, the bishop's mother-in-law, eighty-eight years of age, jumped up and started to dance before the Lord. Then in one great motion, the whole congregation stood and started to dance. It must have been like Miriam, when she led the Israelite women in the victory dance after God had delivered them from Egypt. This went on for a long time.

Eventually, the bishop took the microphone and, weeping, he said that eighteen years before he had been in a service like this and had been asking God for it to happen again. As he was weeping and talking to his congregation, gold dust appeared all over his face.

One of the sisters jumped up. Her handbag was covered with gold dust. Then another and another jumped up, and they all had gold dust on their faces.

During the few days I was there, I had not yet ministered on gold dust, and they had not seen nor experienced this manifestation before. Until that moment, I had not seen gold dust manifest in our services. I had seen it for the first time myself in the Winter Campmeeting in Ashland. Now it was happening in our meetings, too.

The next day, Sunday, more than fifty families were added to the church, and an emergency building program was announced to accommodate the increased crowds.

One of the things that touched my heart most was what God did among the children and young people. They were deeply touched and very hungry for His presence. Night after night they fell on their faces worshipping God and weeping, seeming out of control. God moved so mightily that we ended up staying in that place and ministering for three weeks. To God be the glory!

✳

When our website, www.revivalglory.org, was first up and operating, we were out there by ourselves. Now there are dozens and dozens of pages of testimony at any one time on several Internet sites about this phenomenon. We are aware of three churches in Denmark that have gold dust. It's in France, Belgium and England, and, as you can see, in many other countries as well. This golden glory is breaking forth everywhere and blessing the nations.

Chapter 13

What Brought Us to This Place

Several unusual experiences mark our moving into this new level of signs and wonders in God. The first happened to me in April of 1997, while I was ministering in an Assembly of God church in Mandan, North Dakota, a town that adjoins Bismarck. It was the first night of a series of meetings at the church, and when the pastor introduced me, I rose from the first row of the sanctuary where I had been sitting and started to walk toward the pulpit. Before I could get there, however, I found myself suddenly "frozen in place," unable to move. Not only was I frozen in place, but I was unable to speak, so I could not tell anyone what was happening to me.

The pastor was waiting on the platform for me to come forward, the entire congregation was expecting to hear from me, and there I was stuck between the front row and the altar. I am not sure just how long I stayed there like that, but it seemed like an eternity at the time.

The pastor was looking at me as a father looks at a child just beginning to walk, beckoning me with his eyes to take another step. Finally, the Lord released my

187

Stuck in place.

tongue, and I said, "I'm stuck, I can't move," and, with that, everyone broke into laughter. It was several minutes before the Lord released me to walk the rest of the way to the platform. We had a glorious outpouring of the Spirit of God in Mandan.

A man came that same night and told us that the night before he had been driving by on the highway and had seen a terrible fire in the city. A building was being consumed by flames. He was in a hurry to get somewhere and was unable to stop to see what damage was done to the building. That next morning he came by and was amazed to find that the building he had seen burning was the church building, and it was not damaged at all. There was, in fact, no sign of fire.

When he saw the fire, the people of the church were gathered praying for revival, and God had allowed that great visible manifestation to come to show what He was about to do for them. No wonder I had felt such glory in that place!

From the time I had that experience in Mandan, I was frozen in place many times, usually when I least expected it, sometimes several times in a single service, always for at least a minute or two and sometimes longer.

"Frozen in place" never seemed to me to be a good description of this phenomenon because there was so much of the fire of God involved. "Stuck in place" may be a better description of what we were experiencing.

We had all had experiences through the years of falling out on the floor under the power of God and occasionally being held on the floor by the Lord until He had wrought His work in us. Then He released us to get to our feet. It was a new experience for us to have God do this while we were standing.

In November of that year, in our weekend revival meetings in the Ashland Camp, I stepped up to the pulpit to speak and suddenly could not say a word. I was caught up in what could be described as a standing trance. Other than the experiences of Maria Woodworth-Etter relayed to us by my mother, I had not heard of anyone who went into a trance while standing. I was unable to move, and this went on for about half an hour to forty-five minutes. During that time, <u>I was carried away in the Spirit, feeling myself being rapidly lifted upward to the throne of God, and everything in the meeting came to a standstill.</u>

I was positioned at the pulpit so that it was not convenient for anyone else to step up and continue the service or do anything else, for that matter. The people in the congregation waited in worship and praise for me to come to myself and continue the service.

When I came to myself, there was a rhythm that was going over and over again in my spirit. Very slowly I heard myself saying, "The eyes of the blind shall see, the ears of the deaf shall hear, and the dead shall be raised to life again." Again, "<u>The eyes of the blind shall see, the ears of the deaf shall hear, and the dead shall be raised to life again.</u>"

The congregation had been sitting all this time in the glory, and some later said that it was the greatest glory they had ever experienced. Still, it was a strange, new experience for me. One would naturally wonder that if the Lord had wanted to carry me away in the Spirit, why had He not done it while I was simply sitting on the platform earlier in the service? The fact that He had waited until I was at the pulpit showed me that He obviously wanted everything to come to a stop, for that great glory to come in.

Less than a week later we took several carloads of our camp people to the funeral of a pastor in Fredericksburg, Virginia. Just before the funeral service started, Ruth Carneal, a sister who worked with our ministry for many years and was seated next to me on the front row, turned to me and asked where the rest room was. I pointed it out at the back of the church.

"Would I have time to go before the service begins?" she asked.

"Please do," I answered her.

When she didn't return to the front pew, I assumed that she had taken a seat farther back in the sanctuary.

I am not sure how much time elapsed. I had a part in the service, and several other pastors read scripture portions and prayed. After a time, however (probably fifteen or twenty minutes), someone tapped me on the shoulder and said, "Sister Ruth Carneal is on the floor at the back." I got up and went back quietly, not wanting to disturb the service. When I saw Ruth stretched out on the floor, I knew immediately that she was dead.

My first thought was not to spoil the funeral, so I got two brothers to pick her up quietly, one by the feet and the other by the shoulders and carry her into a side room. It was a small room, and there wasn't enough space to stretch her body out completely, so the men sat her up on a chair. Her head was falling to one side, so I reached over to support her head and neck.

Until that moment, my only concern had been to get her away from the funeral service so that it would not be disturbed. As I placed my hand on Ruth's neck, suddenly those rhythms from the week before returned to my spirit, and the words came within me just as slowly, distinctly and powerfully as they had that night: "The eyes of the blind shall see, the ears of the deaf shall hear, and the dead shall be raised to life again." I was not saying the words out loud. They were going over and over in my spirit. "The eyes of the blind shall see, the ears of the deaf shall hear, and the dead shall be raised to life again." When I said it the second time within myself, Ruth gasped as her spirit came back into her body.

Someone had called an ambulance and, by this time, it had arrived. The paramedics quickly placed Ruth into the ambulance and headed for the hospital. I was able to ride in the front seat of the ambulance with them. In the rear they were doing a preliminary examination of Ruth, and they found that all her vital signs were normal. When we arrived at the Emergency Room and doctors had thoroughly examined her, they discovered that when she had gone to the rest room she had suffered a severe hemorrhage and lost fully a third of her blood. This had caused her to faint and die as she came out of the rest room.

It had been an awesome experience when I was first carried away in the pulpit and again that day when the rhythms of the river came to me. The most amazing thing about this experience, however, came to me later. I had never actually prayed for Ruth to come back to life. The miracle happened in the presence of the glory of God.

The next great sign appeared a few months later. We began to have oil appearing on our hands in the services. This was not a totally new experience to me. It was only new in this day. Mother and Daddy took us to all the revivals that were happening in our childhood, and in the process taught us to keep an open spirit to new things and to have an appreciation for the ministry of others. They taught us to be very careful not to grieve the Holy Spirit, and part of that teaching was to be careful what we said about what God was doing and to walk softly before God. People are much too quick to criticize what they don't understand and have not personally witnessed before. We must not pretend to be authorities on everything that God is doing.

Before we were able to attend the meetings of Brother A.A. Allen for ourselves, we had heard people talking about the strange phenomenon being experienced in his meetings of oil appearing on people's hands and even flowing from their hands. I was in my early teens by then and overheard preachers that I respected making fun of this phenomenon. They said, "It's nothing more than perspiration. They just rub their hands together and make them sweat. This is nothing more than a show. Everybody wants to get up front and be seen, and they will do anything to call attention to themselves."

Our parents never joined in these comments. They were wise enough to withhold judgment until they could see for themselves what was happening. They knew the Holy Spirit, and they were sure they would know the real from the false; so, until they had seen it for themselves, they would offer no opinion. I never heard either

of my parents say anything critical about what someone else was experiencing in God. They were so hungry
for God themselves that it made them open to new
things. They didn't want to do anything that would
hinder the move of God's Spirit.

We traveled from Richmond to Pittsburgh to be in the
Allen meetings, and when we got to the tent, we found
it to be packed with thousands of people. One of the
first people who drew my attention was one of the ushers. He was leaning against a tent pole very near the back.
His hands were behind him, resting on his hips, but he
had his palms upward so that the oil that was coming
from them would not drip onto his pants. He was not
creating any sort of show. He was not waving his hands
or showing them to anyone. He was just leaning against
the pole, weeping and expressing his love to Jesus.

When I saw this, my heart was totally melted. I realized that I had allowed the criticism I heard from others
to get into my heart and affect my feelings about the oil
on people's hands — even before I had personally witnessed it. Once I had seen it, I knew that it was of God.

This man was one of thousands who experienced this
in those meetings, and I believe we will see thousands
again experiencing the same phenomenon.

One night near the end of our Summer Campmeeting
in 1998, a young woman, who, along with her husband,
had been a missionary with Wycliff, came to the meetings. I had never seen her before. After she had been in
the meetings for several days, she came up to me at the
close of the service to say that she would be leaving the
next day and to ask me to pray for her. As I was praying

for her, I looked down and saw that her hands were filled with oil. When we had finished praying, I pointed to her hands and asked her, "Have you ever experienced this before?"

She looked at her hands with astonishment and said, "Never!"

It was after midnight, and there were only a dozen or so people left in the Tabernacle. I said to those remaining, "This sister has oil on her hands. I want her to come and show it to you." She walked the five or six steps to the edge of the platform, and when she got there, she showed her hands to the others. They all wanted to be touched by her hands, but when she reached out her hands to them, some of them were so hungry that they wiped all the oil out of her hands onto their own. When I saw it, I said, "Oh, don't wipe it all off. I want Brother Dwight Jones to see this." (He was the one who had ministered that night, and he was now in the snack bar, visiting with the people.) She started walking back toward me, and by the time she had walked those five or six steps back from the edge of the platform to where I was seated, her hand had again filled with oil. I encouraged her to go to the snack bar and show Brother Jones the supernatural manifestation of oil that was flowing from her hands.

I had experienced oil on my own hands many times, and this is one of the reasons I never used other types of oil to anoint the sick. When the Lord has given us supernatural oil, what else could compare? Many times, when I was preaching, oil would be dripping from my face, and sometimes seems to come from my eyes. Now, however, we began to experience it in a new way.

When I was with Monsignor Walsh at the Presentation Church in Wynnewood, Pennsylvania, that September, I ministered three nights. On one of those nights, the priests commented about the oil they saw dripping from my face as I was ministering. God was giving us wonderful signs and wonders to confirm His Word.

Chapter 14

What Is the Purpose of the Golden Glory?

The first question that comes to many people's minds when they hear about the golden glory or see it for the first time is "Why? What purpose does this serve?" I find that God gives an answer that satisfies each individual, although it is not always the same answer.

One man said the Lord showed him that because Jesus is walking on streets of gold, the appearance of gold dust is an indication that we are getting closer to Him. He has golden dust on His feet from the golden streets of Heaven.

A lady said that she discovered that it was the Hebrew tradition that the bridegroom send a gift of gold to his bride as an indication that he was soon to come for her. She understood from this that the appearance of the gold dust meant that Jesus was coming back soon for us.

Some, remembering that the furniture of the wilderness Tabernacle and the Temple in Jerusalem were overlaid with gold (because God chose to dwell there) and consider it logical that God would cover us with gold, for we are *"earthen vessels"* that bear His glory.

And we are to be in the dust of our rabbi.

Wow!

Others have received very different answers. We don't have all the answers; we're still learning. It is not necessary that we be authorities on everything that happens to us. The important thing is that we are blessed by what God is doing and become a blessing to others.

The Golden Glory
as Anointed Manna from Heaven

Personally, I have sensed that the golden glory is to us as the manna was to the children of Israel in the wilderness. The manna came down from Heaven every day, the children of Israel had to gather it up, and it met their natural needs. In much the same way, God is now sending down the golden dust to meet the spiritual needs of the Body of Christ.

There is an anointing upon this golden glory. This is evident in the number of miracles that take place when it is present. Pastor Bob Shattles told me that when he began getting the oil and the gold dust on his hands, he would show it to everyone who was in the meeting, and they would wipe some of it from his hands into theirs. He allowed them to do this as long as the oil or the golden dust remained. Then one day the Lord told him not to allow the people to wipe away the oil or the gold dust in this way because it was an anointing for that service, and it was not to be dissipated in this way. It was to remain in the service until the end so that there would be a greater anointing in the service for miracles.

At first, as the gold dust was raining down around him, people would come forward and pick it up during the service. Then God told him not to allow the people to pick it up because that gold dust was for the anointing for that service. He was to let it build up during the meeting so that the purposes of God for that service could be fulfilled right up to the end of the service.

We have not seen these showers of the golden dust nearly as much as I would like, but it is happening more and more. When the workers took up the old carpet in the camp Tabernacle to change it before the 1999 Summer Campmeeting, the carpet was saturated with gold dust, and they got it all over themselves. I knew that God was about to do greater things in our midst.

The Golden Glory as a Sign to Confirm the Word and Help Bring in the Great Harvest

The gold dust, the oil and the gold teeth are all signs that follow us and confirm God's presence with us. When the disciples went out to obey the Great Commission, signs and wonders followed them. Why should it be any different with us? God wants more than the preaching of His Word. He wants the demonstration of His Word.

Signs and wonders are God's supernatural help to enable us to reap the end-time harvest. This is God's way of bringing it in. We cannot reap in the same way we have in the past. We have had wonderful anointed preachers for many years, but it isn't enough. We need more to bring in this increased harvest.

The harvest of the end-time will be so great that we will not be able to gather it all in a single day. It will require a daily effort on our part. Just as the children of

Israel gathered manna every day in the wilderness to be fed, we must gather in the harvest of the end days on a daily basis.

It is not just a coincidence that the color of wheat, the color of ripened grain, is golden. God is showing us the importance of the harvest and the importance of His glory among us to enable us to reap it.

Signs were one of the tools given by God to the apostles to evangelize the world:

> *And by the hands of the apostles were MANY SIGNS AND WONDERS wrought among the people ... and believers were the more added to the Lord, multitudes both of men and women.*
>
> Acts 5:12 and 14

Signs and wonders still draw men and women to the feet of Jesus today.

Pastor Bob Shattles has always had a passion for souls, and his church has consistently ranked among the top three percent of Baptist churches all over the world in evangelism. This manifestation of gold dust, however, has given him a greater opportunity to evangelize than anything that has ever happened to him. This manifestation excites the sinner and compels him to come to the Lord. Pastor Bob has many wonderful stories to tell of those who have come to know the Lord because of the gold dust. Pastor Shattles has been keeping a record since this miracle came into his life and ministry, and he alone has won thousands of people to the Lord because of it.

The church has so much competition for people's attention that it costs more and more in advertising dollars to win people to the Lord. We no longer have time for that, nor do we have enough funds to bring in as many as God will in these times. From now until the end of time, signs and wonders will bring in the crowds. In these end times, churches will be packed out, auditoriums will be full and overflowing.

Churches that have tried for many years to build up their congregations will suddenly find themselves with more people than they know how to handle. We have wondered sometimes if our desire for greater crowds might be carnal. It isn't. It is the desire of the heart of God. He wants His house to be full. More people are being saved then ever before. God is doing things differently than we ever imagined. He knows just the right bait to use to bring in the net full of fishes.

This harvest will be reaped quickly and effortlessly in the glory. So many of the methods men encourage us to use are exhausting. That can't be God. His ways are effortless. If the harvest could be reaped through our efforts, it would long ago have been accomplished here in America because great effort has been put forth.

American Christians are great organizers, and we even have programs to organize the organizers. God, however, is doing it His way. He will use the little people and will reap through miracles.

It is time to submit ourselves to the Chief Harvester. The work will be done by His hand, not ours. Join your hand to His and reap the harvest together. This is the time to throw the net on the other side of the boat, the glory side.

The Golden Glory as God's Love Gift to Us

When a girl receives a diamond ring from her boy-friend, she is very excited. It is not, however, the diamond that excites her. If the ring had come from her grandmother, she may not be nearly as excited about it. She is excited about the diamond because it was given to her by the man she loves. That ring represents their loving relationship and the fact that he has asked her to spend the rest of her life with him.

If someone else were to give her the ring, she would appreciate it in a very different way, and because it is a nice ring she would show it off. Nothing could compare, however, with receiving a ring from her beloved. The rest of the week she is touching her hair, touching her face. She has never used that left hand quite so much. She is showing off the diamond, but not just because it is a diamond. It is because of who and what it represents.

She is delighted in the relationship she has with her betrothed, and delighted that he has shown his love for her by choosing her and by giving her the diamond as a token of that love. That's exactly what God is doing for us, and when we show it off, we are declaring His love.

God has chosen us, and His touch of gold proves it to the world. He loves us, and no one can deny it. We are to be part of His beloved Bride, and He is adorning us for the wedding day. He is very excited as that day draws near, and so am I.

The Golden Glory as a Reminder
of God's Presence with Us

This golden glory is a reminder to us and to others that God is with us. That is not just so that people will think highly of us. It gives us confidence, and it also purifies us. The golden glory and similar miracles in which God's presence is seen on our bodies, make us so aware of the Lord's presence that we are more careful of what we say, what we do and even of what we think. It also makes us careful how we respond to each other. The visible sign of God's presence causes us to take hold of the reins of our own spirits and to cause them to be controlled by the power of the Holy Ghost.

This experience purifies us in yet another way. Once you have experienced the golden glory, you don't want to do anything to miss the signs and wonders that God is bringing forth in this day. You become aware that those who say, "I could care less," don't receive these graces, and you don't want to be among them.

This gift is for those who have a desire for God and a desire for His holiness. This blessing is for those who love the Lord and are willing to become a spectacle to the world for His name's sake:

> *Behold, I and the children whom the* Lord *hath given me ARE FOR SIGNS AND FOR WONDERS in Israel from the* Lord *of hosts, which dwelleth in mount Zion.*   Isaiah 8:18

The Golden Glory as a Faith-Builder

Seeing the golden glory is one of the most faith-building experiences anyone can have. Many financial miracles and healing miracles come about because of the presence of the gold dust. The faith it inspires brings a release into our lives. Nothing could compare with having God's glory being seen upon your own body.

My personal life has been greatly enriched in the period since this miracle began to happen for us. It is so wonderful just to know that the Lord loves us so much that He is manifesting His presence in these supernatural ways.

The gold dust is a faith builder, for believers and unbelievers alike. To look at the pores of your own skin and, instead of seeing ordinary perspiration coming forth, to see specks of gold supernaturally appearing, is a life-changing experience. When I see my arms covered with gold dust, I think, *If God can do this, He can do anything,* and there is no room in my life for doubt and unbelief. To have supernatural oil flowing from your hands, your face and your eyes is an awesome experience you can never forget. It changes you forever.

We have believed for healings for many years now, but this is the time of unusual miracles for the entire Body of Christ. Let your faith be raised to new levels through what God is doing. What we are now seeing in measure, we will soon see in immeasurable ways. It will burst forth upon us suddenly.

Healings have happened so easily and so quickly and so often in the poor countries of the world because people there have been less complicated in their faith, and they have known their need of God. Americans became skeptics in many ways and have to be shown before they believe. Our health care system has been so good and it has taken care of so many of our needs that we sometimes have not felt the need of crying out to God for healing. That is all changing. God is performing more and more miracles of healing for us in this country, and we will see an acceleration of that healing activity.

God is raising our faith level by the visible signs and wonders He is giving us, and that has a timely purpose. We will need a stronger faith to see all that He wants to do for us in these days ahead. The Lord said of Mary:

> *And blessed is she that believed: for there shall be a performance of those things which were told her from the Lord.*   Luke 1:45

Our faith will be increased and will produce the performance, the demonstration, that will be necessary to convince the multitudes of lost to turn to Christ.

When people saw Jesus doing miracles, they said of Him:

> *Rabbi, we know that thou art a teacher come from God: for no man can do these miracles that thou doest, except God be with him.*   John 3:2

This same thing will be said of us in the future. Men and women of all ages and of all positions will know that God is with us by the signs and wonders He causes to accompany our lives. We have seen miracles in every generation, but this is the last generation, and we will now see an increase of the miraculous and to produce it, God is giving us an increase of faith.

After my brother had been saved for a short time, he was fasting and praying for God to do miracles through him. One day in the kitchen of our home, Daddy asked my brother, "Son, why are you fasting?"

"I'm fasting for God to heal the sick, to open blind eyes, to open the ears of the deaf," my brother replied. "I'm fasting for miracles."

Daddy had a wonderful sense of humor. He looked around the kitchen and then said, "I don't see any blind people here. I don't see any deaf here. I don't see anyone here who needs a miracle. How do you know that God has not already answered your prayer?" God is giving us an increase of faith, and we must put it to work to accomplish His purposes in the Earth.

My brother always said that the way you develop a healing ministry is by laying your hands on the heads of many sick people. Just find people who need a miracle and lay your hands on them and believe. There may be a time when the miracle does not come instantly, but don't be distressed. Focus on the miracles God does perform for you. Let your faith rise, and put it to work for the Kingdom.

Look at your hands right now and say, "These hands are made for healing; these hands are made for miracles, these hands are made to bless the peoples of the Earth." When you can see gold dust or supernatural oil on them it will help you to believe what you are saying. Then, you must stretch those hands forth and use them, for it is as you stretch forth your hands in faith and lay them upon the sick that the miracles are performed.

When we were young in ministry, we had the idea that it didn't take much faith to pray for somebody with a headache. If you knew that someone had cancer or some other serious illness, however, you wanted to have a serious time of prayer before you laid hands on them. When I was still very young and living as a missionary in Hong Kong, I was asked one day to go pray for a Chinese lady who was in the hospital dying of cancer. This message came as I was teaching English in one of the many rooftop schools in the colony, and as I was on my way to the hospital, I realized that I had not had time to spend in serious prayer about this difficult case. Would I have enough power to heal her of cancer? The Lord spoke to me and said, "I didn't call you to be a reservoir; I called you to be an empty vessel through which My river could flow."

When I got to the hospital and stood by the bedside of the sick lady, I was not feeling especially powerful. I said within my spirit, "Lord, I'm extending my hand in faith. Let my arms be a channel of your blessing, your healing virtue." The moment I extended my hands and laid them on the sick woman, I felt such a surge of the power of God going through them that I was nearly embarrassed by it.

The woman was instantly healed and got up out of the bed. The Chinese custom is that when someone comes to visit you, you walk them to the gate or to the door. The Chinese sister was determined to walk me all the way down the corridor and see me safely into the elevator, and she did.

When I see gold dust and oil on my hands, I become aware that this type of miracle can be accomplished with such ease that we are left amazed.

The Golden Glory as a Monetary Blessing

Does the golden glory have a monetary value? That is not yet clear. While some tests of the substance have come back positive for gold, other tests have been inconclusive or have determined that the substance raining down on us is not of this world and, therefore, has no known monetary value. There are several testimonies, however, that give us reason to think that in the near future God will use this blessing in a monetary way to supply the needs of His children:

A congregation in Spain was having difficulty making the mortgage payment on their building. Some members had already sold jewelry and other items of value to make payments, but they were still behind. God rained down gold dust for two or three days on them, and they gathered it up, took it and sold it, and were able to pay the mortgage off entirely.

A team from Brunswick, Georgia recently visited Mexico and came back with this testimony: A very poor Mexican lady came to the meetings, hoping to find someone to help her financially. She was disappointed that no one seemed to respond to her need. After she got home and was undressing, a gold nugget fell from her clothing. She was able to sell it and pay all of her debts.

More testimonies like this one are sure to come. We
will need supernatural intervention in our affairs in the
days ahead. We must learn to move into the supernatural now while we are in days of ease, so that when the
days of trauma come, we will be ready.

Will God send gold nuggets to all of us to pay our
bills? Probably not! He will send gold dust to attract
more people to the church and they will give more offerings to meet the needs. God knows how to do it.

On Christmas night 1998, a group of us were sitting
in the dining room of our campground, singing and sharing, and one of the sisters gave a prophetic word. I only
remember three words of that prophecy. They were:
"Abundance! Abundance! Abundance!" When that
word came, I had a vision and saw myself with my right
hand on the West Coast of America and my left hand on
the East Coast of America. Suddenly, I began to gather
in, with great sweeps of my hands, all the abundance of
America. It was one of those prophetic acts that change
us forever.

Then, suddenly, I saw myself beginning to disperse
the abundance to the nations of the world for the end-
time harvest. From the East Coast, I was dispersing it
through Europe and Scandinavia, the Middle East, Africa, the subcontinent of India, and all of Asia. With my
right hand, I began to disperse it in South America and
the Pacific Rim nations.

The vision lasted probably no more than a minute, but
in that minute I knew that I had gathered in from the
finances of America everything that would be needed
for the end-time harvest. I did not sense that the money

would necessarily go through my hands, but I knew that the Body of Christ would have everything needed financially for the end-time harvest. There will be no financial lack.

When this vision came, we were believing God for some miracles for our ministry. God had placed in our heart the determination to be totally out of debt by the end of 1998. Although we didn't actually get the check until the first week of January, God paid all the bills of this ministry, and left us debt-free within a few days of the vision.

The interesting thing is that when we were believing God for abundance for everyone else, we never thought to believe for anything for ourselves. We just gathered in from across America and threw the abundance out to the rest of the world, believing for the end-time harvest everywhere. The Lord, however, took care of us.

Then, someone gave us a gift and we were able to completely refurbish our camp tabernacle in time for the summer program. The seats were reupholstered, the floor and ceiling were painted, and new carpet was installed in the aisles, the altar area and the platform. We were so busy getting ready for camp that I failed to check to see how the money was doing. When I asked on the opening night of camp, I was told that our expenses for renovation had been within $2,500.00 of the amount we received to do the work. God had dropped the exact amount into the hearts of those who gave, and the necessary changes had been made.

It is time to go forth everywhere, proclaiming the abundance.

A friend spoke to me by phone around that same time

and said, "You decreed abundance. Will you do it for my ministry?"

Over the phone, I began to proclaim it: "Abundance! Abundance! Abundance!" She told me later that from that moment, her ministry began to increase financially. She has received one miracle after another, some of them hard to believe they are so great.

Take the limits off of God, and you too will see great miracles of supply. It will happen in the glory.

God has told us that in the days to come we will have miracles "of necessity." Even though our Congress is trying hard to preserve Medicare and Social Security and other social programs for the future, much of it will fail in the days to come, and we will not have at our disposal everything the Congress wants to give us. We have nothing to fear. We will know the healing touch of God in this last day as never before, and God will perform unusual miracles for us of financial supply as well.

When my parents first came to the city of Richmond, Virginia, they knew only one lady whom they had met at campmeeting in the Eastern Panhandle of West Virginia. There was no Pentecostal church in Richmond, and they had come to pioneer one. Other than this one lady, they had no contacts. The new church they started was built up through miracles of healing. These were not just little healings. They were great miracles that were "noised abroad," and these attracted the attention of many people. Every person they prayed for received a miracle, and they never lost a case. For many years my father could say that none of his members under the age of sixty-five had ever died.

It was because those were difficult days, and the people knew they needed miracles. We will see it again. In all the developing countries it is the same. Health care is lacking, people are poor and cannot afford medicines, and great miracles are experienced by those who love the Lord. When we get desperate and pour out our hearts to God, we often see these same type of miracles — physically and financially.

The Golden Glory as A Release of "the New"

Finally, the golden glory is sent to us as a release of "the new." When this miracle is experienced, many others follow. This can be confirmed by many of the personal testimonies we have included in this book. The golden glory results in healing from physical and psychological illnesses, financial and marital restoration and every other type of miracle.

Even more important, the appearance of God's presence in any of these manifestations takes us to higher levels of worship, higher levels of anointing and higher levels of effectiveness in the gifts of the Spirit. Everyone I know who has received one or more of these manifestations is doing much more for God than ever before. In fact, the effectiveness of their ministries has multiplied many times.

This phenomenon causes us to be excited about what's coming next. It makes us excited about today, excited about tomorrow and excited about the future. If God is with us, what do we have to worry about?

The appearance of the golden glory makes people excited about going to church, excited about sharing their faith, and excited about growing in faith so that they can do more for the Lord who obviously loves them so much.

What is the purpose of the golden glory? There are too many purposes to address fully, and we will continue to discover more purposes as we go deeper in the experience.

Chapter 15

Who Can Receive This Golden Glory?

The signs and wonders promised by the Lord were for *"them that believe"*:

> *And these signs shall follow them that believe; In my name shall they cast out devils; they shall speak with new tongues.* Mark 16:17

That would seem to eliminate many who have doubted. The Lord, however, is capable of dealing with doubt and unbelief and of raising us up from it.

It is notable that, at one point, the Lord rebuked the disciples and *"upbraided them with their unbelief and hardness of heart."* The story is told in this same chapter of Mark:

> *Afterward he appeared unto the eleven as they sat at meat, and upbraided them with their unbelief and hardness of heart, because they believed not them which had seen him after he was risen.*
> Mark 16:14

The Lord *"upbraided"* or scolded those who failed to receive the testimony of the disciples who had seen Him after His resurrection, and some of those He scolded that day were counted among the most important of the early believers.

That someone would fail to accept God's signs and wonders is nothing new. Even during the time when Jesus was physically walking on the Earth and performing miracles everywhere He went, He spoke of those who would not believe His signs. In His story of the rich man and Hell, He said that some would not repent *"though one rose from the dead"* (Luke 16:31).

The disciples who had seen Jesus after His resurrection were sure of what they had seen, and yet others would not receive their testimony. Jesus Himself had said that He would rise from the dead, so by rejecting the testimony of these disciples, people were also rejecting the testimony of Jesus.

This same easy rejection is evident among some believers today. God has been telling His people for years that He was about to do some great things upon the Earth, but because it is happening in a little different way than most people expected, many are slow to receive it.

Some people, when they have heard about the manifestation of the golden dust, have said to me, "Sister Ruth, the only reason we believe it is because we have confidence in you." I am grateful for their confidence, but in the future we must believe *"for the very works' sake"* (John 14:11). We must recognize the signature of the Lord upon our human situations.

When we first saw the video that Sister Jane brought

back from Brazil — of Sister Silvania with golden dust falling from her hair, of the pastor taking it and using it to anoint the people, and of the miracles that were following — I knew it was God. Although I had never seen anything like it, and although I had not heard of anything like it, I could not help but remember that when I was a girl thousands of believers had oil supernaturally flowing in their hands. There were Pentecostal believers who rejected it then. They could not believe that God would do such things, but I saw it with my own eyes and it was glorious. I never forgot it.

One miracle helps us to believe for another. Maybe we haven't seen the particular miracle God is giving us now, but we have seen enough of God's acts, we have seen enough of the ways He works, that we can accept it as being from Him.

When you have seen God in action, you are not as surprised the next time. When you know God, you know what He sounds like, you know what He smells like, and you know what He looks like. When He is working, you recognize that it is Him.

We learn to know our earthly fathers intimately. We can walk into a room and instantly know if Daddy is there or not. We know the scent of his shaving lotion. If he is not there, we can know if he has been there and how long ago he left. Can we not know our heavenly Father in that same way? If we can know a person after the flesh, we can also know God after the Spirit. We can know all the characteristics of His nature.

One of my associates knew me well enough that when someone would approach her and say, "Sister Ruth said thus and so," she could reply, "No, she didn't."

"What do you mean, she didn't?" they would ask in surprise.

She could answer, "I know the way she thinks, and I know the way she talks, and she wouldn't say that." And she was always right because she knew me so well.

If we can know a friend or a loved one or an associate this well in the natural, surely we can know the Lord so well in the realm of the Spirit that when somebody gives a testimony of the miraculous, we can say: "That sounds just like my God. He is the Miracle Worker." "I wasn't there, but I know that He loves to do miracles." "I have never heard of miracles like that, but He said He would do new things." "We have seen Him do this and this and this, and it would not be any problem for Him to do the other."

We must not be among those who are saturated with unbelief, but let us be those who are saturated with faith. How can we get that way? By letting the Word of God dwell in us richly, by letting the testimony of our fellow believers dwell in our hearts.

Reading good books on miracles is another way to get ready for what God is about to do. The book *Miracles That I Have Seen*, by my uncle, Dr. William A. Ward, has blessed many thousands of people and lifted their faith for the new things God is doing. My mother's book, *God of Miracles*, is another one that will flood your soul with new faith. Both of them experienced miracles from the time they were very small children, and therefore what they have to say carries great weight.

LOL Why would we allow someone who has never seen a miracle convince us that a miracle is not possible? Why would we counsel with those who have never been healed about God's healing? What authority do they have? Their only authority is in the realm of doubt and unbelief. Believe the testimony of those who have lived in the miracle flow of God.

Jesus *"upbraided"* some of the disciples. He had been teaching them by His words and deeds, but some of them had not heard Him well enough. Some had not watched closely enough. They were not yet aware that He could do all things.

What miracle could have been more important than the resurrection of Jesus? What sign meant more to the believers of the early church? Yet some were not open to it.

They had heard Jesus say:

> *Destroy this temple, and in three days I will raise it up.*   John 2:19

The *"temple"* of which He spoke was His own flesh, but when He had fulfilled this prophetic word, some could not believe.

Don't misunderstand, when Jesus *"upbraids,"* His upbraiding is positive. His purpose was not to put them down, but to raise them up. His purpose was not to degrade them, but to challenge them to new heights of faith. He was not rejecting them. He was not saying that they were somehow unworthy to do His work.

With His very next breath, He said to them, *"Go ye,"* and with that command gave the promise of *"signs following"*:

And he said unto them, <u>Go ye into all the world,</u>
<u>and preach the gospel to every creature. He that</u>
<u>believeth and is baptized shall be saved; but he that</u>
<u>believeth not shall be damned. And these signs shall</u>
<u>follow them that believe; In my name shall they cast</u>
<u>out devils; they shall speak with new tongues; They</u>
<u>shall take up serpents; and if they drink any deadly</u>
<u>thing, it shall not hurt them; they shall lay hands</u>
on the sick, and they shall recover.

Mark 16:15-18

Jesus was giving to these disciples the greatest opportunity anyone had known until that time. He wanted them to get out where the action was, where they could develop their faith, where they could see signs following their ministries.

<u>The very best way to know miracles is to be in situations where miracles are needed, where you can pray for others and declare the miraculous into their lives.</u> The stories of others can never inspire you like God working in your own life can. The stories of Dr. Ward and of my mother will inspire you, but the stories you will remember always are the stories that happen to you personally.

In his book, as well as in his preaching and his conversation, Dr. Ward told about miracles that had happened to him years ago, and he told them in great detail. Some wondered how he could even remember the miracle, much less the details of it. <u>When it happens to you, however, you won't soon forget it. When you see it and smell it and feel it and hear it, it will become</u> engraved on the <u>recesses of your soul, and you will never forget it.</u>

As we grow older, sometimes our memories are not as sharp as they have been in other times, but I find that I can still remember the details of miracles God did for me when I was a child and when I was a young person. Get in the miracle flow, and you will lose a lot of your skepticism. God is confirming His Word with signs and wonders, and we must be ready for the unexpected.

God has set miracles as a means of confirming or approving the preaching of His Word, and those who have no miracles have no means of their ministry being approved. They may get a few pats on the back, a few "thank you's" and a few "well done's," but they have no miracle confirmation for their ministry. This is why we will see an acceleration of signs and wonders in the days ahead. God is raising up His people, and He will confirm them to the world through the miraculous.

We invited a young minister, David Piper, to be one of the speakers of our Fall 1999 Men's Convention. He had been saved for less than a year, but I am sensing that God is raising up new ministries among us. David was a cocaine addict for seventeen and a half years and was delivered in a Benny Hinn Crusade in Birmingham, Alabama. I was in the meeting that night. Since that time, he has been following on to know the Lord, seeking after God. He came to our camp and spent a good part of the summer. Gold dust was falling on him, and oil was flowing in his hands.

He is now preaching in prisons (where once he spent time in prison himself), and is having a great impact. He is able to say to those prisoners, "I know what it feels like to wonder what your daughter is telling her friends about where her daddy is. I have been where you are, but God saved me and delivered me." Reports are that hundreds have been born again over this past year through his ministry in prisons and youth detention centers. After camp ended, he called me nearly every day to tell me some new testimony.

Soon after he got back home, he was in another preacher's house one day, and there was a visiting preacher there who was doubtful about the signs that God is doing. When he looked at David's hands, they were covered with gold dust. He didn't believe it was of God and said, "Go and wash it off in the bathroom, and prove to us that it is God."

David didn't feel that he had anything to prove, and he really didn't want to wash it off. When God does something sovereignly, we want to treasure it and keep it as long as possible, not get rid of it. Because the older man had asked him to do it, however, he went to the bathroom and washed all the gold dust off.

When he came back into the room, David's hands were clean. As they sat there together and talked about the things of the Lord, he began to feel a burning sensation in his hand. He looked down and his hands were again filled with gold dust. Seeing it, the visiting preacher jumped up and said, "Now I believe! I believe! I believe!"

God is dealing with our unbelief, and His desire in doing so is to bring forth in us the ability to believe.

At first this man could not believe — even though He was seeing God's miracle before his very eyes. Our skeptical and doubtful minds want to test everything, to prove everything, but God has given us the ultimate way to prove anything and everything. It is in the Spirit.

We are prone to unbelief. We have two options — believe or disbelieve, and why is it that we always disbelieve first?

In the case of the disciples, they had disbelieved several times. First, Mary Magdalene told them what she had seen:

> *And they, when they had heard that he was alive, and had been seen of her, believed not.*
>
> Mark 16:11

When they didn't believe Mary Magdalene, *"two of them,"* probably meaning the two disciples on the road to Emmaus, told them what they had seen:

> *After that he appeared in another form unto two of them, as they walked, and went into the country. And they went and told it unto the residue: neither believed they them.*   Mark 16:12-13

They had not believed Mary Magdalene's testimony, and they had not believed the two men who walked with Jesus on the Emmaus Road. We can understand them not believing a woman, but why could they not believe two men? They had walked with Jesus in the countryside and listened to His teachings. They had sat with Him at the table. Why did the others not believe them?

Now, after these two failures, Jesus appeared *"unto the eleven as they sat at meat."* We are not told exactly how many of the disciples had not believed, but there must have been a good number of them because Jesus did not

address His words to just one or two of them. He upbraided the entire group for their unbelief and hardness
of heart.

We always feel that God must come to us first or what
is happening is not real. If someone else has an experience first, we are slow to believe them.

Again, Jesus was not cutting them off. He did not declare that He would never again do signs and wonders
for them. Just the opposite is true. He said to them, "If
you will go ahead and preach My Gospel in all the world,
I will be there to confirm your preaching." He promised
them signs that would *"follow them."*

The Lord fulfilled His promise:

> *So then after the Lord had spoken unto them, he*
> *was received up into heaven, and sat on the right*
> *hand of God. And they went forth, and preached*
> *every where, the Lord working with them, and con-*
> *firming the word with signs following. Amen.*
>
> Mark 16:19-20

What a glorious day that must have been! And what
a glorious day this is! These are days of miracles, signs
and wonders, and those who believe for them will see
them.

Don't be discouraged because you have not believed.
Let the Holy Ghost lift your faith onto a new level. If
you are of a doubtful mind or doubtful spirit, cultivate
the faith of God and see the signs, the wonders and the
miracles as they flow from your life and your ministry.
God has chosen you to be an instrument of miracles, to

be an instrument of signs and wonders. If you will do the believing, He will do the rest.

Some who have been involved in revival are resisting this new move of signs and wonders, and if they are not careful, they will find themselves remaining where they are presently and not being able to flow on into the new day of the move of the Spirit of God.

Many individuals are insisting that they are not looking for signs and wonders. One young man surprised me during Summer Campmeeting 1999 by saying openly that he did not want the gold. "My wife has experienced it," he said, "but I don't want it. I only want the harvest." If God is giving us the gold for the sake of the harvest, how can we reject it and expect to see the harvest?

The gold is the lure God is using to bring in the lost. It is not for you and me to determine how God can bring them in. That is His prerogative. If we want the harvest bad enough, we will do whatever it takes to get it.

We have no right to tell God how to run His harvest. Our only response must be to say, "Here am I, Lord, use me." Then we must let God do it the way He wants to do it.

God's river is overflowing its banks. It has a mind of its own. It will flow where it will, and nothing we can do will stop it. Just about the time we think we have the river contained in our denomination, it moves on to some denomination or some individual we have never considered worthy of it.

We are moving into the greatest outpouring of the

Spirit the Church has ever known, and God will do unusual things that will amaze all of us.

 Prepare to do some things you don't normally do. Prepare to act in ways you don't normally act. Prepare to say something you wouldn't normally say. These are days of signs and wonders and miracles, and if you are willing, God will forgive your moments of doubt and unbelief and launch you into the worldwide harvest field.

Lord,
I am willing.

Chapter 16

What Should Our Attitude Be Toward This Golden Glory?

I never get concerned when people have a hard time stepping into something new in God. It is normal to require some time to adjust to the new. I do have a hard time, however, when people DON'T WANT to step into new things. I find this attitude difficult to understand. If God has something deeper and richer for us, why would we hesitate to move into it? If God is ready to bless us, why would we resist?

One of my mother's favorite phrases, one that she used often when praying for people, was: "Open up a little more. Open up to God." She had a great prophetic gift, and all of us loved to stand in front of her and hear what God would say through her. She would never speak a word, however, until she felt that people had opened up to what God was about to say to them.

Sometimes, when this happened to me, I felt that I was about as open as I could be, but she would still tell me to open up more. I would be thinking that I was surely the most open and yielded person in the world. How could she insist that I open more? Even if I had been on

225

an extended fast, with much prayer and seeking the face of God, she would say that I needed to open more. In fact, I never remember her praying for me even a single time without first telling me that I needed to open more to God.

One day I remember standing in front of her, crying because I thought I was open as wide as I could open, and she was telling me to open more. Because she was so wide open, she could tell that the rest of us were not quite that open, and now I understand just what she was saying. I lay hands on people, and their heads feel like a hard block of wood. They seem to be resisting with all their might. I call them "blockheads." When I place my hands on open people, they feel as soft as a sponge, and they seem to be pulling in every ounce of glory they possibly can.

I was sure that Mother must be right that day, and I wanted to open more, but I didn't know how. "Lord," I prayed, "I don't know how to open more fully to You. Cause me to be open." Suddenly, as I was standing there, I felt something wonderful begin to happen. It reminded me of playing the accordion. The bellows of an accordion stick together when the instrument has not been played for a while, and it takes a little while to get them fully opened and filled with air. As they open, there is a unique sound they make.

Suddenly, God was filling the depths of my soul, and I seemed to hear parts of me opening to Him in a way that I had never before experienced. God was teaching me how to open to Him, how to yield to His Spirit, how to flow in the greater things.

Lord open me up to the depths of my soul - teach me

When Mother would say, "Open a little more, yield a little more," she was not being critical in any way. She had experienced this need to open herself, and that was why she was able to help others open to God and receive all that He had for them.

Some have taken a lot longer to come into the fullness of their potential than was necessary, and we can learn by their mistakes. Through listening to those who have come in the hard way, we can see how to come in the easy way.

Times have changed. This is a new day, and in this day, we no longer need to come in as Ezekiel did. He was required to pass through the measurement of the waters up to his ankles, then to his knees, then to his loins, then to his chest, until finally he came into *"waters to swim in."* Now, you can just plunge into the wave and start swimming without any preliminaries at all,

In this day, the wave of God's glory comes crashing in and carries you out into the depths of the Spirit. You no longer have to do it by degrees. You no longer have to take all the steps. God is ready to carry you out into His glory and transport you directly and instantly to His throne.

If you forget everything else about the glory, please don't forget the ease it brings. In the glory, it just happens.

That doesn't mean that you necessarily understand what is happening to you. It may take you years to develop enough vocabulary to describe it. You may not be able to explain it well to others at first. That does not, however, make the experience any less valid. In the glory, it just happens, and you are changed and move from glory to glory.

If you can't explain what God is doing for you, it doesn't matter. The Bible describes it as *"joy unspeakable and full of glory."* Taste the glory of God. Stand in it. Experience it. If there are no words to describe it, don't worry about it. It may be *"unspeakable,"* but it surely is life-changing.

Some people have suggested that we must not desire signs. The Lord, however, has commanded us to desire the gifts of the Spirit, (*"Follow after charity, and desire spiritual gifts ... ,"* 1 Corinthians 14:1). I would say that a sign is certainly a spiritual gift, so if we are to *"desire spiritual gifts,"* it surely is fine and acceptable for us to desire signs and wonders. God not only wants to give us signs and wonders. He wants to make us the signs and wonders:

> *Behold, I and the children whom the* Lord *hath given me are for signs and for wonders in Israel from the* Lord *of hosts, which dwelleth in Mount Zion.*   Isaiah 8:18

In the future, we will be the signs; we will be the wonders; the Lord will use us to manifest His glory to the world. So let us be bold to speak of it and fearless to desire and seek more of it.

When gold dust began appearing on us in the campmeeting services, it was not because we had ever asked the Lord for gold dust. We didn't know what to ask for. We just said, "Lord we are willing to be signs and wonders in this last-day move of the Spirit. Whatever it is

that You want to do, and <u>however You want to do it, we</u>
<u>are willing.</u>" The appearance of the gold dust was one
of the results of that prayer.

<u>We understand why people are, at first, skeptical</u>.
Many times, when laughter was first appearing in the
church, I heard people laughing and thought to myself
that it was probably because they had been to some
laughing revival meeting. When I checked out this
theory, however, I found that many of those who were
laughing had never been in a Pentecostal meeting of any
kind. Laughter was just their response to coming into
contact with the powerful life-giving waters of the river.
<u>Holy laughter has become a powerful liberating force</u>
<u>within the current revival</u>. Here is a testimony our Sis-
ter Jane Lowder gave recently in one of our services:

Jane Lowder, Ashland, Virginia:

> *One afternoon, in the three p.m. service, Pastor Wallace*
> *Heflin came to me and said, "A pastor from West Vir-*
> *ginia has come down for just this service. He brought a*
> *young woman who is in the last stages of cancer. Some-*
> *time before you turn the service over to the speaker,*
> *whenever you feel it is the right time, I want you to call*
> *her up and pray for her." He didn't tell me where the*
> *pastor and his guest were sitting or what she looked like.*
> *The Spirit was present in the service, and during the*
> *praise and worship, people were falling out of their seats*
> *with holy laughter. After I had taken the offering, I be-*
> *gan to sense that it was God's time to heal that woman*
> *and I sensed, by the Spirit, the area where she was sit-*
> *ting. I looked that way and declared, "God shows me*

that He is about to do a miracle for a young lady who has come from West Virginia for prayer. Please come forward?"

It took two people to help her get to the front, she was so weak. She was crying, and they were crying. I asked the woman, "Have you ever laughed?"

She said, "No, never."

I said, "You have never laughed in your life?"

She said, "Never!" and with that she bent double in laughter. Then she fell in the Spirit and laughed on the floor for the next two hours. I never did get around to praying a formal prayer of healing over her. She was laughing so much I went ahead and turned the service over to the afternoon speaker, Brother Glenn Garland.

Brother Glenn proceeded to call out a little boy, saying that streams of power and the very presence of God were there to heal and set him free. He said to the boy, "God shows me there is something wrong with your leg, but as you run, God is going to heal it." The boy began to run across the front, and God touched him. We could see his feet straightening as he ran. Brother Glenn called him back and asked him to run again. While all this was going on, none of us knew that this was the son of the woman who had come from West Virginia to be healed of cancer.

When I finally got out of the Tabernacle that day, it was quite late. When I got to the dining hall, however, some people were still there finishing up the evening meal. As I walked from the entrance down to the front where the serving line is located, people began falling from their seats in gales of laughter. The woman from West Vir-

ginia suddenly jumped up. She said, "While I was laughing, all the lumps went out of my breast. All the lumps went out from under my arms. All the pain went out of my body."

"You know," she continued, "when I came up, I looked outside and saw my son climbing a tree ..." She was laughing so hard she had difficulty getting it all out. What she was saying didn't seem to mean anything to me at the time. Then she told us the whole story, and I understood.

Her son had been run over by a car. The person who ran over him backed over him, and then pulled up and ran over him again. The boy's legs were so damaged that they had required metal plates to be inserted in them, and doctors had told them that he would never run again. In fact, he was not to attempt it or he might injure himself worse. His mother kept him indoors and never let him go outside to play.

He certainly was not able to climb a tree, yet there he was outside that afternoon doing just that in the presence and power of God. His legs were again agile and he could move normally.

This mother was delivered from much more than cancer. Through the miracle of holy laughter, her son was healed and she was released from the fear of letting him play like other children. It all happened when that great presence and power of God was there, putting laughter in the people's mouths.

These experiences have taught me not to make judgments about where people are in their Christian experience. God is bringing us into new realms. In a few moment's time, He is doing things in their lives that they never thought they would experience. Who am I to question what God is doing?

If God wants to cover you in gold dust, let Him do it. If He wants to make you a wonder and a sign, let Him do it. It He wants to place upon you the spirit of laughter, let Him do it. Worship the King and let His supernatural replace your natural. Let Him carry you out into the depths. Let Him take you from glory to glory. Let Him pour forth His golden glory on you.

If you have not yet moved into signs and wonders and miracles, then draw a line like I did, and let God know your desire, by jumping over it.

"The new" is nothing to fear. It is always something divine, something that is being birthed from above. You may not be able to put a name on it because it has nothing to do with the will of man. It only has to do with the cooperation of man with the will of God.

In many church circles, people in the congregation have not been given the opportunity even to do the old things, much less "the new." They haven't been allowed to manifest "the old," much less to have liberty to bring forth "the new." If we want all that God has for us, we must embrace what God is doing and move into it.

From the moment I first experienced this sign, I began to declare it, speaking about it all across America and in other countries. Thousands responded to it and received a new touch of glory upon their lives. Others, however, seemed to have a problem with "the new." Even some of those who had come into "the old new" had a problem with this "new new." What they had received was so glorious that they pitched their tents and wanted to stay there, while God was moving on, leading us into even greater things.

Tents were not made for permanency in one location. They were made for moving from place to place. That's why tents have stakes that can be pulled up when it is time to move on. With such a tent, we can move higher and higher up the mountain. God has places of greater revelation for us, places of greater rest. Let us move on into "the new."

Camping is meant to be done in one place only until we understand the next place we should be. Then it is time to move on.

That doesn't mean that "the new" is something temporary. We can make each new experience in God a permanent part of our lives without preventing our moving into ever richer and deeper experiences.

After the Day of Pentecost, it was ten years before the outpouring of the Spirit came again in the same sovereign way, and then it came to the Gentiles for the first time. From the outpouring at Caesarea until the next sovereign outpouring at Ephesus, another ten years went by. Between these sovereign outpourings, however, the believers were not just sitting by waiting for another outpouring to come. They were utilizing what they had already received.

Because we are living in the end-times, things are happening much more rapidly. There is an acceleration of events. You don't have to go on a forty-day fast to receive this glory. It's here.

Trust the Spirit of God. He is the teacher. He is the Guide. Trust what He is doing in your churches. Trust what He is doing in your ministries. Trust what He is doing in your personal lives.

Sometimes when God wants to send us somewhere, we are afraid that the people He is sending us to are not prepared. How inept we imagine God is! When we get to where God has sent us, the people are usually more ready to receive than we are to give.

Stop holding back. Be bold with the new things God is giving us.

Many believe that their friends are not ready for our campmeeting, but we let the Lord get them ready. We let the atmosphere of worship get them ready. When people of every background get into Heaven's atmosphere, they get ready quickly.

It is time to be daring, to move into "the new," to lay aside the former ways and to embrace what God is doing. If some simple phrase is dropped into your spirit, start singing it. If something is given to you, share it with others. Lead others into it. Let God multiply the little you have and make it much. It doesn't take long. In a moment's time God can lift you out of your surroundings and into His presence, into His glory, into a totally new realm of the Spirit.

It's a lot like going to school. By the time you become a senior in high school and feel like you know your way around, you suddenly graduate and become a freshman again. Suddenly you are taken out of your comfortable surroundings and thrust into another world. One minute you are at the top, and the next minute you find yourself back at the bottom, starting all over again.

This can be a terrifying experience for some. They quickly forget that they are climbing ever higher. They suddenly feel so inept, so disoriented and so out of place that trying to find their way around is about all they can accomplish at first. They remember the "good old days" and long for them. They would rather be back in high school feeling confident as a senior than to be in college stumbling around with the freshmen. It's the same way in the Spirit.

One of the difficulties in moving into "the new" is that we constantly want to fall back on the familiar. We long to do the things we excel at. Stumbling around learning some new method is no fun. We must keep in mind, however, that "the new" is not a step backwards. It is always a step into a higher way. It is always a promotion. God is looking for those who are so ready to move into "the new" that they will not mind sounding like novices for a little while. They will not be totally disoriented by the fact that they stumble around a bit at first. They will not be embarrassed by the fact that they don't quite know their way around. They know that they are moving into something more efficient and more rewarding.

It seems that every time the Lord is leading you into something new, He sends some important people to be in your meeting. They witness you stumbling your way into the new thing.

Years ago, when we were worshipping in St. Peter-en-Galicantu, the Catholic Church on Mt. Zion, Brother Ed Miller, from the earlier Argentine revival, came to visit us. He was a great man, and we were very blessed by his presence.

I made the serious mistake (one that I have tried not to make in the years that followed) of telling our people in advance what a great man he was and how honored we were to have him. As a result, they were all nervous and stumbled through their prophecies. After the service, Brother Miller felt he need to give me some good advice. "Sister Ruth," I remember him saying, "I suggest that you use your more mature people to prophesy in the services at St. Peter's, rather than those who are in training. Have them prophesy in your meetings at home."

I laughed. "Those were our more mature people. It was my fault. I made the mistake of telling them who you were, and they became nervous."

Now, if we have the greatest preachers in the world with us, I say nothing to our people in advance. I don't want to make them nervous and prevent them from flowing in "the new," no matter what it might be.

When the Lord first spoke to us about singing the new song, we would do it during our prayer meetings in Bethlehem. For several hours we would sing spontaneously and flow together in the Spirit. When we went to St. Peter's to have our regular services, however, we would have it in the usual way.

Then one day the Lord said to me, "Can't you trust Me? In the prayer meeting, you are quite willing to sing spontaneously and to let My Spirit flow, but in the church you do it just as you have done for many years."

"But Lord," I said, "some of these people have come from ten thousand miles away to attend a single service on Mt. Zion."

He said, "So?"

"Well, Lord," I tried to explain, "when we are in our prayer meeting and we stumble a little, it's all right, but that would not be good for the church service. It's too important. We want to be more smooth there."

The Lord continued to push us toward the new song, until we finally said yes and started singing the new song in every service at St. Peter-en-Galicantu. The Lord honored us for it, and the number of people traveling long distances to be in a single service increased. Now people were coming because they wanted to be in the flow of "the new."

There is a greater anointing upon "the new," even when we are still stumbling, than on the polished old. Again today, God is looking for those who will move forward, without fear, into the unknown.

Some love the old hymns of the church so much that they cannot consider attending a service where new choruses are sung. I feel sorry for them. They are missing so much. It is time to break forth into "the new" and receive all that God has for us in this hour.

We are coming into greater anointings, greater glories, greater signs and wonders. In nearly every service, I feel the supernatural rain coming down, the dew and the mist falling on my arms. God is giving somebody gold teeth in every service. There are those who are having gold dust in every service. In every service we are receiving creative miracles of healing. In every service, God is beginning to bring forth "the new."

As we sing the old year out this December 31 and sing the new year in, we can expect great things in God. As we dance the old year out and dance the new year in, we can look forward to greatness in Him. As we rejoice over the blessing of the old year and look forward to the promise of the new, we will expect the greatest harvest ever and experiences beyond any we have ever known before.

So what should our attitude be toward this golden glory? God said He would declare new things unto us *"before they spring forth,"* and when He declares them, we must too. John the Revelator was not afraid or ashamed to speak of the signs he saw:

> *And I saw ANOTHER SIGN in heaven, great and marvellous, seven angels having the seven last plagues; for in them is filled up the wrath of God.*
> Revelation 15:1

When God gives us signs and wonders, we must not hide them. They are for people to see. John spoke of the sign he saw and was not silent about it. He wrote about it. He wanted everyone to know what he had seen. The rest of the apostles were not silent about the signs that followed their ministries. They spoke boldly of them. They knew it was the signs that would convince the hearts of men.

When we first began to experience the gold dust, we, too, had a little of that old thinking, that we should not look at signs, but only at Jesus. We had to be careful not to re-peat those worn-out cliches. If the Lord had not wanted us to notice His signs, He would never have put them in our meetings. If He did not want people to have their minds on the sign, He would not have spotlighted them.

Should we talk about these things? The Lord has showed me that when we talk about them, they happen. So if we fail to speak of them, they may cease.

I talk about signs and wonders because I am believing for them more and more. I am not satisfied with one gold tooth or a few people with gold dust on their hands and faces. I want to see a deluge of signs and wonders coming into our meetings, so much so that everybody present goes back to his home with a new touch of God on his life.

Not everyone is ready to declare these new signs and wonders. Brother and Sister Maltese, who pastor in New Jersey, told me this story:

Around September or October of 1998 someone gave them a copy of the video of Silvania that was made here at the camp that summer. When they had seen it, they called two or three of their mature believers to come and watch it also. They all agreed that what they were seeing was of God, but Pastor Maltese counseled the others to caution. They should not tell the other members about it, he felt, because they surely would not understand.

October 18 was Sister Maltese's birthday, and she and her husband invited a couple from the church to go out to lunch with them. The man was one of the more conservative members of the church and one of the more successful businessmen of the congregation. As they were eating lunch together, the wife of this gentleman noticed something on him that looked to her like perspiration.

"Why are you perspiring so much?" she asked.

"I'm not perspiring," he replied.

"Yes you are," she insisted. "Just look at you."

With this, everyone's attention was drawn to the man, and they all saw beads of oil on his forehead. He reached up to brush away what he thought was perspiration, and gold dust appeared under the oil. The well-kept secret was suddenly out of the box.

This brother had been born with one kidney deformed. It had never functioned, had atrophied and become the size of a nut. This had overworked the other kidney all his life. Not long before this, he had learned that his good kidney was so diseased that he would have to undergo a kidney transplant. When he returned to the doctor a few days later, to make a final decision about what to do in this regard, his doctors found that he had two perfect kidneys.

God is doing it — whether we like it or not. He is performing signs, wonders and miracles, and we must be bold to declare them to the world. Gold teeth, supernatural oil, raining gold dust, miracles of healing, creative miracles, multiplying money ... He is doing it all today. Don't be ashamed of it, and don't try to hide it. It is all for the purpose of glorifying God and bringing men and women into His Kingdom.

Become supple and pliable in the Lord's hands. Let Him melt you and shape you into the image He desires. Be tender in His hands. Let Him remove inflexibility from your life.

God is manifesting His presence in ways we have never experienced before, and He wants us to be excited about it. Get excited about what God is doing, and you won't have to worry about talking about His signs and wonders. You will not be able to keep silent.

Chapter 17

What Should We Expect in the Future?

What we are seeing now is only the beginning of the great things God is about to do. In the near future, we will see more and greater manifestations of God's glory.

I have been watching this phenomenon, and the most exciting thing I find about it is that God is doing it a little differently each time. He wants the sense of the unexpected to be in our spirits. We must believe Him, not only for the gold dust and the oil, but for other signs and wonders. He is about to do many great things for us.

The promise of the Lord to those who would be His disciples was:

And THESE SIGNS SHALL FOLLOW THEM THAT BELIEVE ... .   Mark 16:17

The beginnings of the fulfillment of this promise is recorded in the same passage and in the opening chapters of the book of Acts:

So then after the Lord had spoken unto them, he

*was received up into heaven, and sat on the right
hand of God. And they went forth, and preached
every where, the Lord working with them, and confirming the word WITH SIGNS FOLLOWING.*

Mark 16:19-20

*Then they that gladly received his word were bap-
tized: and the same day there were added unto them
about three thousand souls. And they continued
stedfastly in the apostles' doctrine and fellowship,
and in breaking of bread, and in prayers. And fear
came upon every soul: and MANY WONDERS
AND SIGNS WERE DONE BY THE APOSTLES.*

Acts 2:41-43

When God commissioned His disciples to do His work
in the Earth, He promised to be with them in visible
ways. He did not tell them to look for one specific sign
or wonder or for two or three signs and wonders as proof
of His presence. He told them that He had destined them
to experience a life of great signs and wonders.

Once the disciples had received the power of the Holy
Spirit at Pentecost and had gone out and begun to live
out the life of signs and wonders, the biblical record
sometimes did name a particular sign or wonder that
occurred in their midst. The verses that follow these, for
example, speak of a miracle that happened with a
crippled man who had been laid daily at the Gate of the
Temple so that he could ask alms of those who went in
and out. As the disciples came by one morning, this man
experienced a touch of the glorious anointing that was

on them, and he who had been crippled from birth suddenly went *"walking and leaping and praising God"* (Acts 3:8). This one miracle alone was responsible for thousands more being spiritually transformed that day.

For the most part, however, the Bible does not name the specific signs and wonders that were seen by the early church. They were far too numerous for that. It says simply, *"And MANY wonders and signs were done by the apostles."* God did MANY signs and wonders then, and He wants to do MANY signs and wonders now.

The Scriptures say of the ministry of Jesus:

> *And many other signs truly did Jesus in the presence of his disciples, which are not written in this book: But these are written, that ye might believe that Jesus is the Christ, the Son of God; and that believing ye might have life through his name.*
>
> John 20:30-31

If Jesus did *"MANY OTHER SIGNS,"* surely we can expect to see MANY OTHER SIGNS in our ministries as well.

Healing is clearly one of the signs we should expect to see God doing in our midst. He is willing not only to heal headaches and stomach problems and cancers and other incurable or difficult diseases, but He is showing us that it is time for more creative miracles, such as those experienced in the time of Jesus and the Apostles.

Healing is much less controversial these days. Many Christians have come to accept miraculous healing as an expected manifestation among us. Now, there are many other signs and wonders that God wants to do among us, and He is finding resistance among some Christians. If a certain sign or wonder is not specifically named in the Scriptures, these believers find it difficult to accept it as being from God. But we cannot deny the fact that *"MANY wonders and signs were done by the apostles,"* and God has not changed. His desire is to do MANY wonders and signs for us, too, so we need to be ready for it.

The manifestation of gold dust and gold teeth, as dramatic as it is, has not gotten the attention of some. They have, until now, successfully ignored it. God has said, however, that His glory will now come to us like a sandstorm so that people will no longer be able to ignore it.

Until recently we didn't know anyone who had the gold dust come so profusely out of their hair like it does with Sister Silvania, but in one of Brother Eddie Rogers' meetings this past summer a lady suddenly began to have gold dust fall from her hair in much the same way.

Elizabeth Stamford, from Pastor Ron Smith's church in Eatonton, Georgia, received a gold tooth immediately after Evangelist Eddie Rogers prayed for her in that revival meeting. The next day, while listening to praise and worship music, blue and green and gold flakes began to pour from her scalp. This manifestation has increased to the point that Pastor Smith says it looks like ground-up diamonds falling profusely from her as she praises and worships God. Miracles follow. In just sixteen weeks, more than two hundred have been saved because of this sign in the small town of Eatonton, and she accompanies Pastor Smith to other towns to give her testimony.

In the future, there will be hundreds of people, even thousands, who have similar manifestations and demonstrations. Yes, this in only the beginning of greater things to come.

This present revival will be marked by the miraculous, by signs and wonders. It will not happen because of our state-of-the-art equipment, but because the Miracle Worker is present and is allowed to work. It will happen because of the expectation of our spirits and because we let God's Spirit flow in the midst of us.

As we have seen, God fully intends to make US the signs and wonders. The outpouring of His golden glory upon us is a sign to the world that we are His, and many more such signs can be expected in the future.

Are we ready for "the new"? Are we ready for the new wave of God's glory? Are we willing to step from "the old" so that we can embrace "the new"? Even if we don't know fully what the new entails, we are saying to God, "We trust You, Lord. We know that all that You do, You do well. You do it in Your glory, You do it in Your power."

Because we have been afraid of the unknown, we have only begun to see what God can do for us. He desires to carry us out so quickly into the depths of His Spirit, that we will be amazed.

Don't wait any longer for the outpouring of God's Spirit. It is here. This is the day of the glorious outpouring of the Spirit spoken of in the Scriptures. This is the day in which the glory of God is being revealed. Don't let a day go by without experiencing a new and different touch than you ever had before. Don't let even twenty-four hours pass without coming into a realm in the Spirit that you have never been in before.

What should we expect in the future? After I visited Pastor Shattles' church and he began receiving supernatural oil in both of his hands, the Lord spoke to him and said, "From this night on, I don't want you to ever use man's oil to anoint anybody," and he hasn't. He is still a Southern Baptist in good standing, but he never takes his bottle of anointing oil to the pulpit anymore. God puts oil in his hand with which to anoint the sick, and many unusual miracles are happening as he prays for the sick.

Gold dust appears in every one of his services, and great creative miracles are taking place. People are having organs which were not functioning healed, and even organs that have been removed are being restored. God is giving people new organs. I believe that shortly there will be thousands raised up with a similar anointing for healings and miracles.

I am not making a bold prediction. I have seen it happen. During the 1960s, God raised up, seemingly overnight, thousands of men and women with great miracle ministries. Since we are living in the last days, it will happen in the coming months in even a greater way. We are about to see a spiritual explosion. What began in America with Azusa Street will end with every street in the nation being aflame for the Kingdom of God. I know we haven't seen it yet, but this is the time of "the new."

In many ways, we have not yet reached, in this current revival, the intensity of the revivals of the 1950s and 60s, and even some aspects of the revival of the 1970s. We know, however, that this revival will eventually be much greater than any of those revivals and maybe of all of them put together.

I remember as a child going directly from school to the church, where a prayer meeting was in progress. There would be such a great presence of the Lord in those meetings that we would just stand and weep at the overwhelming sense of the presence of God. I am not minimizing what God is already doing today, but it definitely will get greater.

Recently, Brother Garland Pemberton and Pastor Gary Ladd came to visit with me. Brother Pemberton told me, "Sister Ruth, in those meetings up in Detroit years ago the fire department came once a week and ordered everybody out of the building to fumigate it because there were three thousand people there constantly fasting and praying. They would leave the auditorium just long enough to go to the rest room because they were afraid to lose their seat. They stayed in the presence of God day and night. Even when the fire department came in and moved everybody out, it was just long enough to fumigate the building."

We have not experienced it just in that way yet in this current revival, but we will. The Lord has showed us that our campground would one day have services around the clock and that, at times, we would have to let people sleep in shifts so that everyone could rest in the available beds. It's coming. God is creating a hunger within us.

I never tire of telling the story of my friend Jimmy Smith. In one of his meetings in Ireland, he prayed for a young lady who was born as a thalidomide baby. Those who were affected by that widely-prescribed drug taken by their mothers were often born with partially formed limbs. This lady had small hands that dangled from her shoulders. All her life she had only one desire, to some-day be able to reach down and touch her waist.

Jimmy laid hands on her in the service, she fell out under the power, and her little arms began to jerk. As her arms jerked, they began to extend further and fur-ther until, by the time she got up off the floor, her arms were a normal length. She was able to touch her waist for the first time in her life.

That's the type of miracle God wants to do more of in these days, creative miracles with the eyes, creative miracles with face structure and with parts of the body that have been missing or deformed, either through birth defects or accidents. More and more of God's servants are experiencing this type of miracle in their meetings. Get ready for it, and when it comes, embrace it joyfully.

A friend of mine has a weekly Thursday morning miracle service in Phoenix. Recently a child with Downs syndrome was healed. The facial features of the child shifted and became normal as everything else in his sys-tem also returned to normal.

Aside from gold dust and gold teeth and money mul-tiplying, we have already experienced many unusual signs and wonders in this revival:

We had a visiting youth choir from Washington, D.C. come and sing for us in our campmeeting. Because of the constraints of time, we sent word to them only to sing one song. When the group had finished their one song, however, all of them stayed in their places. No one moved. The choir director was motioning with his hands, with his eyes and with his lips and telling the members of the choir that they should return to their seats. Still they all stayed where they were. After a few moments, when the director had gotten no response, he started another song, and we were blessed by that one as well.

The next day the lady who had brought the choir came to me and began to apologize. "I'm sorry," she said. "We got the message to sing only one song, but … ."

I didn't want her to feel badly. We had all enjoyed their music. "It was so beautiful," I told her, "that I was expecting one of our leaders to step up and say, 'Please, sing another one.' I was glad your young people did it without our having to ask."

"No," she protested, "you don't understand … . I want to tell you why everyone continued to stand there when they knew ahead of time that they were to sing just one song. <u>Such glory came on them while they were singing that when they were finished, none of them could move.</u>"

She was talking about a group of teenagers. They had been so caught up in God that they could not physically move from their places. They were stuck in place, and this is happening more and more these days. God is doing unusual things to show His presence with His people.

Why are we surprised when men and women get

drunk in the Spirit in our services? The same thing happened on the Day of Pentecost.

Why should it surprise us when people are taken out of their bodies and lifted up into the presence of God? These signs and wonders are the evidence that God is with us, and they have been seen in the Church throughout the centuries.

Many of us have fallen under the power of God and not been able to get up when we tried. It is happening increasingly under those circumstances, but also when we are standing or sitting because of the increased presence of God's glory in our midst and His desire to perform signs and wonders for us.

One night during our 1998 Summer Campmeeting one of the young girls in attendance was out under the power of God and, when one of the brothers was called to help her get up from the floor, he found that he couldn't move her — as much as he tried. She was very petite, smaller than his own four daughters, but she seemed to weigh four hundred pounds or more with the weight of glory that was upon her. It was much later before he was able to get her up.

Several years ago, I was in Pretoria, South Africa. I had been invited to speak three nights at a certain church on the subject of Praise, Worship and Glory. There was a good crowd of about a thousand or more people present and we enjoyed God's presence together.

The third night, when I spoke on the Glory and invited people forward to experience it, I was expecting us to have a rather quiet standing-in-the-glory, seeing-visions-of-the-Lord and visions-of-the-heavenlies night.

This seemed to be the type of altar service that was in keeping with my teaching that night. But as the people gathered around the altar, something very different began to unfold. To my right, I saw the cloud of God's glory coming into our midst. The pastor was standing several steps below me, and I called him to come quickly and see what I was seeing.

He rushed back up to the platform, and I pointed toward the glory cloud and said to him, "Look!" No sooner had I uttered that word than a group of some fifty to a hundred people fell under the power of God. As the cloud made its way toward us, in a zigzag pattern, more and more people fell under its power, in small groups. No one had prayed for them; it was a sovereign act of God as that glory cloud came in.

No sooner had people fallen in the Spirit than they began to burst forth in a most amazing laughter. This was new to them, and I had not spoken about it, nor had I anticipated it happening in this way. This went on for a very long time, and hours later people were still trying to find their legs and arms, and gather themselves up and get up off the floor. One very sophisticated lady told me at lunch the next day that she had been forced to crawl to a pole so that she could pull herself up. She seemed to be incapable of getting up any other way, such an amazing power of God had been flowing through her body.

That amazing night proved to be, for me in South Africa, just the first of many amazing nights. Everywhere I went God was doing something that amazed us all. One night I was singing and suddenly noticed that I had lost my accompaniment. Amanda Vanderholt, who had accompanied me from Jerusalem, was still seated at the piano, but she had now slumped over the instrument, overwhelmed by the power of God. One hand was moving up and down over the keyboard, but she was making no contact with the keys. I had never seen her like that, and we have laughed about it many times since.

When I was in Utenhaag, right across from Port Elizabeth, I saw an article on the front page of the South African newspaper about the wife of a pastor in Port Elizabeth and the unusual revival that was taking place at their church. I arranged to have lunch with her so that I could learn what they were experiencing. She told me that her husband and a group of the elders from the church had flown to Singapore to attend a seminar on church growth. While they were away, the One who knows more about church growth than anyone else in the world visited the church, and those who were present experienced a sovereign work of the Holy Spirit. It was so startling that she called her husband and asked what they should do. "Don't let it stop," he said. "Keep doing whatever you're doing until we get back."

The woman was very short and, because the Lord instructed her to lay hands on the heads of all the people who were attending and pray for them, she had to have a chair that she moved along with her, standing up on it in order to reach the heads of the people. This didn't prevent them from falling under the power or receiving the deep joy that God was pouring out upon the people of South Africa.

I spoke that night in a rather conservative Pentecostal church. My hostess, a member of the Dutch Reformed congregation, accompanied me. The South African people are very social, and my hostess was always beautifully and meticulously dressed. Her purse and shoes always matched her outfit, which she changed several times a day.

After the message and a time of waiting in the glory, I invited those who had received some vision or revelation to come forward and share it with the others. After sharing her revelation, this sister fell under the power of God right on the platform, and this was fine — until she tried to get up. Every part of her body was able to get up except her chin, which stuck to the platform. She was a very delicate and graceful person, and she now moved herself this way and that, trying to get her chin unstuck. What a funny sight she was! And we all laughed and laughed together as she struggled to free herself. We were laughing with the joy of the Lord.

That sister was so drunk with joy that we had to carry her home after the meeting, and all through the night I could hear her laughing. The next morning she looked twenty years younger, as if she had received a total face lift. I saw her the next year in a conference in Jerusalem, and she told me that her experience that night had been life-changing. She has never been the same. As she told it, joy and laughter broke out in our midst and many others experienced being stuck.

This experience, the supernatural move of the Spirit,

happened in place after place throughout South Africa where God sent us. In one service, God gave me a word of knowledge about someone who had one leg shorter than the other. When I called it out from the platform, a man way in the back of the church instantly had his leg lengthened. It had been, it turned out, not just a little shorter, but a lot shorter, and now it was the same length as the other.

The signs and wonders we are experiencing today are nothing more than the fruit of revival. God is pouring out His Spirit upon His people, and the natural result of that outpouring are the miraculous deeds He does in the midst of us.

Why should we be hesitant about anything God wants to do for us? Why would we not joyfully reach out and appropriate every manifestation of His power available to us?

Yes, we are experiencing some new and unusual things, some of which have not been reported regularly in the history of the Church. That's because we are moving into new levels of faith, into new realms of God's glory. That's because we are in the last days, and God is preparing us to live with Him forever.

These signs and wonders are not something that we have thought up ourselves or decided to do. This is God confirming His Word. This is God showing forth His power. This is God confirming His goodness. He is the miracle-worker. Signs and wonders are a natural fruit of His very nature.

God is doing so many great things that we cannot keep up with them. Many testimonies are heard only years

Jesus was revealed by signs & wonders

later. It would be impossible to record all that God does. His wonders are boundless, endless, innumerable. Jesus had MANY, the disciples had MANY, and we are having MANY.

Signs and wonders are a natural result of the preaching of God's Word. We should expect them to be there. And we should not expect just one or two. One miracle should lead to another miracle. God wants to give us an increasing progression of the miraculous, until we come into the supernatural, the realm of the miraculous.

Some people seem to be super-spiritual. "We're not looking for signs," they say. "We are more mature now, and we no longer need signs to believe." They have it all backward. Jesus said if you believe signs will follow you, not the other way around. We will never get so full of faith that we no longer require miracles. Faith produces miracles. It always has, and it always will.

It's not the Christians who need the signs to help them believe; it's the world. So when the Christian increases in faith, there will be an accompanying increase of the miraculous as well. We will never grow beyond signs and wonders. They will only increase as we mature in God.

Are we more mature than the apostles of the first-century? Of course not, and yet they had many wonders and signs accompanying their ministries. Stop being so super-spiritual. Believing for signs and wonders is not a sign of immaturity. Just the opposite is true.

If Jesus had to be *"approved ... by miracles and wonders and signs, which God did by him in the midst of [the people]"* (Acts 2:22), should we not expect the same?

Every once in a while, the Lord speaks to us to expect an increase in signs and wonders, and we reach out and embrace the opportunity to glorify Him more. We are thrilled with the privilege of showing His glory to the world.

"Aren't you afraid that people will misunderstand?" some ask. Oh, there have always been those who misunderstand, but that didn't prevent the apostles from believing for signs and wonders, and it must not stop us either.

The wonders we are witnessing are a fruit of the transforming graces of the sovereign Lord at work. Stop resisting His work, and let it happen.

Why should we be afraid of the unusual? God has always done the unusual. If you don't want to be unusual in this world, how can you even be a Christian? Christians are unusual by definition.

If something is not unusual, how could it even qualify as a sign or wonder? That's what signs and wonders are — unusual and unexpected happenings. So if we expect to see God's glory, we must be prepared for the unusual.

God is giving us new organs and causing limbs to grow where none existed before. Why should we be surprised by this?

If we are not comfortable with what God has done so far, how will we be able to receive what is to come?

Once, when I had just returned to Jerusalem from an overseas trip, I walked into our fellowship, and I felt the glory of God as I had never felt it before. It was absolutely awesome! In that moment, I suddenly knew how easy it is to raise the dead and to heal all manner of sickness and disease. How easy it is in that realm of glory! How easy to see people leaping out of wheelchairs and off of stretchers! How easy to see blind eyes opened and deaf ears unstopped! In that glory realm, nothing is impossible.

That glory stayed with us for several hours, as God was giving us a foretaste, as He often does, of a greater day, so that we could encourage ourselves and others to move into the glory realm.

There were no visible miracles that day because there were no sick people among us, but God was giving us a foretaste of the glory to come.

We must not come to God's house with any sense of indifference. We must come totally focused on what He is about to do in our midst. I get excited every time I get ready for another service. I know that God is going to do great things.

Time is quickly advancing and the wave of God's glory is upon us. We are on the verge of something great. The signs and wonders of the early Church were done *"by the hands of the apostles"* and it is time for signs and wonders to be done by our hands too:

> *And by the hands of the apostles were many signs and wonders wrought among the people.*
>
> Acts 5:12

I grew up seeing such miracles. I watched as cancers fell into my father's hand as we prayed. When he laid hands on people, he didn't expect to see God answer his prayer a week later or a month later. He expected a miracle at that moment, and he got it.

Let your faith be raised to receive it today as well. If you pray and something doesn't happen, never be discouraged. Pray again.

Right after Daddy died, the Lord told me not to receive any of his natural inheritance and I told Mother that I wanted only my father's spiritual inheritance. The only thing I have that belonged to my father is a neck scarf. After I was back in America and the responsibility of our camp and church ministries fell on my shoulders, I realized that I needed to move more fully into my father's inheritance. He contended for the miraculous, and I was determined to press into it more fully.

I am convinced that Jesus wants us all to do this. He is saddened when we are indifferent or unconcerned.

Don't let someone else do it for you. If others are doing it, that's fine, but you do it too. When you see others doing it, let God know that you expect it as well.

We have the opportunity today to see not only the same signs and wonders evident at the birth of the Church, but even greater things, because we need to bring in the last-day harvest. This harvest will dwarf the harvest of the first century and will be the greatest of all times.

There are more people alive on Earth today than in all previous centuries combined. All other generations saw only a measure of what we will now see. All other generations had only a glimpse of what we will now experience.

God has raised us up for this glorious day and hour, and He will use you and me to declare His glory in these last days.

It was our privilege to help, from the start, the now-famous Christian celebration of the Feast of Tabernacles in Jerusalem, and we have always attended. A couple of years ago, however, I was invited to speak in one of the services on the glory realm. The night before I was to speak the Lord gave me a wonderful song on my way to the Conference Center. He showed me that the glory realm is "the realm where the angels sing," and "the realm of the heavenly King."

When I was introduced, I got up and sang the song the Lord had given me and read my scripture and, before I realized what was happening, the glory began to break forth in our midst in laughter, something which did not normally happen in that auditorium. Now, there are times when we want this to happen, and there are other times when we might prefer that God would do it in a different way, but God takes it out of the hands of the preacher and lets us know that He is still sovereign over all. By the end of the service a number of very conservative people were stretched out on the seats on the huge platform, and they were laughing uncontrollably. Nobody laid hands on them to pray for them, but they were being touched by the glory. God is doing things differently, and we must be willing to let Him do things His way. God told me that if I would be willing for the Spirit to work as He willed, He would put me on the great platforms of the Earth, and He has fulfilled His promises.

Chapter 18

Raising Up the Foundations
of Many Generations

We are the most privileged generation that has ever lived on the face of the Earth, and we are marching into a new century and a new millennium with a glory that has never been manifested before. Every day from now until Jesus comes will be an exciting one. God's glory will only increase in the Earth.

Every revival comes in on the wings of fasting. For the revival of 1948, God raised up a brother by the name of Franklin Hall. He traveled from church to church across America with only one message — fasting and seeking the face of God.

Franklin Hall had a great anointing that went with the message. I watched him preach and saw that people who had never sacrificed a single meal for spiritual reasons were suddenly launching into a forty-day fast. People who had never gone by a place of refreshment without stopping were suddenly doing lengthy fasts.

These fasts brought in the great move of God which shook America and much of the world. We are still enjoying the results of it today. In like manner, Bill Bright's book, *The Coming Revival: America's Call to Fast, Pray and Seek God's Face* (New Life Publications, 1995), was used of God to help spark this present revival. Since the publication of the book, many prominent Christian leaders have been giving more time to fasting and prayer than they did in the past. We are experiencing a new wave of seeking God, and that is producing the new wave of His glory among us. My friend Mahesh Chavda's new book, *The Hidden Power of Prayer and Fasting* has become one of the fastest selling books on the Internet.

I love the teaching of Isaiah 58:

> *And they that shall be of thee shall build the old waste places; thou shalt raise up the foundations of many generations; and thou shalt be called, The repairer of the breach, The restorer of paths to dwell in.*
> Isaiah 58:12

This is part of the great promises made to those who are willing to deny themselves the pleasure of eating for a spiritual purpose. I love to fast, and I love to preach about fasting — not, however, from the standpoint of what a fast signifies to most people. When we think of fasting only in the context of sacrifice, we miss what God is saying. We must look at fasting from the standpoint of the benefits it brings us. When we do, it becomes easy to fast. When we only think of fasting as denial, it is difficult, but when we can see it as feasting, it becomes enjoyable.

The thing I like most about fasting is that it is "fast." It is a fast way of touching the heart of God. What we can get through years of ordinary seeking after God, can be accomplished "fast" (quickly) through a good fast. Through fasting, we are elevated into a new place in God.

Sometimes it seems that we are standing on tiptoes, and yet our fingertips cannot quite reach what we are desiring in God. It is just in front of us, and we can almost reach it, but not quite. We are just ready to step into something new, but we can't quite understand what type of step to take. This is when fasting can bless us by pushing us over the top. Through fasting we are propelled from one realm into another, and we need never go back to the former.

This is not a short visit or a momentary touch of God's glory. God is lifting us up into something new.

Every single one of the promises of Isaiah 58 are wonderful, but one seems to me to be particularly pertinent to us today. *Thou shalt raise up the foundations of many generations.*

During periods of spiritual darkness which have come upon the face of the Earth, God has touched individual men and women and begun to use them, not only to bless their own generation, but to raise up the foundations of former generations which have crumbled and are lying dormant. This is what God wants to do in our day and hour, and He intends that when the outpouring of His Spirit reaches its climax, it will be a complete restoration of former things for His children.

For example, the miracle recorded in the Bible of the shadow of the disciples passing over the sick and bringing them healing has largely lain dormant for many generations. Christians have not expected to receive the same miracle, and it has not happened, for the most part. Now God is raising this sign up again for the end-times, and we will all witness it.

The miracle the evangelist Philip experienced, being miraculously transported from one place to another is one that we should expect to see again.

Even in Old Testament times, the prophets Elijah and Elisha were used of God to "heal" water unfit for human consumption, call down fire on the prophets of Baal and raise the dead. When they were in need, God sent ravens to feed them. They declared plenty to one widow who found meal in her barrel and oil in her cruse every day during a period of drought and lack and to another widow who borrowed vessels from her neighbors and them proceeded to fill them all with oil from a single vessel, so that her bills were paid and her sons spared from slavery.

There are many other such foundations that God will raise up through this revival. When my mother was a child, for example, she had the privilege of being in Maria Woodworth-Etter's meeting at a time when the great evangelist was being frozen in place for days at a time. She would be preaching, and then suddenly stop in mid-sentence and speak nothing more for several days. When she began to speak again several days later, she would take up with the next words of the sentence begun days before. God is about to do this same miracle and many other ones similar to it for us again.

Mother also told us that in the early days of Pentecost people would act out their prophecies. For instance, someone would be picking clusters of heavenly grapes from the vine and would eat them individually. As they did, they would be acting out the glories they were experiencing in the heavenlies.

We are still much too earthbound, and we all need to break through into that heavenly realm. It's so easy for it to happen. We make it much too difficult. Half of the battle is getting our reasoning minds to stop reasoning and just get lost in the river.

In June of 1999, I had the privilege of speaking at two different meetings in connection with the Catholic revival. I spoke at the priest's conference in Malvern, Pennsylvania, at a retreat center, and then the following week I spoke at the Fire Conference at Presentation Church in Wynnwood. Something wonderful happened there. One of the priests, Father Ed, suddenly began acting out a prophecy, rather than speaking it, as we normally do. He began as if he were preparing to swim, and then started diving into the water. It was obvious to anyone who watched what was happening, as he began to experience the river. Great joy broke forth in our midst that day. It reminded me of the Azusa Street Revival.

Recently, someone was reminding me of the ministry of John G. Lake in Washington and Oregon. Thousands were healed because of the great miracle flow in his ministry there, and one of the cities in that area was soon considered to be the healthiest city in America because of the miracles the faith of this one man had brought to pass.

Entire cities and villages were changed in the time of

Jesus, in the time of the apostles, and through the ministry of other great men and women of God through the
centuries, and it will happen again very soon.

Many of the signs and wonders of former years are
unknown in our time. We have never even heard about
them because they happened so long ago, but we will
soon see them happening again and on a regular basis.
God's will is for us to go continually forward, never backward. There should be an increase of God's power with
every generation. We can reach back and take hold of
that which we are not presently flowing in and bring
them into this present day.

When I first heard of what God was doing with Sister
Silvania and saw the video, it was the first I had heard
of this particular sign. Since then I have heard that the
golden glory was falling in the Argentine revival and
that it became so common that people no longer commented on it. So many people received gold teeth that if
a person did not have three or more, he or she was not
even given a chance to publicly testify of it. So many
had received the miracle that testimonies had to be limited. It was just that common. I had never heard about
that before, but now God is doing it everywhere.

We are beginning to tap into realms in the Spirit that
previous generations experienced, but which were later
abandoned. I firmly believe that anything experienced
by any man or woman of God in previous generations
can be ours today as well — and should be.

You and I have the privilege of raising up the fallen
foundations of every glorious thing that God has done
in a former day. God is willing to do it for us, if our ex-

pectations are high enough. If we are content to be touched and blessed personally, we put limits on what God can do for us. If, on the other hand, we say, "Lord, have Your way in me. Raise up the foundations of that which You did in former generations — whether it is something I have heard about and agree with or not," God will amaze us all with what He does.

In previous generations, God did such amazing things in India, in Africa, in Asia, and in every other part of the world. Let us believe for it to happen HERE and NOW for the glory of God and for the sake of the end-time harvest. Let us call out to God, "Lord, raise up the fallen foundations. Restore signs and wonders to Your people. Glorify Yourself as in days gone by, and do it through ME."

In Jerusalem, we live around the corner from the British School of Archeology, on the same block as the British and Greek Consulates, and near many of the other consulates. Some years ago we became good friends with a particular British Consul General. After he was absent from the city for a period, one day we learned that he was returning and would be lecturing at the British School of Archeology. He sent us an invitation to attend.

The theme of the lecture he gave was how the British first came to Jerusalem, and there were many interesting historical aspects to it. What touched us most that night was to learn that it was the preaching of John and Charles Wesley that had caused the hearts of the British people to be stirred toward Jerusalem. The British had gone to Jerusalem with Messianic expectations, and the government had opened a consular office, not with forethought, but to look after the many British citizens who had gone there for these spiritual reasons.

When he was living in Jerusalem, the Consul General had not been known as a particularly religious man, but I was blessed to hear him speak now of the revival in Britain attributed to the efforts of the Wesley brothers. "These two men," he said, "single-handedly kept Britain from civil war, as the French had experienced." We are going to see God shake whole nations again and turn them around overnight through spiritual revival. We can be free of civil strife and free of racial division through the power of the living God. And the peace we bring to our localities and our nations will be a sign to the people of our times.

Revival brings men to their knees, it convicts sinners and turns them to Christ. May the revelation of the glory of God in the souls of men cause enemy forces to be pushed back, and may we claim our nations for revival, not violent revolution.

Is fasting that powerful? Just read any verse from Isaiah 58 and your soul will be stirred by the promises it contains for those who fast. Fasting helps you crucify your flesh and move into the Spirit realm, and once you have moved into the Spirit realm, anything at all is possible.

When I stood to speak at the Pentagon in June of 1999, I began having visions of that impressive building. I had driven by the Pentagon many times, and it had always seemed like an impenetrable fortress. Now, however, I saw parts of the foundations missing and in need of repair. Parts of the walls needed to be restored, and I began to declare it. I saw that God wants our Pentagon to be kept as a fortress, that He does not want outsiders to take up positions of authority there. He allowed me, in the Spirit, to speak restoration to its foundations and to its walls.

Through Isaiah, God promised:

> They ... shall build the old waste places.
> Thou shalt raise up the foundations of many generations.
> Thou shalt be called, The repairer of the breach, The restorer of paths to dwell in.

Let us believe for it and begin to exercise it in the Spirit.

One night during Summer Campmeeting 1999, I had a great vision of the East Coast of America. I saw some towers, taller than skyscrapers and taller than television towers. I didn't have time to count them, but as I later thought about it, there seemed to have been somewhere between three and six towers situated along the East Coast. These were spiritual towers that God was raising up on the coast as a bulwark against the enemy's intentions.

We are not just to hear prophecies and then sit back. God is warning us so that we can be stirred to raise up a hand against the enemy, to say, "Thus far and no farther." God has given us the authority to do this.

If we were to see a thief coming to our houses, we would not sit still and let him have his way. Even if we were to see it happening to our neighbor's house, we could not sit still and do nothing. We would be compelled to run over there and try to do something.

If we were able to do nothing more than shout to try to frighten the thief away, at least we would do that much. It would be the least we could do.

God wants to place His authority within you, an authority to raise up fallen foundations, to repair breaches, and to raise up paths where people may dwell.

Fasting changes you more than anything else. It prepares the ground, so that when God drops a word in your spirit it will germinate and bring forth fruit.

When Jesus was teaching concerning putting new cloth into old garments and new wine into old wineskins, He said it could not be done:

> No man putteth a piece of new cloth unto an old garment, for that which is put in to fill it up taketh from the garment, and the rent is made worse. Neither do men put new wine into old bottles: else the bottles break, and the wine runneth out, and the bottles perish: but they put new wine into new bottles, and both are preserved.
>
> Matthew 9:16-17

The logical conclusion is that we need a new wineskin. But how do we get a new one? The preceding verse speaks of fasting:

> And Jesus said unto them, Can the children of the bridechamber mourn, as long as the bridegroom is with them? but the days will come, when the bridegroom shall be taken from them, and then shall they fast.
>
> Matthew 9:15

Fasting renews your wineskin and prepares you for the new wine.

For many years, we required that all our camp staff fast on Wednesdays and Fridays. What we learned, however, was that when people fast and they have no choice in the matter and they don't want to be fasting, they receive no benefit from it. It looks good because we have one hundred percent compliance. We're all fasting, but that's all it does.

If we can catch sight of what God will do for us through fasting, we will make an effort to do it.

Fasting is difficult for most of us, and it doesn't get easier until four or five days into the fast, but do what you can. The next time, you will be able to do more.

Any one of the promises of Isaiah 58 is enough to make you want to fast, but if you can develop the godly habit of fasting, all these promises can be yours.

My uncle, Dr. William A. Ward, was blessed to be taken to Heaven several times years before his death. He told us that when he came back one of the few regrets he had was that he hadn't given more. I somehow imagine that we might also have some regrets that we have not fasted more.

When we see that we can move automatically into new realms of the Spirit of God, when we see that we can have new authority in the Spirit, that we can extend ourselves, reaching back and taking hold of things in the past and bringing them into the present, why should we not do more of it?

This revival will be beyond anything we can imagine.

To me the proof is that when the Holy Ghost speaks to us about it, it is with one superlative after another.

Uncle Bill, who went home to be with the Lord in July of this year, visited a leprosarium in the Bahamas. The head doctor considered the patients to be so contagious that he did not permit Uncle Bill to go inside. Instead, fifty-six of the occupants were permitted to come outside to receive his prayer. Even then, he could only pray for them from a safe distance of fifty feet. After Uncle Bill had prayed for the fifty-six leprous men and women, he prayed for those who were still inside and had not been allowed out because they were the worst cases. He decreed that everyone within the sound of his voice would be healed.

Sometime later he was in a meeting here in America and David Nunn in his sermon was telling a story about a leprosarium in the Bahamian Islands where one hundred lepers had been healed. He knew it was the same case. "I was the evangelist," he told Brother Nunn later, "but I didn't know there were that many healed. I didn't even know I had prayed for a hundred lepers."

He called the missionary in the Bahamas to confirm the matter and was told that even those inside the building that day had been healed, and the leper colony had closed. That's what I want to see all over the world, and I know we will see it, as we press on into this new wave of signs, wonders and miracles in the Spirit.

Stop and think of every great story you have ever heard of the miracle power of God at work — regardless of when and where it happened. Whether it was in the first century in Jerusalem, in the pioneer days of

America, somewhere on the mission fields of the world or in the early days of the twentieth century, it makes no difference. Begin to declare what God says, that we will build up *"the old waste places,"* that we will raise up the fallen foundations of previous generations, that we will become repairers of the breach and restorers *"of paths to dwell in."* If you can believe for it, God will surely bring it to pass.

Several years ago I was in Jerusalem and was sharing with the people the miracle of what God was doing through satellite television. A young Jewish man came up to me and said, "Sister Ruth, I want to tell you of a way to reach people that is even more powerful than television."

I was curious and asked him what that was, and he said, "You need to get a website, because the Internet is growing faster than any other means of communication. Soon there will be two hundred million people on-line."

I asked the young man to secure us a website and soon he was setting it up for us: www.revivalglory.org. It has been amazing to see how much response we have received through our website. Aside from informing people about our meetings in Jerusalem and America, the site has served many other purposes. We put prophecies on the site. We have our books available there for people to read in many languages and also in portable file format (PDF) that can be downloaded in remote locations of the world. We also have sound files of my songs that can be played.

Sometime in the near future, I am told, we should be able to broadcast live from our campground in Ashland,

Virginia, to the whole world, and I believe God will do that for us.

I sense a multiplication, an abundance, in the movings of the Spirit of God. I feel the stirrings of God in my soul, and am sure that we will all be amazed at what He does for us in the days to come.

If your faith has grown a little rusty, ask God to stir you up. Ask Him to erase limitations from your mind. Refuse to be limited by what you have heard in the past. This is a new day.

God has called us for this day and hour and has given us the authority of His name. He is sending His glory upon us and causing us to see it descend. It is coming as a cloud, as rain, as golden dust, as oil, as a mist, and the whole world will be amazed at what He will do and how He will do it in these days of *Golden Glory*.

The wonderful thing is that He wants to do it through YOU. He wants YOU to serve up miracles to the world. He wants them to come from YOUR hand. He wants them to come from YOUR mouth, and they will.

Hallelujah!

A Prophetic Word by Ruth Ward Heflin

I shall do greater things for thee than you have considered. There is glory which is yet to be revealed. You
shall not only see it come from the pores of your skin,
but you shall see it rain down from the heavenlies. It
shall fall from the heavens, even upon the people.

You will be in gatherings where you will see the rain
falling inside the building. You will be in meetings where
you will see gold dust beginning to fall upon the people.
I shall do it from within, but I shall also do it from without. I shall do exploits in these last days.

I am working on your faith, for faith must be more
than a doctrine. Faith must be an experience day by day,
so that when you will see the signs and wonders and
miracles I send, you will believe without question.

I am giving you simplicity of faith, and you will walk
in it. You will raise the dead. Many of you shall be used
in this way also in these last days.

Greater miracles, greater signs and greater wonders
are just ahead. Even this day I shall perform miracles
for you, My people. I shall do signs among you, I shall
do wonders, and I shall do it by my Spirit.

I shall cause an awesome sense of My presence to come
into your life, that shall abide with you even from this
day forward. And you will walk softly, softly, softly ...
You will walk softly before Me, and thus you will not
miss out on what I am doing in the Earth.

— Thus saith the Lord!

Appendix:

Excerpts from Newspaper and Magazine Articles About the Golden Glory

Under the byline of Sibella C. Giorello, a Richmond Times-Dispatch staff writer, the following article appeared on Sunday, August 22, 1999. It was accompanied by full color photographs taken during Silvania's meetings in the camp.

The woman with the short auburn hair walks onstage wearing a bright red dress over an ample frame. She does not carry a purse, and during more than five hours of religious services, she does not excuse herself to use the restroom. These are the two things Silvania Machado stopped when the signs and wonders began: carrying purses and excusing herself from services, no matter how urgent the call. "Too many skeptics are ready to pounce," she says, "too many people want to throw stones."

"It is easy to judge," she says.

A Brazilian woman in her mid-forties, Silvania, as she is known, stands before 1,500 people at Calvary Pentecostal Tabernacle in Ashland earlier this month. It is a Friday night and the air under the Tabernacle roof compresses summer humidity and the funk of superheated humanity.

People have driven from New Mexico, Florida and California to be here, to dance in the humid night, to praise God, and to watch Silvania.

On the stage, Silvania lowers her head and closes her eyes. Occasionally she raises her olive-skinned hands to the black night. She sings and sways to the music. The dancing continues for nearly an hour. Sweat rolls down backs.

Suddenly Silvania looks up. One hand quietly moves to a place near her heart. Nodding, assenting to some inaudible voice, she leans forward over an open Bible and runs a hand over her head, her fingers strumming her short hair.

Gold dust rains. It pours from her head, scattering over Scripture. A yellow iridescence paints her face and each time she turns her head, sparks fly.

The crowd cries, "Hallelujah!"

"Amen!"

"Praise God!"

Sister Silvania's miracle has come again.

* * *

Silvania Machado is said to have suffered from three types of cancer — liver, bone and leukemia. As the cancers progressed for more than a decade, green bile emanated from her orifices and pores. She vomited throughout the day. Too weak to leave her home, and too ashamed of her appearance, her life was bound by her husband, Luiz, and their four children.

One spring day in 1995, Silvania says, Luiz brought home a friend.

"Please, take Silvania to an evangelical church," the friend said. "Let them pray for her."

Catholics through South American culture, Silvania and Luiz went to the evangelical church nearby, which was associated with a church in North Carolina. The minister asked Silvania, "Do you give Jesus thirty days to change your life?"

"I have been sick twelve years," Silvania said. "What is thirty days more?"

This was on a Friday in early April 1995. The church prayed for Silvania three more times in the next three days and by Monday night, Silvania was certain the end was near. She says it was one of the longest nights of her more than four thousand nights of illness. She closed her eyes, and begged death to cease her suffering.

Tuesday morning Silvania woke up. Luiz said her skin looked different. It was no longer green. Silvania acknowledged that she felt better, much better than she could ever remember. Several days later, they say, they went to the doctor, who said Silvania was healed.

No more cancer.

"I know Jesus healed me," Silvania says, sitting in a room at the Comfort Inn in Ashland, an hour before the Friday evening service at Calvary. Her interpreter sits near and an open book, *Uno Deus*, lies on the double bed.

"And I don't believe the healing was all in my mind. I don't believe in that at all," she says, her dark eyes widening. "Cancer comes from hell. It comes from the devil. Jesus heals."

About a year after her healing, Silvania says, she attended a prayer vigil. Luiz says that they did not know what a prayer vigil was, and that Silvania had dressed for a night on the town. But during the vigil, something strange happened.

"What is this?" Silvania asked her pastor. She lifted her hands. Oil dripped from her palms.

At another prayer vigil, her face sparkled with tiny flecks of gold. Sometimes the gold would not wash off.

In March 1996, a missionary from Calvary Pentecostal, Jane Lowder, traveled to Brazil. Lowder's interpreter was the sister of the church's pastor. As she customarily does, Lowder prayed and preached with the congregation, and she baptized Silvania with the Holy Ghost — a Pentecostal anointing that comes when one receives the Holy Spirit and begins to speak in tongues. Lowder stared at the woman with the golddusted face. *Why does she put that on her face?* Lowder wondered. *She's prettier without it.*

Later, the pastor explained: Gold had come to Silvania during prayer. They could not explain it, except to say that Silvania had been ill and Jesus healed her and now these signs and wonders like gold and oil were appearing and they were certain it was the work of God.

In December 1997 Lowder returned to the Brazilian church and brought back to Calvary a videotape. Lowder wanted to show Silvania's miracle to the Rev. Ruth Heflin, director of Calvary.

Heflin, whose parents started the religious camp forty-five years ago, had just returned from Brownsville, Florida, where a revival was drawing national attention. Even the secular press — Newsweek and The Washington Post among them — featured reports on speculation that a supernatural, end-times, religious revival was sweeping America.

Heflin invited Silvania to come to Calvary. She wanted to see the signs and wonders for herself.

In August of last year, Silvania and Luiz attended services at Calvary for the first time. Heflin wept. The gold fell on her. It stayed for days, months. And it seemed to propagate. Wherever Heflin traveled to other churches after Silvania's visit, the gold came to people.

"It comes through your skin and sits on you," Heflin says. "You see sparkles, it recedes and then comes out again with perspiration. It just keeps reproducing."

* * *

Some who have witnessed Silvania's supernatural out-pouring have Scotch-taped the gold dust into their Bibles. Others have reportedly taken it for analysis. Results apparently varied: One test found the dust was similar to platinum; another said it was oil between gold flakes; another claimed it was monetarily worthless.

Many of those who believe Silvania's miracle say the chemical components in the dust are meaningless to their faith. "The gold doesn't have to do with how man measures metal," says Debbie Kendrick, a Calvary member who has seen Silvania preach several times.

"And if this is a substance created miraculously, if it's cre-ated supernaturally, then you're subjecting it to manmade instruments in a lab and comparing it to substances we know of in the Periodic Table. It might not be anything we've ever seen before. It's more like manna from heaven."

Heflin claims she's also seen other miraculous manifesta-tions of the gold: gold teeth appearing during services; a

Baptist preacher in Atlanta who has gold dust falling on him from above during sermons.

Heflin says ... "I'd never heard of gold myself, but I think it's because the coming of the Lord is so near. We, the church, are his bride, and He is an oriental bridegroom and they always bedeck the bride in gold before the ceremony.

"Other people say they've had visions of the white horse Jesus is coming back on, and that the horse is pawing the streets of gold in heaven with impatience and the gold is raining down."

* * *

Silvania maintains the gold and oil are incidental.

"Even without them, wouldn't my testimony be enough?" she asks through her interpreter. "Wouldn't that be worthwhile?

"There's no reason I'd want to lie when the Lord has done so much for me. What do I have to gain from that? My goal is not to travel the world and show the gold. My goal is to open my mouth and speak of Jesus, the salvation I received, how he healed me and the signs that followed."

Silvania and Luiz have recently returned to America from travels in England, Switzerland, Germany, France and Belgium, where they say more than seven hundred and fifty people came to call Jesus their savior, at their behest. Silvania also says that the metal detector beeped in one airport as she passed through security, but officials could find nothing on her that would trigger the system — except the gold on her face; she didn't have time to shower after the service.

Her financial compensation comes from donations. Heflin says the camp in the past has given her "the smallest type of honorarium you would expect if you were on a speaking circuit," or several thousand dollars.

"But she preaches in places where she doesn't get paid," Heflin says. "This is more like the kind of offering you give missionaries. They have no money themselves; they lost it all paying her doctor bills. We have missionaries down there who see how they live, and it's humble. When Silvania arrived this weekend, I gave her my credit card to go buy a dress because the dress she was wearing was very humble. It was the same one she wore when she came last year."

* * *

After an hour of giving her testimony on stage through her interpreter, with her face glinting in the floodlights, Silvania offers to pray for people.

She says that she has seen miracles in healing when she lays hands and prays — a deaf and mute child who started speaking; a blind woman who told her she "shined like the sun, because she saw the gold."

The air is thick and hot, but more than a thousand people file orderly to the stage. Silvania takes out her vial of oil, collected from her skin while she prays in private, she says, and anoints foreheads. Laying hands on the people, she murmurs in their ears. Some people fall out, and are caught by Calvary security and laid on the tabernacle floor.

For more than two hours, Silvania prays. She touches each person tenderly, including a man in a wheelchair with a basket that holds a book, *Hell's Best Kept Secret.*

His name is Rick Goff. He came to Calvary from Morehead City, North Carolina, after watching a fifteen-second video clip on the Internet showing the gold dust falling from Silvania's hair (www.revivalglory.org). Goff says his first reaction arose from skepticism.

"I said, 'This is foolish.' But then I thought, 'If it can get people to think more about God, it can't be foolish.' It's got to be of God because it's good. People are seeing signs and wonders. Look at my hands."

He lifts them high. They are curled with paralysis.

"The gold dust is on me," he says. "Everybody's looking for God's outpouring of the Spirit to believe, and some people see it and still don't believe. But the real sign and wonder is when I get out of this chair. His mercy is going to lift me right out of it."

Djimlor Brown of Petersburg is among the few people who did not stay under the tabernacle roof. Sitting in a lawn chair next to the covered seats, she watches the crowds pulse forward as a light breeze furls the hem of her cotton dress.

"I don't have to go forward," Brown says. "I was here last year when she came. It's been a year now and gold still comes. A few weeks ago it came up out of my skin. She's all the way in Brazil and I'm here."

She nods.

"So it's real," she says. "I know it's real."

* * *

Under the byline of David Eames in the Fredericksburg, Virginia, Free Lance-Star, the following article appeared on September 12, 1999:

It is a recent early morning and I sit at my computer and stare at the blank screen. My usually busy fingers are frozen in place. How do I write it? How do I begin? How do I present the facts so it doesn't sound like science fiction? And am I going to lose any credibility I have gained as a writer? Who will I alienate? Who will I offend?

I stand up, walk over to my window and look outside. It is black except for a neighbor's porch light. Sunrise is hours away. I sit back down at the computer.

Sometimes writing is very hard because you want it to be so very right. Maybe if I just tell it the way it has been presented to me ...

Silvania Machado, a Brazilian woman in her mid-40s, had been in constant pain for well over a decade. She had been diagnosed with leukemia, liver cancer and bone cancer. In the final months of her disease, green bile escaped from her rotting liver and came through the pores of her skin and orifices. She was a walking dead person, far beyond the reach of medical science.

In early May, Silvania, raised as a Catholic, was prayed for by members of a nearby evangelical church. Silvania woke one morning soon thereafter, and her pain was gone. Her husband remarked that her skin looked different. It was no longer green. The doctors shook their heads in amazement and told her that her cancer had disappeared. Her liver, spleen and stomach had been rebuilt. It was nothing short of a verifiable modern-day miracle.

I stop typing for a minute and lean back in my chair.

Maybe I should end this woman's story right here. Everyone knows about sickness and suffering. Everyone will rejoice with Silvania in her restored health, whether attributing it to God, to prayer or to the power of suggestion. After all, many people have been miraculously healed before.

Once again I get up and look out of the window. The branches of a young oak are swaying in the wind. A storm is passing by. I hear the sound of thunder.

Someone once told me that God is easily pleased but not easily satisfied.

He is the ultimate personal trainer. Just when we think we have stretched ourselves to our limit, when we have believed beyond our capacity, when we have stood before some mirror and flexed our little faith muscles and admired our spiritual progress, then our trainer comes along and asks us to go a little further, lift a little more, believe a little deeper.

I fold my arms and think how people might react. Some readers will finish this column and say, "That is the most ridiculous thing ever to appear on the pages of this hallowed newspaper. Pure poppycock. Let me turn away from this foolishness and cast my eyes on something I can trust, like our government's account of the Waco tragedy on Page 1."

Others will turn up their noses and smell something slightly sulfuric about it all.

And still others will take a deep breath, bend from the knees, and approach it with skepticism or maybe just plain curiosity — but approach it nonetheless ...

One year after her dramatic healing, during a prayer vigil at the same evangelical church in Brazil, Silvania noticed an oil emanating from the palms of her hands.

"David, the oil has a very faint fragrance," our friend Kathie Fette of Bowling Green told me after hearing Silvania speak last month in Ashland, Hanover County. "Slightly sweet. I've never smelled anything like it before."

Now, three years after it first occurred, Silvania still collects oil from the palms of her hands and uses it to anoint those who come to her for prayer for healing.

But even more unusual and more controversial than the appearance of the oil is the manifestation of gold dust that began about the same time. It is a substance that surfaces on Silvania's skin continually, despite daily washings. A substance that has set off metal detectors in airports. A substance that when she brushes her hair, a cloud of golden glitter falls around her.

"The gold dust was very apparent even from a distance," Kathie told me. "When I saw her close up, I was trying so hard to be prayerful and reverent and not ogle her, but curiosity got the better of me. She had a lot of gold on her face. It was also in her hair, on her hands, and some on her clothes. Her face just sparkled. I was so skeptical when I went. I am sure that there is a lot of counterfeit stuff going on in the name of revival. But what changed my mind about her was her testimony. She is very simple and just exudes genuine love and caring."

Since Silvania's first visit to Virginia last August, the gold dust phenomena has happened to many others. The director of the religious facility in Ashland has experienced it for months at a time. It has occurred to people in at least one church in Fredericksburg.

I mentioned Silvania's story and the meetings in Ashland to my son, who went to a church conference in North Carolina recently. He wasn't unduly impressed.

"Dad, it happened to a lot of people there at the conference. Some of my friends found gold dust appearing on their hands. God is just doing some very strange things to get people's attention."

The hows and the whys of it all are certainly a mystery to even the most devoted believer. Some are convinced it is just one part of a supernatural religious revival beginning to sweep over the world. Other believers are concerned that people are paying too much attention to these "signs and wonders."

But whether it serves as an object of ridicule or a subject of praise, this much is certain: Silvania Machado's story and ministry are attracting a great deal of attention. They can scarcely do otherwise.

So, maybe my son's evaluation is right: Maybe God is just trying to get people's attention. God — or maybe I should say, gold — has a way of doing that.

I read what I have written again and again. I consider the weight of each word. I try to purge the bile and polish the gold. I look out my window. The storm has now passed and the eastern sky is beginning to lighten.

The long night in just about over.

* * *

In the August issue of End-Time Handmaidens Magazine, founder Gwen Shaw wrote:

There's Gold in the Glory

"It's golden rain, and there's always gold in it."

When I wrote those prophetic words in one of my earlier books called *The Parable of the Golden Rain,* I never could have dreamed that one day the actual gold of Heaven would visibly fall from Heaven upon us in such an abundance that we would see it with our natural eyes from the last row of seats in a great auditorium. But that is exactly what happened at the End-Time Handmaidens and Servants 24th World Convention in Dallas this July. There was gold in such abundance that no matter how often the women would come and collect it with Scotch tape, there would still be sparkles of it on the steps leading to the platform and all over the platform. We found it on our clothes, our skin, our hands, our shoes — everywhere. We all watched in amazement when our speaker, Rev. Robert Shattles, the pastor of Friendship Baptist Church in Austell, Georgia, told us how God has brought revival in his ministry that was accompanied with supernatural signs of gold and mystic oil.

I kept reminding myself of the Scripture, "... *neither have entered into the heart of man, the things which God hath prepared for them that love him*" (1 Corinthians 2:9).

I first saw the "gold dust" (which also looks like tiny diamond chips) when I was in Jerusalem in April. Sister Nancy, Ruth Heflin's co-worker, gave me a little which I sprinkled in my Bible. I have treasured it and felt that it was a wonderful reminder of the greatness of God. But other than that, I did not see any — until ...

Until our World Convention in the first week of July. Then it appeared suddenly in Rev. Shattles' meeting. His black suit became covered with it around the collar and down the front as he was praising the Lord down among the people before he went up to the platform to speak. After that, it started appearing on many different people all over the hotel, and continued to do so after the convention was over.

We have just received a letter from one of the End-Time Handmaidens who was at the meeting. She writes: "I thoroughly enjoyed the convention. I still have gold dust on me. I baby-sat a baby today, and before I knew it, the gold dust was on her face. After I wiped her mouth, I showed one friend some gold dust on a tape. She touched the gold dust and the tips of her fingers were covered with it.

"I had that gold dust all over me after Ruth Heflin prayed for us. I rushed back to Oklahoma to rub it on my kids. By the time I got back to Lawton, it was all in my car. It was all over my banner and my T-shirt. I taped it off of my T-shirt to give to people and it keeps reappearing! Everybody I told went wild.

"I went to the church and told Pastor P. While I was there gold dust specks fell in the chapel. He said the city was blocking his building project again. Twenty-four hours after the gold flakes fell, everything went through, and a quarter of the steel frame has been put up for the new sanctuary! Now that's God. This is all so glorious. I laughed and laughed. I don't understand it all, but it has good fruit." (Karen S., Oklahoma)

Another sister dropped us a line at the convention. "Last December when Ruth Heflin spoke in Florida, the gold dust was 'everywhere.' My husband did not speak against it, but only said, as we drove back to Orlando, that he would 'have to think about this gold dust happening.' Several weeks later, on Saturday, December 19, a few of us met in a home to pray for Israel and America, since President Clinton had just arrived in Israel for the peace negotiations. Upon returning home at 11 p.m., while eating a cheese sandwich, I thought I saw two 'sparkles' on his forehead and told him it was gold dust. Disbelieving, he went to the bathroom mirror to look. As he turned his head, gold dust appeared on his cheeks, in his beard, and all over the back of his neck. We were sobbing to think that the 'Lord of Glory' would reveal this 'shimmer' of His presence in such a way after we had been praying for His City of Gold." (Georgean H., Apopka, Florida)

Another amazing report came to us even before the convention was over: "We have an End-Time Handmaiden that needed to leave Thursday morning. She took home a video of Tuesday night's session when Robert Shattles spoke. She showed it to her group last night and one of the girls in her group had 'glory dust' all over her. The girl called her sister to tell her what had happened. Her sister is a believer, but her husband is not. The sister told her husband about the 'glory dust' and the unbelieving husband said that it was strange because when he had looked in the mirror that night at about the same time the video was being shown, he had 'glitter' all over his face. It is still there this morning! Praise the Lord!" (Marie G., Texarkana)

Since returning from the Convention, we received the following letter: "Dear Sister Gwen, I came to Dallas to the Convention on the invitation of Mary S. after the homegoing of a mutual friend. It was a financial sacrifice to come, but I knew it was what God wanted me to do.

"Believing for a healing at this outpouring, I came with open mind and great faith. When the gold was first mentioned, observing flakes on me and Mary, I looked around for machines in the ceiling to be blowing this around (doubting Thomas) or ushers to be sprinkling as they moved about. I saw nothing.

"Tuesday, I observed the amassment of the 'glitter' and the 'aura' around the evening speaker, Robert Shattles. The more he spoke, the brighter he became. God had previously healed me of cancer, MS, and a torn-up knee. So, when it was announced that those with bone problems were healed and that they should get up and run, I obeyed and ran. After a lap around the ballroom, I made my way back to my seat praising Father for healing my 80% missing disc. All of a sudden, I got a 'whamo' in the lower back. It was just like something was whacked into place that it barely fit into. The pain was severe and I kept praising Him for the healing. My lower area became so hot, I noted it to Mary, and she felt the heat of the healing as well as others around me. The pain vanished as the heat increased. I became covered in gold. I was then directed by God to ask a lady behind me, 'What prayer need do you have?' She told me that she had asthma and said that no one had ever asked that of her before. The next night she told me she was healed. Praise God! May childlike faith never vanish in the obedient followers of Christ."

The day before the gold dust appeared at the convention, Rev. Esther Cherry, from Ontario, Canada, received this amazing prophetic word from the Lord, and handed it to us on the platform: " 'Behold, I stand at the open window of Heaven,' saith the Lord. 'My eyes have seen, and my ears have heard your worship, and I am well pleased. Behold, do a new thing, even now! I have begun to pour out My glory, My maximum glory. My golden glory shall fall on all who are ready and seeking Me. Yea, and I will shake the nations. All that is not Mine will fall. But all that is Mine will be built up and glorified. I will exalt My faithful servants, and I will guide and direct your steps. Expect great things! Look for them! Pray for them! And you shall receive!' "

* * *

Under the byline of Andy Butcher, the following article appeared on the Charisma Internet newsservice.

Gold Dust Phenomenon Stirs Up Questions among Charismatics

While gold dust keeps appearing in Charismatic meetings in the United States and abroad, metal tests puzzle those who say the substance is falling from heaven. A Brazilian evangelist at the center of the "gold dust" phenomenon being reported at Charismatic churches across the United States and Europe says she is unfazed by scientific reports suggesting that all that glitters is not what it seems.

Two independent tests on samples of the gold-colored dust that falls from Silvania Machado's head during services have found the substance to be more like plastic glitter, with no gold content.

But Machado, who attributes the manifestation to her divine healing from cancer, is untroubled by the conclusions of the analyses carried out on behalf of "Charisma" magazine. "To me, it doesn't matter what it is as long as it's from God," she said. "Some people focus on the signs instead of the fruit. I must continue to share with the world what God has done in my life and the life of my family."

Speaking through an interpreter, Machado tells packed churches how after more than ten years of sickness, during which she desperately sought a cure, she was finally healed after being prayed for by Christians. Now when she prays for others, gold-colored flecks start to rain from her head.

The curious occurrence is happening elsewhere. Revivalist Ruth Heflin — who first brought Machado to the United States after hearing about her ministry — regularly sees the same manifestation at her meetings. She believes the dust is a sign of God's glory.

"The Lord loves for us to show off the gold dust because of His relationship with us," said Heflin, whose ministry is based in Ashland, Virginia. "We couldn't do this ourselves. He is doing it because His coming is so near."

These days Machado avoids carrying a handbag to or stepping down from the platform at her meetings to avoid accusations that she is faking the phenomenon, reported "The Richmond Times-Dispatch" recently. One of those attending a meeting at Heflin's Calvary Pentecostal Tabernacle told the newspaper that chemical components of the dust were meaningless to her faith.

"The gold doesn't have to do with how man measures metal," said Debbie Kendrick. "It might not be anything we've ever seen before. It's more like manna from heaven."

Meanwhile, churches also are reporting incidents in which people's silver fillings are being miraculously renewed or even replaced by gold ones. A number of cases have been documented and verified at Toronto Airport Christian Fellowship.

Heflin stands by Machado. It was God's presence, not the gold dust, that first convinced her Machado was genuine, she said. "I began to weep because of the wonderful sense of His presence," Heflin said of Machado's meetings. "Perhaps we should call it 'glory dust' instead of 'gold dust.'"

A full report on the gold dust and gold teeth phenomena will appear in the November 1999 issue of "Charisma." The article contains an account — documented by dental records — of an Oklahoma woman who received seven gold crowns during a healing service in Tulsa six months ago.

* * *

Under the byline of Kimberly Winston, the following article (accompanied by photos of Bob Shattles and Renny McLean) appeared in The Dallas Morning News, October 10, 1999.

Gold Rush: Glitter-like dust is latest proof of God's presence, Pentecostals say

As Pentecostal services go, this one seemed typical: dozens of people "slain in the Spirit," some falling as slowly as trees, others dropping like rag dolls. Holy laughter punctuated the prayers, and here and there people shook as with a seizure.

The Rev. Bob Shattles, an avuncular man with graying hair, moved among the eight hundred people gathered at Christ for the Nations Institute in Dallas, laying on hands here, listening there, praying everywhere. And then, the gold dust came — a scattering of tiny spangles that appeared on Mr. Shattles' shirt and pants and soon sparkled on the clothes of those nearest to him. Several people used black "prayer cloths" to brush at him, gently folding the dust inside. Still glittering, Mr. Shattles told the crowd how, beginning last November, God began sending gold dust to him every time he prays. "I wouldn't care if it was bird feathers falling on me, as long as God's doing it supernaturally," preached Mr. Shattles, a Southern Baptist pastor visiting from Atlanta. "It's not about gold dust. It's not about crowds. It's about lost souls."

For a year, a handful of itinerant Charismatic-Pentecostal preachers such as Mr. Shattles have traveled North America, leaving trails of what looks like gold dust wherever they go. Last week it fell in a Deer Park church outside Houston. Last month it shone in a Tulsa congregation. In the past year, gold dust has glittered in churches in Ohio, Georgia, Oklahoma, Montana, Florida, Washington, D.C., Virginia and Canada. It has been particularly widespread in the Houston area. And where it falls, both believers and skeptics speak out in its wake.

"God is doing a new thing," said Deborah Peregrine, a Houston woman who says she has seen the gold dust in a dozen Texas churches. "It is a manifestation of God's glory. And people are being healed, but not by man's hands."

Religion sociologists are just beginning to learn of this latest development in the Charismatic-Pentecostal movement, which has an estimated 450 million adherents worldwide. It is a movement that has grown beyond its blue-collar origins in fundamentalism to touch every economic class and Christian denomination, including Catholicism. But Charismatic-Pentecostals are united in their belief that the Bible is the true Word of God and that in it He promises proof of His power and love. Many point to the Gospel of John 4:48 to explain the gold dust: *"Then Jesus said to them: unless you see signs and wonders, you will not believe."* Mr. Shattles also points to Psalm 68:13, where the wings of a dove are covered with gold.

Margaret Poloma, a religion sociologist at Vanguard University, a Pentecostal school in California, has seen the gold dust appear in her own church. Believers say it is "a special sign of God's presence," she says. "They have a whole different world view where the supernatural is natural," she said of her fellow Charismatic Christians. "There is an intuitive way of knowing and expecting miracles. It is another paradigm and requires a paradigm shift."

Benny Hinn, the television evangelist who recently moved his headquarters to Dallas, reported on the September 10 broadcast of "Praise the Lord" that he had experienced gold dust. Paul Crouch, his co-host and Trinity Broadcasting Network's president, described seeing the dust on Mr. Hinn's face, hands and jacket. "I think Heaven's door opened a crack and a little of the street dirt came down on you," Mr. Crouch told him before an international audience. "I did not invent it, I did not ask for it," Mr. Hinn replied.

Another Dallas-based evangelist says his ministry has been blessed with the gold dust for the past year. The Rev. Renny McLean said he first experienced the gold dust last October in Tulsa while he was preaching at Abundant Life Church, an Assemblies of God congregation. Since then, he says, the gold dust has shone everywhere he has preached. "It is not man," he said during a return trip to Tulsa in August. "I just outright say that. It is not us at all. It is God. We are just His people, His servants. It is a sovereign movement of God."

According to the Rev. Kenneth Sturgill, who brought Mr. McLean to his Big Stone Gap, Virginia, church in January, Mr. McLean told the congregation to "expect a miracle." He then asked people to pray that the gold dust would come, and it soon did. Mr. Sturgill counted eighty-five people with gold on them that first night, and he says the gold has returned to every meeting since then. But he met unbelief when he tried to share his church's joy with other pastors. "Each season, each revelation that comes along, there are those who receive it and those who are skeptics," he said.

Wherever the gold dust falls, stories of healing and prosperity follow. Mr. Shattles says that he has seen a crippled girl's legs straighten before his eyes when covered with the dust and that others have been cured of cancer. Mr. McLean tells of a Virginia woman whose eyesight was restored, a Harlingen man whose $400,000 debt was "erased" and a Cleveland woman who grew a new liver.

So far, no one associated with the dust is claiming that it is real gold. Believers say it doesn't matter what the dust is — glitter, tinsel or the purest gold — because its composition is beside the point. The crucial factor, they hold, is that the dust is a manifestation of God's presence, a sign of His devotion to His people. "I never considered to have it tested," said Dr. Jerome Parker, leader of Church of the Living Word in Akron, Ohio, where the gold dust has appeared on the faces, hands, hair and clothes of his congregants twice a week since Mr. McLean's visit there last March. "I just believe God. I don't doubt it. I don't see him as fabricating something. I don't view him that way."

The gold dust came a long way before falling in Akron. Its first appearance is thought to have been in the 1980s in Argentina, a country that, like much of Latin America, has been experiencing a Charismatic-Pentecostal revival for a number of years. It was first reported in North America late last year when Silvania Machado made a guest appearance at the Toronto Airport Fellowship Church, the church that reported nightly bouts of "holy laughter" in 1994 and the appearance of gold tooth fillings in people's mouths last March. Ruth Ward Heflin, a traveling evangelist based in Ashland, Virginia, and an associate of Ms. Machado's, is thought to be the first person on whom the dust appeared in this country.

Witnesses say it appears on her skin and clothes in tiny bars, stars and scrolls. "You can't even feel it," said Norma Powers Marlowe, who hosted Ms. Heflin in her Kingwood home when the evangelist made a three-week preaching visit to Houston.

"It comes out of the pores of her skin. It is awesome." Mr. McLean says the gold dust was bestowed on his ministry during a visit to Ms. Heflin last fall. Mr. Shattles, too, says the dust began to appear in his ministry after he was "laid out" — struck by the Holy Spirit — as Ms. Heflin sang a song. He had a vision, he said, that he was in the Lord's throne room and God told him he was saddened by empty churches. God told him, "I'm going to put an anointing on you that's going to stop the lost from walking away from you," he said.

In a fax sent from her ministry's headquarters, Ms. Heflin said of her Houston trip: "Every place we went, the gold dust came. The exciting thing was that it didn't happen while we were there but would come afterward." She described several incidents, including a thick fall of gold dust on plants at the base of a church podium she preached from, and a woman who reported that her purse was "full of gold" when she returned home from one of Ms. Heflin's appearances.

Staff writer Jeffrey Weiss contributed to this report.

* * *

Under the byline of Sandra K. Chambers, the following article appeared in Charisma magazine in March of 1999:

/1997

Pentecostal Evangelist Calls Christians to Expect the Unusual when Revival Hits
Ruth Heflin challenges churches to stop limiting what God can do

Two years ago, Ruth Ward Heflin heard God's heart cry for America and gave up an international ministry to focus on what has become her passion: the coming spiritual revival in this country. Returning to her home base near Ashland, Virginia, she now travels and ministers in churches and conferences across the nation.

After her brother's death in December 1996, Heflin saw an outline of the United States on a banner dropping down from Heaven. Lights began to come on all across the country on this banner until there was not a city, town or village where the light could not be seen.

"I knew God was showing us the pattern of the coming revival," says the fifty-nine-year-old preacher.

Author of three books, *Glory*, *River Glory* and *Revival Glory*, published by McDougal Publishing, Heflin has spent the last thirty-nine years traveling to every country in the world. She founded a church in Jerusalem, Mt. Zion Fellowship, and currently serves as pastor of Calvary Pentecostal Tabernacle in Richmond, Virginia. She's also director of Calvary Pentecostal Camp, a family campground in Ashland, where people gather in the summer and weekends throughout the year to focus on prayer and revival.

"When I first returned to the [United States]," Heflin told *Charisma*, "the Lord gave me a vision of some cornfields and a lone country house in the middle of them. He said He was sending me to the heartland of America."

Though quite a change from her former globe-hopping lifestyle, Heflin found in these small towns and small churches a deep hunger for God and for a move of the Holy Spirit.

"I know revival is coming," Heflin said, "because I see unity developing in the Body of Christ. People are so hungry for God that they're willing to forget their doctrinal differences and come together."

Heflin believes all mainline churches will be involved in the coming revival, and she has even ministered recently in a Roman Catholic church in Philadelphia. Her passion for revival was born during prayer meetings she attended as a child.

"I've always had a burden for our nation's capital, and I believe when revival hits Washington, D.C., it will be the head and not the tail," she told *Charisma*. "I believe the glory of God will flow from the Capitol to the Pentagon, from the White House to the State Department."

Currently, she says, our nation is being shaken by God. "But I don't feel distressed about what is happening in Washington, D.C., because God is working through everything." Referring to President Clinton's impeachment, she urges

Christians to pray for Clinton rather than criticize him, and she views the current White House scandal as "a mirror for everybody's heart" that should cause every person to examine his or her own sins.

Heflin believes the church in the United States will begin to experience more supernatural signs and wonders as we move closer to a season of revival.

"We are beginning to see more miracles at our camp meetings in Virginia," she said. "In addition to healings, we've seen oil appear on people's hands and have literally felt the rain of the Holy Spirit come down during a service. Sometimes I've looked to see if there were pipes leaking!"

In recent meetings, Heflin has claimed that people sometimes see what looks like gold dust falling on them during worship. The dust supposedly sticks to people's hands, faces or clothing and later vanishes. While there is no verification that this alleged miracle is legitimate, Heflin and her audiences believe it is tangible evidence of God's presence.

During the Latter Rain revival of the 1950s, those involved in similar meetings said anointing oil sometimes appeared on worshipers' hands; people also smelled perfume-like fragrances and even saw "clouds of glory" hovering over congregations. Critics dismissed such reports, but Heflin says Christians shouldn't limit God.

"People tend to run away from anything that might be new or a little controversial," she says, "but there are a lot of people who need signs. And God's going to send them as part of the coming revival."

Under the byline of Elizabeth Moll Stalcup, the following article appeared in the November 1999 issue of Charisma magazine:

When the Glory Comes Down

Recently many American churches have reported unusual manifestations of God's presence, including the appearance of gold dust and reports of dental healings involving gold fillings. What is God saying through these miracles?

When I pulled into the wooded parking lot next to Calvary Pentecostal Tabernacle in Ashland, Virginia, I could hear lively praise music coming from the meeting house — a wooden structure that seats more than fifteen hundred people. Although it was a sweltering summer night — with no air conditioning in the place — people were singing, clapping their hands and even dancing in the aisles.

I grabbed my seat in the second row and looked around to find Ruth Heflin, a fifty-nine-year-old Pentecostal minister whose family has preached at this camp meeting for forty-five years. I scrutinized her, searching for any trace of the supernatural gold dust she says has been falling on people for months in these meetings.

Despite the heat, Heflin was wearing a long-sleeved black dress. I watched her closely as she worshiped, and I saw no metallic gleam anywhere. But as the service progressed, tiny specks of gold began to appear, first on her face and then on her clothes. I remembered what she had told me about the gold dust when we talked on the phone the day before: "It falls like rain, or it just suddenly appears."

I searched the air over Heflin's head. With its high ceiling and theater-style seats, the Tabernacle was open on all sides to the surrounding woods. Occasionally I thought I saw something floating in the air, but each time it turned out to be a buzzing insect drawn to the bright lights.

As I watched, more gold appeared on Heflin and on some of the women in the music team. I was skeptical. After all, I had worked as a geologist for the federal government for seventeen years. My scientific training told me this was impossible.

"Lord," I prayed silently, "If this is of You, I want to know."

A few minutes later I saw flecks of gold on the face of a teenage girl a few seats away. Later, I spotted two tiny bits of gold on my wrist. Baffled, I held my wrist up to the light and twisted my hand back and forth so I could see the gold as it sparkled. This was hard to believe. Was God really manifesting the glory of His presence in a tangible way?

Excerpts from Articles About the Golden Glory 297

Sparkles From Heaven?

For about six months, *Charisma*'s offices have been flooded by fax and e-mail reports of gold dust falling on people during worship, as well as accounts of believers receiving supernatural dental healings. Silver amalgam fillings or crowns have turned to gold or platinum, or even to white enamel. In other cases, people claim their dark amalgam fillings have miraculously turned to shiny silver. Others claim they received new fillings or crowns that appeared in their mouths where they had had no previous dental work. And some say whole teeth have turned to gold.

According to church growth expert, C. Peter Wagner, miracles like these are not new. In Argentina's revival in the mid 1970s, teeth were mostly being filled "with a hard, white substance that dentists could not identify" Wagner recalls.

Wagner and his wife, Doris, first heard of the dental miracles in the early 1980s when they encountered the ministry of Omar Cabrera. "Today," Wagner says, "there is hardly a church that I have been to in Argentina where numbers of people haven't had supernatural dental work."

In services conducted by Argentine evangelist Carlos Anacondia, Wagner adds, "People can only give a public testimony if they've had three or more teeth filled. If they've just had two teeth filled, that is considered normal."

The dental miracles spread to Brazil in the early 1990s, where the first reports of gold dust also originated. Although there have been isolated reports of gold fillings in North America even in the late 1800s, the phenomenon only became widespread in 1999.

Heflin says she saw gold dust for the first time in February 1998, after some of her associates visited Brazil. The daughter of Pentecostal pioneers, Heflin says she never doubted that the gold was a miracle from God. Within a few days of hearing the reports, people began to see flecks of gold on Heflin's face when she preached.

By April 1998, Heflin began seeing gold on the faces of others. Once, a gold nugget the size of a dime fell out of a woman's dress during a women's convention where Heflin preached. At the same conference, tiny flecks of gold appeared on the face of a guest speaker. It seemed the more Heflin talked about the phenomenon, the more it occurred.

Because so many pastors were uncomfortable with the idea of God putting gold dust on people's skin, when Heflin traveled she was careful how she reported it. She kept quiet if the pastor asked her not to mention the gold. But she still saw gold dust appear on faces in the congregation, even when no one had said a word about it.

Pastors admonished Heflin to "focus on the Giver and not the gift," she says. But finally she decided that to stop talking about it would dishonor God — because she believes it is a sign of His glory.

"The Lord loves for us to show off the gold dust because of His relationship with us. We couldn't do this ourselves. He is doing it because His coming is so near," Heflin says.

Whenever Heflin talks about the gold dust, it falls on someone nearby. In November 1998, Pastor Bob Shattles of Friendship Baptist Church in Austell, Georgia, asked Heflin to minister to his congregation. When she prayed for him, he felt overcome by the Holy Spirit's power and saw an extended vision.

The next morning, Shattles says, oil began flowing from his hands, and by the evening service, gold dust appeared on his neck and face. He says he received an unusual anointing for evangelism that day — and he now claims that he has led more than two thousand people to Christ since the encounter.

Heflin finally decided she wouldn't minister in a place where she is not allowed to talk about the gold.

"I had a major speaking invitation canceled because of it — but I never felt bad because when you've got the gold dust, you don't care," she says. "It is like a sovereign sign from Heaven that is so glorious that you don't care about the approval of people because you know you have God's approval, and that is all that matters."

By the end of last year Heflin had gold dust on her face almost every time she preached. Soon she was not alone. In March, during a conference at the Toronto Airport Christian Fellowship (TACF), almost seven hundred people claimed they received gold or silver fillings. The church put the story in their newsletter and posted it on their web site, and almost simultaneously reports of gold manifestations began occurring in Oklahoma, California, Florida, Montana, Tennessee, Kansas, North Carolina, Ohio and outside the United States.

A Contagious Phenomenon

Everywhere that Heflin or Shattles preached, gold miracles were reported. The phenomenon spread from Toronto, too, as well as from South Africa, where it had actually occurred a few months earlier. "It is highly contagious," says Marc Dupont of Fort Wayne (Indiana) Vineyard Christian Fellowship.

After the conference in Toronto, TACF pastor John Arnott excitedly called Ché Ahn, pastor of Harvest Rock Church in Pasadena, California, to tell him about the miracles. Although it was 11:30 at night in California, Ahn asked Arnott to pray for him over the phone when he heard about the gold fillings.

The next morning, Ahn noticed that all his dark gray amalgam fillings had turned to shiny silver. "They were bright," Ahn says. "I just said, 'Wow.' It gave me enough faith that God was up to something."

Ahn already was scheduled to speak at churches in Oklahoma and Tennessee that week, so he shared the story of the gold miracles in both places. People received gold crowns and fillings at each location, and the miracles were repeated at his home church in Pasadena and at a church in Pennsylvania when he visited there the next week. Since then Ahn has seen the miracle duplicated in Indonesia, the Philippines and Hong Kong.

But what does it mean? Why would God put gold in people's mouths and sprinkle gold dust on church audiences? Everyone involved in this unusual movement has a different opinion: Some say it is a sign that Jesus is coming soon or that revival is near or that God is simply displaying His extravagant love.

"I believe this is a sign to make people wonder," says Trevor Pearce of St. Martin's Episcopal Church in Bergyliet, South Africa. Using his distinctive Anglican terminology, he says the gold is "an outward and visible sign of an inward and spiritual grace." He advises his parishioners not to pass the sign or stop at it, but to "follow the sign to God and hear what He is saying."

Ahn agrees, noting that God always uses signs and wonders to attract the curious. Recently, a man who visited Ahn's church told God he would become a Christian if he received a gold tooth. Says Ahn: "He didn't get a gold tooth, but he came expecting it. He heard the Gospel and came under conviction, and he gave his life to Jesus later that week."

Wagner notes that dental miracles seem to attract even more attention than healings from diseases such as cancer. "Perhaps because it is something you can measure, something that dentists can confirm," he says. "Not that you can't confirm other healings, but somehow this seems to be more spectacular."

The skeptics are receiving gold teeth, too. In Ahn's church, someone brought a non-Christian friend to her college fellowship meeting. "She received a gold filling, and it freaked her out," Ahn says.

Joel Budd, pastor of Open Bible Fellowship in Tulsa, Oklahoma, says a fourteen-year-old boy came to his church after telling his parents that he could get his teeth fixed at Open Bible. His father scoffed at him, but the boy countered by making a deal with his dad: "If God heals my mouth, you have to stop drinking and start attending church too," he told him. The father reluctantly agreed.

"The boy was a brand new Christian from a rough family,"

Budd says. "Yet he received two gold teeth." The father was reportedly astonished.

Last spring, Dupont prayed for a man in El Cajon, California, who was scheduled to have surgery to correct serious dental problems caused by an automobile accident. The young Baptist testified in front of hundreds of people: "The pain is all gone, my teeth are right, and I didn't even believe God did these things ten minutes ago."

In some unusual cases, entire crowns made of porcelain and metal turned to gold, with "fairly good evidence from dental records, lab reports, plus personal testimony that they weren't there before," Pastor John Arnott noted.

Others also have seen entire teeth turn to gold. Last spring, after Marc Dupont prayed for pastor Rich Oliver of Family Christian Center in Sacramento, California, Oliver got a huge gold tooth. "There is absolutely no white showing," Dupont says. Oliver's current dentist and his previous one confirmed that he never had any gold teeth before.

No one knows what is happening when people's amalgam fillings become shiny, but Arnott speculates that God may be removing mercury in the fillings. A friend of Arnott's who owns a dental lab recently told him that amalgam, which is a mixture of silver and mercury, is tricky to mix.

"If there is too much mercury in it, it bleeds out," Arnott says. Mercury is toxic, so surplus mercury can be harmful to the body. "I could see where God would take mercury out of a person's mouth — to heal them of mercury poisoning," Arnott adds.

Wagner, who says he has no problem believing that God is performing these miracles, notes that they should catch the attention of the secular world. "Alchemists have been trying to turn other elements into gold for a millennia," he says. "They haven't been successful, but God has."

To keep the focus on Jesus and not on the sensation, Dupont says he never prays specifically for people to receive gold fillings or gold teeth. "I pray for God to heal their mouth, teeth and gums," he says. "I don't pray for manifestations, but when they take place they are signs and wonders."

In most cases where the gold dust has appeared recently in the United States, no one has tested the substance, and some pastors said they wouldn't feel right about testing it anyway because they saw the flecks appear out of nowhere.

"We know it is a supernatural occurrence, whether or not it is gold," says pastor Bill Ligon of Christian Renewal Church in Brunswick, Georgia. His church began witnessing the gold dust phenomenon early this year. "The fact remains that God is sending a supernatural sign in our midst that He is using to win the lost, heal the sick and deliver the oppressed," Ligon says.

And that is what most people involved in this movement contend: If people are being healed or converted to Christ, or if their faith is being strengthened, or if they are becoming more zealous in evangelism as a result of gold dust or gold fillings, then God is at work no matter how bizarre these miracles seem or how much they offend human reasoning.

The real "acid test," says Anglican minister Trevor Pearce, is whether people affected by these miracles grow closer to the Lord, develop greater faith in His power and become more serious about the things of God. Notes Pearce: "Satan doesn't do those things."

Several related articles appeared in the November 1999 issue of Charisma:

Glory Dust From Heaven?

Charismatics around the world today say gold dust has appeared on their faces, hands and clothing during worship. Most say the dust is like a fine golden mist — tiny pinpoints of gold that look like they fell from Heaven's throne.

But the gold dust in Silvania Machado's meetings is different. A Brazilian who has ministered widely in the United States this year, Machado gets so much gold that it covers almost all of her face and rains from the top of her head. Although she doesn't speak English, she's been invited to minister in churches across America because of the remarkable phenomenon.

Many believe this unusual occurrence is tied to Machado's testimony. According to her pastor, three years ago she was dying of several kinds of cancer, including leukemia. She was so sick that foul-smelling bile oozed out of her pores. She tried everything to rid herself of the disease.

Finally she went to a church where the pastor asked her if she was willing to give God thirty days to heal her. Machado said yes, but just five days later she experienced a complete healing. A year later, she says, oil began to pour from her hands when she prayed.

Jane Lowder, who has worked with Bible teacher Ruth Heflin in Virginia for twenty-three years, saw the oil pour from Machado's hands in 1996 when Lowder traveled to Brazil with the late Wallace Heflin, Ruth Heflin's brother. While Lowder was in Brazil, she laid hands on Machado and prayed for her to receive the baptism of the Holy Spirit. A short time later, gold began to appear on Machado's face during the worship service.

In a service videotaped in Brazil, viewers can watch as the gold appears on Machado. After about fifteen minutes, the gold particles literally pour from the top of her head, and her pastor takes some of it and uses it to anoint people who are standing in line for prayer.

This video has been shown widely in Charismatic circles in the United States, but many questions have arisen from it: Why would God do something so strange? Why would anyone want to be anointed with a substance that comes from another person?

And most important — Is it really gold?

Heflin and Lowder insist that Machado is not a fraud. While Lowder was in Brazil, she checked Machado's scalp before each service to make sure she wasn't hiding glitter in her hair.

Heflin says it was a strong sense of God's presence, not the gold dust, that convinced her Machado was for real. "The gold wasn't even visible [the first night I saw her], but the pres-

ence was. I began to weep because of the wonderful sense of
His presence. Silvania prays with great love for everyone who
wants prayer in every meeting."

"Perhaps," Heflin adds, "we should call it 'glory dust' instead of 'gold dust.' "

Some people who believe the gold particles are from God
say it is like manna in the Bible, an unknown substance that
may not even be on the periodic chart of earthly elements.
Heflin says she has seen dust that resembles tiny diamond
shavings and colored dust that looks like emerald, ruby or
sapphire particles. To her, it is simply evidence of God's tangible glory.

'It Happened Before Our Eyes'

*In March, Oklahoma pastors Joel and Linda Budd
watched Linda's mother supernaturally receive
seven gold fillings.*

Elda Munce knew God could fix her crumbling teeth by
giving her gold fillings. The eighty-one-year-old woman, who
had serious dental problems, came to the altar during a
Wednesday evening service at Open Bible Fellowship in Tulsa,
Oklahoma, in March. After receiving prayer, she stretched her
mouth open with her little fingers and asked her son-in-law,
"Do I have any yet?"

Joel Budd, pastor of the church, looked at his mother-in-
law in amazement. He and his wife, Linda, peered into Elda's
mouth. She asked again, "Do I have any yet?"

The altar call that night was not for people who needed
gold teeth. Ché Ahn, a visiting pastor from the Los Angeles
area, had simply invited people to come forward for healing
of any kind.

Joel and Linda knew Elda needed dental work. They had
moved her from South Dakota six months before so she could
live near them in an assisted-living facility. When she arrived,

she told them she needed to see a dentist because her teeth were cracking.

"We never thought of asking God to heal Elda's teeth," Joel told *Charisma*. But tonight they would see a miracle occur right in front of their eyes.

As the Budds watched in amazement, gold crowns began to form in Elda's mouth. "I saw this big glob of gold material on the top of one of her teeth," Joel said. "I started to say, 'I can't believe this!' but I stopped myself Then I asked, 'Did you have gold in your mouth before?' "

Elda started laughing and told Joel, "You know I can't afford gold!" The gold globule moved down the side of Elda's tooth and was covered with a translucent film that looked like clear Jell-O, Joel says. The gold fluid then moved to the tooth beside it. When Joel told his mother-in-law that she was receiving a gold filling, she began laughing and crying at the same time.

People surged forward to see Elda's teeth, and Joel and Linda were pushed aside in the rush. When Joel looked in her mouth an hour later she had five gold crowns.

The next morning when Linda called her mother. Elda reported that she had received two more gold teeth — bringing the total to seven. "My mouth feels so clean," Elda told her daughter. "I had so much tartar built up. It's all gone. It's like I've been to the dentist, and it is totally clean."

Today, people at the church line up to see Elda's teeth, and many of her senior citizen friends have come to the church and received healings.

Two weeks after Elda got the gold crowns, Joel struggled with unbelief and called Elda's dentist in South Dakota — the same dentist she visited for fifteen years — and talked with a staff hygienist. Records showed that Elda had only one gold crown in her dental history, and it had fallen off years before. In fact, the hygienist found the gold crown in a plastic pouch in her file.

The Budds, who also have seen the gold dust in their services, say they don't sensationalize the gold miracles. They are more excited about the documented healings that have occurred since the gold phenomena began.

"To actually see miracles with my own eyes has been humbling," Joel says. "It has given me a much simpler faith. While I am still careful in terms of not calling everything a miracle, I will more readily pray for people's healing now."

That's a good thing, now that people are lining up for prayer at Open Bible's revival services. Says Linda: "God is trying to give us all a gift of faith and shake us away from our unbelief so He can bring a major revival of healing."

A Mouthful of Miracles

Jack Winter started sharing his faith with new boldness after he got two gold crowns during a worship service.

Jack Winter was enjoying the Palm Sunday service at Harvest Rock Church in Pasadena, California, in March when his pastor, Ché Ahn, described how God was giving people gold and silver crowns and fillings. As Winter listened to the reports of dental miracles, he prayed silently, "God, I'd like to get in on this."

Winter joined a crowd of people who went to the altar later that morning. Because so many people were waiting for Ahn to pray for them, Winter approached Debbie Malouff, one of the pastors' wives at Harvest Rock.

Winter says he felt no sensation in his mouth during prayer, so he didn't even check his teeth. But the next morning he discovered two gold crowns on his lower left jaw and a gold filling on the upper left side. The gold crowns, which extended all the way to the gum line, had replaced two old silver amalgam crowns — which typically turn dark gray with age.

Winter visited his dentist the next morning. After studying X rays and dental records, the dentist looked at the gold crowns and announced, "I didn't do that."

But that wasn't the end of the miracles. On the other side

of his mouth, Winter had some amalgam fillings that were cracked and needed to be replaced. But after God touched his mouth, he noticed what looked like silver streaks in the old fillings.

"I said, 'God, maybe You're filling the right side of my mouth, too,' " Winter told *Charisma*. A second dentist told him that it looked like the cracks in the dark amalgam had been filled with fresh silver.

Winter, 68, says a profound change occurred in his spiritual life after the dental miracle. Although he is the director of an international ministry, The Father Heart of God, and has ministered in thirty-two nations, he struggled to share his faith one-on-one.

His lack of boldness bothered him. "Sometimes I've sat on an airplane and wanted to start talking to somebody, but I didn't. Afterward, I would be disappointed. I've said to God, 'I need to be free to witness.' "

The day after Winter received his gold teeth, he shared Jesus with sixty-five people, most of them total strangers. He told his story to almost everyone he met that day.

At the doctor's office the next day, he shared his story with his doctor and the doctor's staff, two nurses and with people in the waiting room. He even prayed for a woman in the elevator. He soon realized he was free from his timidity.

Shortly after he received his gold crowns, Winter traveled to Germany and South Korea, and people in those meetings reportedly received dental miracles, too. In July, when he visited Poland, Winter said the anointing on his ministry was unusually strong.

"It was a remarkable time," Winter said. "The Father's love and the depth of God's healing was imparted." Perhaps those who received gold fillings in Winter's meetings will be as eager as he is to share their stories.

Books by Ruth Ward Heflin

Glory	English Edition	ISBN 1-884369-00-6	$10.00
	Spanish Edition	ISBN 1-884369-15-4	10.00
	French Edition	ISBN 1-884369-41-3	10.00
	German Edition	ISBN 1-884369-16-2	10.00
	Swedish Edition	ISBN 1-884369-38-3	10.00
	Finnish Edition	ISBN 1-884369-75-8	10.00

Revival Glory	ISBN 1-884369-80-4	13.00
River Glory	ISBN 1-884369-87-1	13.00
Golden Glory	ISBN 1-581580-001-0	13.00
Harvest Glory	ISBN 1-884369-81-2	25.00

Jerusalem, Zion, Israel and the Nations

ISBN 1-884369-65-0   13.00

Ask for them at your favorite bookstore or from:

Calvary Books
11352 Heflin Lane
Ashland, VA 23005
(804) 798-7756

www.revivalglory.org

The BESTSELLING:

GLORY

by
Ruth Ward Heflin

What is Glory?

- *It is the realm of eternity.*
- *It is the revelation of the presence of God.*
- *He is the glory! As air is the atmosphere of the Earth, so glory is the atmosphere of Heaven.*

Praise ... until the spirit of worship comes. Worship ... until the glory comes. Then ... stand in the glory. If you can capture the basic principles of praise, worship and glory which are outlined in this book — so simple that we often miss them — you can have anything else you want in God.

ISBN 1-884369-00-6 $10.00

Ask for it at your favorite bookstore or from:

Calvary Books
11352 Heflin Lane
Ashland, VA 23005
(804) 798-7756
www.revivalglory.org

The BESTSELLING:
REVIVAL GLORY

by
Ruth Ward Heflin

What is Revival Glory?

- *It is standing in the cloud and ministering directly from the cloud unto the people.*
- *It is seeing in to the eternal realm and declaring what you are seeing.*
- *It is gathering in the harvest, using only the tools of the Spirit.*
- *It is, ultimately, the revelation of Jesus Christ.*

One cannot have revival without the glory or the glory without having revival.

ISBN 1-884369-80-4 $13.00

Ask for it at your favorite bookstore or from:

Calvary Books
11352 Heflin Lane
Ashland, VA 23005
(804) 798-7756
www.revivalglory.org

The BESTSELLING:
RIVER GLORY

by
Ruth Ward Heflin

What is River Glory?

> *Through the analogy of the river, God has given us a whole new consciousness of His Spirit. Because He wants us to know the Spirit, He is showing us the river. When we see the Spirit of God as a great flowing river, we can better understand how to step into it and how to flow with its currents. The river is the Holy Spirit and the flow of the river is the outpouring of the Spirit. Whatever brings us to the river, if we can all get into it, every need will be supplied.*

ISBN 1-884369-87-1 $13.00

Ask for it at your favorite bookstore or from:

Calvary Books
*11352 Heflin Lane
Ashland, VA 23005
(804) 798-7756
www.revivalglory.org*

The BESTSELLING:
HARVEST GLORY

by
Ruth Ward Heflin

What is Harvest Glory?

We are called for this day and this hour. Born for it. Destined for it. The time of Harvest Glory.

You and I are making ourselves available as threshing instruments to bring in the end-time harvest, the harvest of the world.

Strengthened together in God, we shall bring all the harvest into the barn. Not one grain shall be lost. This is Harvest Glory.

Hardback edition; 432 pages with 40 pages of photographs.

ISBN 1-884369-81-2 $25.00

Ask for it at your favorite bookstore or from:

Calvary Books
11352 Heflin Lane
Ashland, VA 23005
(804) 798-7756
www.revivalglory.org

Jerusalem, Zion, Israel and the Nations

by
Ruth Ward Heflin

"God is returning the focus once again to Jerusalem. The place of beginnings is also the place of endings. And God's endings are always glorious.

"This overview is by no means definitive but an unfolding of scriptures coming into prominence in these days. As Moses saw the Promised Land from Nebo, one sees the world from Jerusalem."

— Ruth Heflin

ISBN 1-884369-65-0 $13.00

Ask for it at your favorite bookstore or from:

Calvary Books
11352 Heflin Lane
Ashland, VA 23005
(804) 798-7756
www.revivalglory.org

God of Miracles
Eighty Years of the Miraculous

by
Edith Ward Heflin

"My life has been very exciting because I was always looking forward to the next miracle, the next answer to prayer, the next thing Jesus would do for me. I expect I have lived twenty lifetimes within these eighty years. The God of all miracles has been so good and so very gracious to me."

— Edith Heflin

As you become witness to a life that has spanned the period from Azusa Street to this next great revival, the life of a unique woman who has known the great ministries of our century and has herself lived the life of the miraculous, you too will encounter the God of Miracles.

ISBN 1-56043-043-5 $10.00

Ask for it at your favorite bookstore or from:

Calvary Books
11352 Heflin Lane
Ashland, VA 23005
(804) 798-7756
www.revivalglory.org

Hear the Voice of God

by
Wallace H. Heflin, Jr.

* Does God still speak to His people as He did to the prophets of old?
* If so, how does He speak?
* Can we actually hear His voice?
* What can we do to become more sensitive to God's voice?

Wallace Heflin, Jr. spent a lifetime hearing the voice of God and following God's directives in dynamic ministry to the people of this nation and the world. In this manuscript, the last one that he prepared before his death in December of 1996, he challenges us that not only is it possible to hear the voice of God, but that God actually extends to every one of us an invitation to commune with Him.

ISBN 1-884369-36-7 $13.00

Ask for it at your favorite bookstore or from:

Calvary Books
11352 Heflin Lane
Ashland, VA 23005
(804) 798-7756
www.revivalglory.org

The Power of Prophecy

by
Wallace H. Heflin, Jr.

"Of all the nine gifts of the Spirit, prophecy is the gift that God is using most to bring in the revival of the end-time. Because of that, it is prophecy that is being opposed now more than any other gift. I want to declare that it is time to take the limits off the gift of prophecy and off the prophets God has raised up for this hour. It is time to move into God's plan of action to declare His will prophetically to this, the final generation."

— Rev. Wallace Heflin, Jr.

- What is prophecy?
- What does it accomplish?
- Who can prophesy?
- How can YOU get started prophesying?

These and many other important questions are answered in this unique and timely volume.

ISBN 1-884369-22-7 $10.00

Ask for it at your favorite bookstore or from:

Calvary Books
11352 Heflin Lane
Ashland, VA 23005
(804) 798-7756
www.revivalglory.org

Other books
by
Rev. Wallace H. Heflin, Jr.

A Pocket Full of Miracles	0-914903-23-3	$7.00
Bride, The	1-884369-10-3	$7.00
Jacob and Esau	1-884369-01-4	$7.00
The Potter's House	1-884369-61-8	$9.00
Power In Your Hand	1-884369-60-X	$8.00
Power In Your Hand *(Spanish Edition)*	1-884369-04-9	$6.00

Ask for them at your favorite bookstore or from:

Calvary Books
11352 Heflin Lane
Ashland, VA 23005
(804) 798-7756
www.revivalglory.org

Books by Dr. William A. Ward

Miracles That I Have Seen	1-884369-79-0	$13.00
God Can Turn Things Around	1-56043-014-1	12.00
On the Edge of Time	0-91490347-0	15.00
Get Off the Ash Heap	1-884369-20-0	9.00
Christian Cybernetics	1-884369-19-7	10.00
How to Be Successful		10.00

By Bob Shattles

Revival Fire and Glory	1-884369-84-7	$12.00

Ask for them at your favorite bookstore or from:

Calvary Books
11352 Heflin Lane
Ashland, VA 23005
(804) 798-7756
www.revivalglory.org

Mount Zion Miracle Prayer Chapel

13 Ragheb Nashashibi
P.O. Box 20897
Sheikh Jarrah
Jerusalem, Israel

Tel. 972-2-5828964
Fax. 972-2-5824725
www.revivalglory.org

Prayer Meetings:

2:00 – 3:00 P.M. Daily
Monday – Thursday

Services:

Friday, Saturday and Sunday
10:30 A.M.
7:30 P.M.
Pre-meeting praise 7:00 P.M.

Come and worship with us in Jerusalem!

Calvary Pentecostal Tabernacle

11352 Heflin Lane
Ashland, VA 23005

Tel. (804) 798-7756
Fax. (804) 752-2163
www.revivalglory.org

8 ½ Weeks of Summer Campmeeting 2000

Friday night, June 30 – Sunday night, August 27
With two great services daily, 11 A.M. & 8 P.M.

Ruth Heflin will be speaking nightly the first ten days and each
Friday and Saturday night during Summer Campmeeting

Winter Campmeeting 2000

February 4 – 27

Ruth Heflin will be speaking nightly the first week and each
Friday and Saturday night during Winter Campmeeting

Revival Meetings

Each Friday night, Saturday morning, Saturday night and
Sunday night with Sister Ruth Heflin in all other months

Ministry tapes and song tapes are also available upon request.